From Civil to Political Religion

The Intersection of Culture, Religion and Politics

From Civil to Political Religion

The Intersection of Culture, Religion and Politics

Marcela Cristi

Wilfrid Laurier University Press

This book has been published with the help of a grant from the Humanities and Social Sciences Federation of Canada, using funds provided by the Social Sciences and Humanities Research Council of Canada. We acknowledge the financial support of the Government of Canada through the Book Publishing Industry Development Program for our publishing activities.

National Library of Canada Cataloguing in Publication Data

Cristi, Marcela
  From civil to political religion : the intersection of culture, religion and politics

Includes bibliographical references and index.
ISBN 0-88920-368-7

1. Civil religion. I. Title.

BL98.5.C74 2001   322'.1   C2001-930472-2

© 2001 Wilfrid Laurier University Press
Waterloo, Ontario, Canada   N2L 3C5

Chapter 5, written with Lorne L. Dawson, was originally published as "Civil Religion in Comparative Perspective: Chile under Pinochet (1978-1989)" in *Social Compass* 43, 3 (Sept. 1996). Reproduced here with minor modifications, courtesy of *Social Compass*, Collège Jacques Leclercq, Louvain-la-Neuve, Belgium.

Cover design by Leslie Macredie.
Photograph by Andrés Gómez, courtesy of
Reuters / Andrés Gómez / Hulton / Archive.

Printed in Canada

TABLE OF CONTENTS

INTRODUCTION

I n "Civil Religion in America," published in the winter 1967 issue of *Daedalus,* Robert N. Bellah affirmed: "few have realized that there actually exists alongside of and rather clearly differentiated from the churches an elaborate and well institutionalized civil religion in America" (1967: 1). Quoting from John Kennedy's and Lyndon Johnson's inaugural addresses, Bellah argued that these speeches, and those of the founding fathers, provided a clue to understanding the relationship between religion and politics in the United States. The speeches, which often mentioned God, revealed a profound religious spirit in American society. "What we have," Bellah noted, "is a collection of beliefs, symbols, and rituals with respect to sacred things and institutionalized in a collectivity" (1967: 8).

Bellah observed that civil religion in the United States was independent of religious and political institutions and, at the same time, not in competition with either church or state. While this religion included many Christian symbols and themes, it was "neither sectarian nor in any specific sense Christian" (1967: 8). An important aspect of the American political tradition, he observed, is the belief that Americans, individually and collectively, have an "obligation...to carry out God's will on earth" (5). Bellah claimed that since the early days of the Republic, Americans have interpreted their history essentially in religious terms. In his view, civil religion served and still serves "as a genuine vehicle of national religious self-understanding" (8). Bellah concluded that civil religion provided a "transcendent goal for the political process" and contributed to the unity and collective identity of Americans as a national community (4). The principal effect of U.S. civil religion had been to generate powerful symbols of national solidarity and to encourage Americans to achieve national aspirations and goals.

Bellah's article galvanized many in the scholarly community and resulted in scores of subsequent articles about his thesis, initiating a debate over civil religion in the United States. Others before him had advanced similar ideas, and had spoken of the "religion of the Republic," "the religion of the American Way of Life," even of "American Shinto," but they failed to provoke substantial discussions or analysis (Bellah, 1974b: 255; Jones and Richey, 1974: 3-4). As Bellah himself acknowledges, it was the expression "civil religion in America" that acquired "a life of its own, that [was] picked up by *The New York Times* and by the popular news weeklies, that has inspired books, essays and symposia" (1974b: 255). Bellah's interpretation of a "national faith," or of a religious dimension of American society, generated concerns about the actual meaning and definition of the term, its applicability as a sociological concept, and whether it could be considered a religion or not (Gehrig, 1981a: 51; 1981b: 1). After the publication of Bellah's article, the sociological landscape (particularly the sociology of religion) divided in two camps: those who enthusiastically accepted Bellah's thesis, and those who simply dismissed the notion of civil religion. The latter not only questioned Bellah's interpretation, but doubted the very existence of a civil religion in America (Bellah, 1974b: 255).

More than three decades after Bellah's publication, the notion of civil religion remains ambiguous and ill-defined. On the one hand, the term "civil religion" has been applied to a wide range of phenomena, as will be explained in chapter 2. On the other hand, the idea of civil religion appears under a variety of different terms, such as public religion, public philosophy, public theology, political religion, republican religion, civic faith, and so on. I understand civil religion in terms similar to John Wilson's, but with a fundamental modification. Civil religion as a concept, Wilson notes (1986: 111), "concerns the possibility that specific social and cultural beliefs, behaviors, and institutions constitute a positive religion concerned with civil order in the society." This definition leaves aside the political dimension, which I consider essential for an understanding of the civil religion phenomenon. Thus, while agreeing with Wilson, I expand his definition and argue instead that civil religion is concerned with both the social *and* the political order. Civil religion tends to sacralize certain aspects of civic life by means of public rituals and collective ceremonies. In so doing, beliefs and behaviours, acquire a "religious" dimension. As such, civil religion may be considered a belief system or, a surrogate religion, that expresses the self-identity of a collectivity. Yet, like secular ideologies of different kinds, civil religion may also attempt to force group identity and to legitimize an existing political order, by injecting a transcendental dimension or a religious gloss on the justification. This latter manifestation I call political religion.

It seems to me that any acute reader of the theoretical developments and disputes engendered by the civil religion thesis will be forced to recognize that the concept, as used by Bellah and other American sociologists, is often not useful for the study of civil religion in other countries, nor for the study of certain types of civil religion in democratic societies, including the United States. Bellah's notion is especially difficult to apply in cases where the state seeks to use civil religion as a political tool to further national policies or programs. The same reader will probably find that many of the claims on which the notion of civil religion rests do not always hold true. Again, this is particularly evident in authoritarian societies, but to a lesser extent in democracies as well.

The central focus of Bellah's thesis is that there is a set of national symbols and rituals in the United States that transcends and neutralizes differences in beliefs and values of American citizens, irrespective of their religion or social position. From Bellah's standpoint, civil religion effectively balances, or even deactivates, the multiplicity of religious, ethnic, political, and ideological discourses found in America.

If one accepts Bellah's theoretical position, as we will later see, it becomes extremely difficult to discern ideological types of civil religion, or to analyze variations within and among societies with regard to the way they tie their political experiences to religion (Markoff and Regan, 1982: 334). Frank Reynolds's work on Thailand is a case in point. His research led him to conclude that there was a significant difference, in "certain important respects," between the Thai situation and Bellah's theoretical position. As a result, he chose to dispense with the notion of civil religion and opted to identify the Thai religious expression as "civic" rather than "civil" to distinguish it from the American phenomenon (1977: 268, 281).

I believe that problems such as the one encountered by Reynolds could be resolved by conceptualizing civil religion as a phenomenon that manifests itself in two forms: as "culture" (the Durkheimian "civil" approach) and as "ideology" (the Rousseauan "political" approach). These forms are not opposites; they are part of a continuum. This means that they are distinguishable conceptually but cannot be separated in reality. Thus conceptualized, civil religion may be seen either as a phenomenon expressing an inward conviction on the part of members of a certain group (implicit culture), or as a political resource, a form of external compulsion or force used to support an existing political order. In the former case, civil religion is assumed to be a "cultural given" (Demerath, 1994: 113) or an "emergent property of social life itself" (Hammond, 1980c: 138). In the latter, it is a premeditated political ideology, constructed by the state and its political leaders, which members of a collectivity are expected or even forced to accept. In line with my understanding that civil religion can be conceived as a political resource at the service of the state, I briefly examine, in chapter 4, some cases of state-directed civil religions from a comparative perspective, in different societies, and at different times.

This book should be read as a critique of civil religion, particularly as interpreted by American scholars, who have set the tone and established the direction of the civil religion debate. I believe that their interpretation of civil religion (the way it has been portrayed as operating in the United States) has been unifocal and, to a certain degree, incorrect. American scholars have tended to concentrate primarily on value consensus, to the relative neglect of conflict, exclusion, and disharmony.

A review of the literature indicates that the notion of civil religion as used by Bellah and others rests on some basic and broadly accepted assumptions that stem from the Durkheimian tradition. This perspective seeks to explain religion in terms of an alleged integrative role. Thus, the <u>integrative function</u> of civil ⟵ religion has been considered crucial to understanding the civil religious experience in the United States and elsewhere. It should be noted that when dealing with the civil religion issue, neither Bellah nor the most representative scholars in this field (such as John Coleman or Phillip Hammond, among others) have restricted their focus to the United States. Expressions of the civil religion phenomenon have been said to exist in different societies (Markoff and Regan, 1982: 334). But despite Bellah's or Hammond's good intentions in developing cross-cultural research (see, for example, Bellah's discussion of civil religion in Japan [1980d], and Hammond's [1980a] comparison of Mexico and the United States), and despite Coleman's (1969) equally good intention to formulate "a more universal civil religion typology," their basic approach to other forms of civil religion has been elaborated primarily in relation to the American case (Reynolds, 1977: 282). Indeed, the American case has been taken to be the paradigm of civil religion. But the concepts and theoretical logic characteristic of the Durkheimian tradition are of limited use when we try to understand how civil religion works.

Hammond, for example, locates civil religion in the "modern" stage of religious evolution, which is characterized by a differentiation of religious and political organizations (Markoff and Regan, 1982: 334). Modern, advanced societies, especially the United States, would exhibit a fully independent civil religion (or belief system) controlled neither by the church nor by the state. This position dismisses, in one sweep, the political, ideological, and sometimes coercive potential of civil religion, and wrongly relegates the coercive type (i.e., political religion, whose theology is dependent on the state) to Third World countries (essentially "premodern" societies). I reject the claim that political religions belong to communist regimes or dictatorships found in the Third World, while civil religions are an expression of modern industrialized societies (Zuo, 1991). I also disagree with those who claim that the political religions of totalitarian regimes are not civil religions (Giner, 1993).

The term *civil religion* was coined by Jean-Jacques Rousseau, so it is not surprising that almost all theoretical or empirical studies on civil religion start by mentioning his name. In his original article, Bellah (1967: 5) acknowledged that the term "is, of course, Rousseau's," and mentioned, in passing, that *The Social Contract* outlines the dogmas of the civil religion. While not necessarily arguing "for the particular influence of Rousseau" on the founding fathers and presidents of the United States, Bellah claimed that "similar ideas" to the ones advanced by Rousseau were part of the political and cultural climate not only of eighteenth-century America, but of the contemporary United States as well. He was referring, in particular, to references to God made by public officials and political authorities, and to the "active" role God was supposed to play in American political life.

To be sure, the belief in a divinity is the first dogma of Rousseau's civil religion, but civil religion as understood by him involves much more than this. Rousseau's intention was to create a religion that would not be attached to any particular religious belief or organized church. Rather, it should be a religion designed and controlled by the state. It is particularly important to keep the latter point in mind, for the Rousseauan version is fundamental to an understanding of why civil religion may be consciously used in democratic societies for political ends. In a true Rousseauan sense, civil religion is essentially a coercive political device—a fact that most sociologists have been either unable or unwilling to fully understand.[1] However, the emergence of civil religion, as Rousseau understood it, is not a phenomenon peculiar to authoritarian regimes or to developing nations alone.

By contrast, Durkheim conceives civil religion as essentially a *spontaneous* phenomenon, whose natural "function" is to provide a people with a common morality and loyalty to the group. Durkheim holds that every relatively healthy society is based on a set of shared beliefs, rituals, and symbols that express its most fundamental values. These values, Durkheim argues, acquire a transcendental meaning, for they are considered sacred by members of the group. They serve to bring the community together. In so doing, they "naturally" provide for the order, stability, and integration of the society as a whole. In Durkheim's terms, civil religion *acts* upon the individual.

Although Bellah mentions Rousseau, he has been strongly influenced by Durkheim. Most students of civil religion, in turn, have opted to take the Bellah/Durkhemian route. As a result, the sociological literature shows a serious lack of understanding concerning the full political implications of a Rousseauan type of civil religion. This oversight has produced a conceptual and theoretical impasse "obscuring almost all contemporary analyses of modern-day civil religion" (Hammond, 1980c: 138). Not surprisingly, many aspects of civil religion have simply been taken for granted, and many others inherent in the notion of civil religion have never been made problematic in theory.

Indeed, hundreds of articles and books make vague references to Rousseau, but these give little evidence of an effort to comprehend what he really meant by civil religion. Most authors seem content to quote him on this issue, or to start their publications with remarkably similar sentences, acknowledging that Rousseau coined the term civil religion. They then take a solidly

Durkheimian approach (see, e.g., Bourg 1976: 141; Coleman, 1969: 67; Gehrig, 1981a: 51; Zuo, 1991: 99). As far as I know, in a truly voluminous literature, only one scholar explicitly acknowledges that Rousseau conceived civil religion "in a way that was fundamentally different from Bellah's understanding" (Wilson, 1971: 14). And, although a distinction between Rousseau's and Durkheim's theories is implicit in the works of some writers (Casanova, 1994; Giner, 1993; Luke, 1987), only a few scholars such as Willaime (1993), Demerath and Williams (1985), or Hammond (1980c) briefly attempt to discuss what this difference entails. It is my conviction that a theoretical clarification of these two traditions is absolutely essential, for most other problems and deficiencies in the literature stem from the failure to make this distinction.

Simply put, American students of civil religion have hardly ever directed their attention to the ideological, manipulative intent (or potential) of civil religion. They have not only accepted the Durkheimian proposition that a stable society is based on a commonality of shared beliefs and symbols, but have also embraced the idea that the general integrative function of civil religion is capable of transcending any particular social structure, political regime, and even historical circumstances. As I indicate in chapters 2 and 3, the Bellah tradition neither considers the possibility that the state (or its political and intellectual leaders) may shape the direction of civil religion, nor does it confront the likelihood that civil religion or religious beliefs may help legitimize the domination of the most powerful cultural or social group in society.[2] In other words, the idea that the state may use civil religion politically is absent from the traditional theories and models of civil religion. With theorists unilaterally adopting the classic "consensual" tradition, the question of legitimation and integration, often considered an essential part of the civil religion phenomenon, has been disengaged from issues of power and conflict associated with the problem of order.

In short, the overemphasis given to the Durkheimian conception of civil religion has left the civil religion thesis open to fundamental criticism. This book questions, or at least makes problematic, the cohesiveness attributed to civil religion in the United States and its inevitable, spontaneous nature. It addresses the possibility that civil religion can exist as a consciously orchestrated and state-controlled political phenomenon. It also calls into question the idea that there is a highly differentiated civil religion in America. At the heart of my criticism is the question of the underlying and widely accepted assumptions on which the traditional civil religion thesis rests. These assumptions clearly illustrate the pre-eminence scholars have given to Durkheim's account of religion. Although a critique of these assumptions (which are intimately related and to some degree overlapping) will reappear throughout this work, I will here briefly summarize some of them and indicate my difficulties with them.

First, civil religion is assumed to be, by definition, an essentially integrative force in society. I dispute the idea that civil religion is a set of religious symbols which *by definition* serves to integrate society. Civil religion may give rise, under certain conditions, to social conflict, tension, and division. Its values and its ritual manifestations may be meaningful only to certain segments of the population, or they may benefit certain groups at the expense of others. Allegiance to certain types of civil religion may also conflict with social cohesion. In other words, civil religion is more likely to produce a "qualified consensus" rather than total social integration (Wimberley and Christenson, 1981: 98). The Durkheim/Bellah interpretation of civil religion does not adequately allow for either the potentially abusive nature of civil religion or for the potentially conflictual diversity (ideological, social, ethnic) of modern society.

Second, civil religion is assumed to reflect the values and beliefs of the society as a whole. This implies that, by definition, civil religion is a national religion. However, civil religion need not be *per force* a national religion. Here the objection I raise against Bellah's thesis is its implicit identification of American civil religion with the alleged religious self-definition of the American people as a whole.

Third, civil religion is assumed to provide legitimating functions. To be sure, while the legitimating capacity of civil religion may not be too significant, or even too effective, there seems to be enough evidence indicating that civil religion is used as an instrument of legitimation, both in democratic and undemocratic societies. Bellah (1974b: 255) claims that civil religion, at least in the United States, performs the function of a "higher law." The nation is subordinated to, and judged by higher ethical principles that transcend it. Thus, in Bellah's view, civil religion explains and justifies society and the political order in transcendental terms (i.e., in terms of an ultimate set of values). Other scholars agree and claim that the nation is the "primary agent of God's meaningful activity in history" (Coleman, 1969: 74). The assumption here is that civil religion not only legitimizes the social order but, at the same time, acts as a check against deviations by confronting the nation and reminding its citizens to uphold its most fundamental moral ideals. If we accept this proposition, civil religion can be only upright or morally justified—a conclusion that contradicts the role civil religion may have in different polities, or at different times within the same polity.

To be sure, in its Durkheimian variety civil religion may be what some authors refer to as a "potentially enduring form of overarching cultural legitimation," at least for some groups in society (Gehrig, 1981b: 36). But I reject the assumption that civil religion is always a positive force favouring cultural integration and pluralistic ethics. Analyses of civil religion, both in the United States and in the comparative cases which I discuss in chapters 4 and 5, belie such a formulation. The coercive, divisive side of civil religion will be discussed at various points in the book. It will be argued that civil religion, as an ideological and political tool, rather than being a permanent legitimator of power and authority in the polity, may be seen as an "episodic" phenomenon emerging during unsettled political times in response to crises of legitimation, both national or international (see Marty, 1974; Purdy, 1982; Regan, 1976).

Fourth, civil religion is assumed to be a spontaneous social phenomenon. In reference to its alleged spontaneity (Durkheim's idea), I contend that we need to confront the issue of the imposed nature of civil religion as well (Rousseau's idea). Western democracies, characterized by a high degree of pluralism and institutional differentiation, are undoubtedly less likely to develop a totalitarian political religion than those societies in the process of modernization or ruled by an autocratic and monolithic state. Clearly, the latter are often confronted with the urgent necessity of legitimating the state before the people. In such cases, the governing elite may be more willing to manipulate cultural and religious symbols to arouse mass support. Having said this, it should also be emphasized that the democratic or anti-democratic potential of civil religion is grounded in the political processes and the uses of civil religion by particular political figures, at particular times, and not in the stages of cultural or religious evolution as some scholars have argued (Bellah, 1980a; Coleman, 1969). One has only to think of Hitler, Franco or Mussolini. This suggests that there is no such a thing as a simple developmental progression or evolution of civil religion, with the most advanced societies having the most advanced levels of civil religion (a structurally differentiated symbol system). Rather, the way civil religion operates has more to do with the type of politics and the type of government under consideration, and less to do with the level of religious development.

Finally, civil religion is assumed to be (in the United States) a belief system fully differentiated from church and state—that is, not tied to any particular denomination or ruling regime. I reject the alleged structural differentiation of American civil religion. In chapter 3, I demonstrate that civil religion in the United States has been closely associated with social and political institutions such as the educational, political, and legal system.

In other words, the notion of civil religion, as it appears in the literature, has been too narrowly conceived. An understanding of the civil religion phenomenon in all its complexity is essential if it is to be applied cross-culturally, or from one era to another within the same society.

In seeking to facilitate the analysis of civil religion, I offer a model that orders civil religion in a continuum in terms of its theoretical sources and its cultural or political significance.[3] The continuum is understood in the Weberian sense of two "ideal types." At one end of the spectrum is the classical Durkheimian position which asserts that each collectivity has a common religion. At the other end, civil religion is conceived in terms of a particular political order, as advocated by Rousseau.

A Durkheimian type of civil religion exhibits strong cultural elements and seems to be, to some degree, more spontaneous than that posited by Rousseau. There is no centrally regulated apparatus to ensure compliance with the tenets of faith. Within the Durkheimian framework, civil religion is the product of collective thought. Moral understandings, beliefs, and values would "make sense" to the collectivity. Civil religion would be a "natural" expression of group life (whether of the nation or a smaller collectivity or group). In this sense, we can refer to civil religion as a cultural force. One may say that as a cultural phenomenon, civil religion only gradually takes on form and becomes institutionalized.

A Rousseauan type of civil religion, by contrast, is a consciously "designed" religion that leaders have to create and encourage. It is intended to exert strong control over the citizenry. Despite Rousseau's democratic intentions, this type of civil religion appears to be closely associated with particular unstable political situations, or with authoritarian and despotic governments. As a political phenomenon, civil religion may be used as a conscious tool to further political purposes (e.g., to foster national integration, to restore social and political stability, and/or to legitimize a particular political order). This implies that civil religion has the potential to be an *imposed* phenomenon rather than a permanent *spontaneous* force in society. The nature of the state and of society are crucial factors determining the character and shape civil religion may assume in a particular society at a particular time.

My work does not imply that Durkheim's and Bellah's theories should be dismissed. Rather, it suggests that students of civil religion (in particular American scholars) have not done their homework properly. By neglecting to understand civil religion as originally intended by Rousseau, they have unintentionally encouraged a misinterpretation of this phenomenon. If the notion of civil religion is to remain a useful sociological concept, we need to stop conceiving it in exclusively Durkheimian terms—as something that springs spontaneously from the culture itself, and spontaneously binds people together. The notion of civil religion needs to be framed at a higher level of generality—that is, as a phenomenon that is neither just civil, nor just religious, but also essentially political. By conceptualizing civil religion this way, and by using it in its dual manifestation—as *culture* and as *ideology*, many of the problems encountered in the literature may be avoided. It is my hope that this broadened conception will enrich the study of civil religion by providing a better sociological tool with which to compare shades and types of civil religion both within societies and between them. I stand with Michael W. Hughey, who, in reexamining the Durkheimian theory of religion wrote: "it is with the limits of the conclusions reached, not their falsity, that the present study is concerned" (1983: xvi).

CHAPTER ONE

Theoretical Foundations

One European Pedigree, Two Different Traditions

The notion of civil religion, as Hammond (1976: 169) has noted, has been of interest throughout the history of Western political thought, for "in a broad sense it is the question of legitimacy or of 'good citizenship.'" Some scholars would argue that, in one form or another, the phenomenon we now know as civil religion is "as old as political society" (Henry, 1979: 1). However, the term itself was first used by Rousseau in *The Social Contract* ([1762] 1973). Civil religion, in Rousseau's terms, refers to a civic faith to be created and imposed by the sovereign as a way of promoting civic virtues and political unity. "Now that there is and can be no longer an exclusive national religion," Rousseau writes, "tolerance should be given to all religions that tolerate others, so long as their dogmas contain nothing contrary to the duties of citizenship" ([1762] 1973: 277).

Notes to Chapter 1 are on pp. 244-46.

Rousseau's purpose was to design a religion that would elicit feelings of civic membership and enforce the duties of citizenship in national communities no longer bonded by traditional religious links. This religion, Rousseau believed, was essential to foster social discipline in a modern liberal polity, and to bind all individuals to the state. Rousseau makes a clear distinction between civil religion and supernatural or denominational religions. I will return to this point later.

Durkheim's classic study *The Elementary Forms of Religious Life* ([1912] 1961), is also an essential part of the civil religion literature. In this work Durkheim deals specifically with primitive religion, but draws conclusions pertaining to modern industrialized society as well. Durkheim, who never used the term civil religion, conceptualizes the totemic practices of the Arunta—a group of Australian aborigines—as a spontaneous religious phenomenon arising from the very depths of the social group itself. In Durkheim's view, "the very existence of society" presupposes a common (civil) religion (Hammond, 1980c: 139). Conversely, any religion is something eminently social, for beliefs in the supernatural and the sacred are essentially collective, social realities. So, even when religion seems to spring from the inner depth of the individual, the actual source on which it feeds is still to be found in society (Durkheim, [1912] 1961: 472). As such, any religion is, in the last analysis, a social phenomenon.

Strictly speaking, as I will discuss later, while Rousseau coined the term *civil religion*, he conceived, in fact, the notion of *political religion*.[1] Rousseau advocates a state religion comprising a simple set of civic-religious dogmas that every citizen must subscribe to, on pain of exile or death. Civil religion in this sense is constitutive of a state or political community. Unlike Rousseau, Durkheim neither conceives civil religion as an instrumental political process to secure loyalty to a particular social order, nor is he interested in the political utility of civil religion. His approach to civil religion implies a spontaneous, non-coercive civic faith uniting all individuals into one single moral community. In a Durkheimian sense, civil religion is truly "civil," in that it belongs to civil society not to the state or political authorities.[2]

These differences between Rousseau and Durkheim are critical for an understanding of the civil religion concept. What follows is a more detailed analysis of their theoretical positions.

Rousseau on Civil Religion

Rousseau's notion of civil religion has to be placed in the context of his broader theoretical preoccupation with legitimacy and the nature of a "good society." Indeed, his overall concern in the *Social Contract*, and other political writings, is to provide practical political principles by which to evaluate a legitimate social order. His objective is twofold: to provide a rational explanation concerning the legitimacy of the social order; and to indicate the basis, justification, and limitation of political obligation and political authority. More specifically, Rousseau's main concern is to justify the "authority to set jurisdictional boundaries and invoke transcendental sanctions." In order to solve these problems, Rousseau turns to civil religion (Hammond, 1980a: 43).

Rousseau claims that the power of the state derives not from force but from moral grounds that legitimize it, and that "no State has ever been founded without a religious basis" ([1762] 1973: 272). In pagan times, Rousseau argues, cult and government were one and the same thing. Each state had its own gods and did not distinguish between "its god and its laws." Political wars were of necessity theological—"the provinces of the gods were, so to speak, fixed by the boundaries of nations" (269). Rousseau observes that Christianity, by setting up the kingdom of God, separated the theological from the political order, made the state "no longer one, and brought about the internal divisions which have never ceased to trouble Christian peoples" (270). Jurisdictional confrontations between ecclesiastical and temporal authorities endangered forever the unity of society. The spirit of Christianity, Rousseau argues, introduced not only "the most violent of earthly despotisms" but also a "conflict of jurisdiction" and a division of power that have made "all good polity impossible in Christian States." Ever since the sacred cult and the state became independent systems, Rousseau contends, "men have never succeeded in finding out whether they were bound to obey the master or the priest" (270). Rousseau charges that, among many Christian writers, only Hobbes had the necessary vision to understand this problem. Hobbes "dared to propose the reunion of the two heads of the eagle," and the reestablishment of political unity, "without which no State or government will ever be rightly constituted" (271). But, according to Rousseau, this vision was destined to fail: Hobbes identified the problem and proposed a solution (the fusion of church and state), but faltered in trying to harmonize Christianity with the needs and interests of the political order, for, with its "'domineering spirit,' Christianity would never consent to be subordinate to the State" (Henry, 1979: 150).

So Rousseau, who like Hobbes addresses the politico-religious problem, starts with two basic assumptions. First, that the state needs a religious foundation, and second that the "law of Christianity" not only weakens but harms the constitution of the state (Rousseau, [1762] 1973: 272). Rousseau distinguishes three varieties of religion: the religion of the citizen, the religion of the priest, and that of man.[3] The religion of the citizen, "codified in a single country," has its dogmas, rites, and cults ordained by law. It has its "own tutelary patrons" and divinities. Duties and rights are circumscribed to a particular nation. Borrowing directly from Machiavelli, Rousseau argues that the religion of the citizen is politically beneficial for it "teaches them [citizens] that service done to the State is service done to its tutelary god" (272).[4] This religion instills a love of the laws and makes the country the object of adoration. By sacralizing the state and the nation, it produces loyal citizens (Casanova, 1994: 59). However, it is based on "lies and error." It is potentially tyrannous and restrictive and may lead to intolerance and national fanaticism. It places people in a constant state of alert, or war, with respect to all others, deeply endangering its security. It is harmful, again, Rousseau notes, when it "breathes fire," incites people to be "bloodthirsty," and "regards as a sacred act" the slaughter of those who do not accept its gods (Rousseau, [1762] 1973: 273).

The religion of the priest divides people's loyalties. It gives the individual "two codes of legislation, two rulers, and two countries." Rousseau places in this category Roman Christianity, and "the religions of the Lamas and of the Japanese," all of them leading, according to him, to a sort of "mixed and antisocial" frame of mind. When the individual is torn between allegiance to the church and allegiance to the state, and is thus subject to different authorities, his moral and political obligations collide. He cannot be "faithful both to religion and to citizenship" (Rousseau, [1762] 1973: 272). Rousseau tells us that the religion of the priest is so "clearly" harmful that he finds "it is a waste of time" to try to prove it. It destroys social unity and "all that destroys social unity is worthless." Moreover, it confuses and agitates man. It forces him to enter into a turmoil of contradictions. Rousseau admonishes that any social institution that sets man at odds with himself is also "worthless." The dual sovereignty model of priestly religions is also politically disloyal, for "the priestly interest would always be stronger than that of the State" (271). While in theory authority is divided between church and state, in pragmatic terms "it means that priests are tempted to usurp temporal authority for themselves, and to this extent undercut the established authority of the state" (Beiner, 1993: 618).[5]

Finally, Rousseau speaks of the religion of man, or Christianity, but not the corrupted Christianity of his day. This religion, Rousseau notes, is eternal and universal, it unites all men as brothers insofar as they are all children of God. It is the true natural "religion of the Gospel pure and simple." Without "altars," "temples," or "rites," it is solely devoted to the cult of God. But Rousseau perceives a difficulty here as well. The religion of man, while certainly trustworthy, does not bind all men to the state. On the contrary, it has the effect of removing them from worldly affairs, for "the country of the Christian is not of this world" (Rousseau, [1762] 1973: 272, 274). But Rousseau finds yet another problem. The religion of man is essentially a religion of salvation. Because resignation is indispensable to achieving salvation, this religion "preaches only servitude and dependence" and, as a logical necessity, it engenders servile and dependent subjects (274-75).[6] It may be morally attractive and religiously true, but it is politically ineffective (Beiner, 1993: 618).

Long before Rousseau, Machiavelli had noticed the antipolitical nature of Christianity and had proposed some sort of "anti-Christian politics" that he thought could be achieved by going back to Roman paganism (Beiner, 1993:619). Rousseau agrees with the diagnosis of the problem, but rejects Machiavelli's solution. Christianity is an entirely spiritual, other worldly religion. Assume or imagine, Rousseau tells us, "your Christian republic face to face with Sparta or Rome: the pious Christians will be beaten, crushed, destroyed" (Rousseau, [1762] 1973: 274). And he further adds, "the soldiers of Fabius" swore and kept their vow "not to conquer or die, but to come back victorious." Rousseau insists that Christians could never have made such a commitment, they could never have been truly good and glorious soldiers for "they would have looked on it as tempting God" (275). It is an either/or proposition. One is either a citizen of the republic or a citizen of the Church. As Bellah has pointed out, Rousseau's concern has been shared by most of the great republican theorists of the Western world, from Machiavelli to de Tocqueville, who have also speculated whether Christianity could ever produce trustworthy citizens (Bellah, 1978: 16).

In short, the main purpose of Rousseau's chapter on civil religion in the *Social Contract* is to show that the reconciliation of Christianity with the demands of politics is a futile endeavour (Beiner, 1993: 619). The notion of a Christian republic, Rousseau contends, is an absurdity; the two words "are mutually exclusive." By preaching servitude, the essence of Christianity is "favourable to tyranny" for devout Christians are "made to be slaves, and they know it and do not much mind" (Rousseau, [1762] 1973: 275).

While Rousseau is convinced that religion is the very foundation of the state, he understands at the same time that all three existing forms of religion are not conducive to a "good polity" (Casanova, 1994: 59). Considered politically, all three religions are flawed. At the same time, he is aware that the "Age of Reason" is inevitably leading towards the secularization of the world. However, while most Enlightenment thinkers agreed that religion was destined to disappear with the collapse of the old regime, Rousseau does not celebrate its demise. On the contrary, he fears the long-term effects and political repercussions of a social order without some kind of religion (Casanova, 1994: 32; Demerath and Williams, 1985: 155). Agreeing with Machiavelli, for whom religion has a profound political (i.e., practical) significance, Rousseau insists that religion, even in the era of enlightenment, is still valuable to the body politic.[7] He suggests, in fact, that there is an unquestionable affinity between religion and political stability: "As soon as men live in society, they require a religion to maintain them there. Never have a people continued nor will they ever continue without religion" (cited in Vaughan, [1915] 1962, 1: 499). Simply put, Rousseau assumes that religion is politically indispensable for it is the base on which the state is legitimately anchored. With religion providing a source of transcendent morality, the authority of the state is perceived as if ordained by God. Civic duties become moral obligations. Rousseau's solution to the incompatibility of Christianity and the state is not to go back to Roman paganism, but to create instead a civic creed.

Rousseau is writing in an age when the feudal order is rapidly decaying. The Christian faith has been, to a large extent, shattered by the forces of the Enlightenment. The modern nation-state is beginning to emerge, and religion appears to be losing its legitimating capacity. Whereas medieval philosophers had interpreted the universe in theological terms, reason and science are replacing the traditional authority of the church. A new legitimation mechanism is needed to secure social cohesion. Once again, Machiavelli's work helps Rousseau on this issue. Machiavelli points out in his *Discourses* that "new religions are 'due to men' rather than 'due to heaven,' that innovations in, and transformations of, religious belief and practice are legitimate objects of statecraft" (Beiner, 1993: 630). Rousseau agrees. His philosophical project entails the creation of a new religious belief made useful for politics. It is in this context that he introduces the idea of a civil creed as a necessary element of the modern polity.

As a liberal, Rousseau concedes that each citizen is free to believe, worship, or express his own religious convictions as he wishes. Quoting the Marquis d'Angerson, he agrees that each individual is "perfectly free in what does not harm others." But he also insists that subjects are accountable for their opinions and beliefs when "they matter to the community." To this he adds that "it matters very much to the community that each citizen should have a religion. That will make him love his duty." Hence, the dogmas of such religion "concern the State and its members" only when they refer to the duties that bind each citizen to all others and to the state (Rousseau, [1762] 1973: 275-76). Rousseau is not interested in issues of the after life or of personal salvation. Those are spiritual and private duties left to the conscience of each individual, for the "Sovereign has no authority in the other world." But he is concerned with the "good citizens in this life" (276). This is a political and public matter that Rousseau leaves to the care of the state.

Given the fact that, throughout history, political institutions have relied or even depended upon religious legitimacy, Rousseau postulates the need for a new religion, a "purely civil profession of faith." The articles of such religion should be dictated by the sovereign, "not exactly as religious dogmas," but rather as "social sentiments without which a man cannot be a good citizen or a faithful subject" (276). These canons of faith "ought to be few, simple, and exactly worded, without explanation or commentary. The existence of a mighty, intelligent, and beneficent Divinity, possessed of foresight and providence, the life to come, the happiness of the just, the punishment of the wicked, the sanctity of the social contract and the laws: these are its positive dogmas. Its negative dogmas I would confine to one—intolerance, which is a part of the cults we have rejected" (276).

Rousseau explicitly sets apart these articles of faith from every kind of religious dogmatism (Merquior, 1980: 37). Members of the social contract are not held accountable for their opinions, or for their specific religious orientation, but only for their moral obligations and civic duties. But, by decreeing the "sanctity of the social contract and the law," Rousseau transforms civic responsibility into "a spiritual duty" (Macfarlane, 1970: 68). The social effects of civil religion are to be similar, though not identical, to the role that Christianity had fulfilled in Europe in previous centuries, especially its role in fomenting social integration and morale (Wilson, 1971: 14). In short, Rousseau's civil religion was intended as a kind of surrogate religion, but one that concerns itself with moral and civic duties to other individuals. Whatever beliefs individuals have pertaining to their own redemption is of no interest to Rousseau. In fact, civil religion "is silent concerning man's duties toward himself" (Masters, 1968:88). It is only when individuals' lives "are touched by the requirements of the common good, [that] they must accommodate their personal views to public needs" (DeLue, 1997: 157). In such a case, everyone is asked to accept and support the doctrines of civil religion, for without a religion civil society becomes extremely vulnerable. Its dogmas are a "minimum requirement" of good citizenship (Macfarlane, 1970: 68). Individuals who violate civic responsibilities and citizen norms can be removed from society. Rousseau decrees that those who break the social compact "must be removed by exile as a violator of the compact, or by death as a public enemy" (Rousseau, [1762] 1973: 190).

From Rousseau's standpoint, civil religion would define a common morality and help maintain a sense of community and cohesiveness among members of a society. It would make possible a common basis "that could sustain a community's quest to define and to maintain the general good" (DeLue, 1997: 157). Civil religion would inspire feelings conducive to civic virtue. It would affirm and foment, in short, those sentiments that motivate individuals "to respect and uphold the contract and its laws" (Noone, 1980: 140).

Having distinguished between traditional religion or religions of salvation (a personal and purely private faith satisfying individual needs) and the civic creed (a national, public faith for the common good), Rousseau leaves no doubt that the latter has to be imposed. It is the responsibility of the state to have its cult, to fix its dogmas, and to force them upon its citizens without "explanation or comment." This is necessary to minimize social division, and to maximize social stability and social solidarity. Civil religion in a Rousseauan sense, is essentially a political religion whose function is to act as the cult of the civic community, and as the pillar of the state. Rousseau, in fact, conceives civil religion essentially an instrumental political phenomenon to "secure loyalty to a contingent social order" (Wilson, 1971: 17).

Rousseau suggests that a belief in God is essential for the common good.[8] It instills both the fear that evil will be punished and the hope that virtue will be rewarded. In this sense, his notion of civil religion is "religious." However, it is also religious in another sense. It declares the sanctity of the social contract, the sacredness of the law, and citizens' obligation to be religiously disposed to "love their duties." The notion of the sanctity of the contract presupposes not only "a belief in a God who sanctifies it" (Noone, 1980: 49), but also a transcendent source of political obligation, and a transcendent source of public morality. However, as Hammond has noted (1980a: 43), it is at the same time "civil" because it forces or encourages feelings of sociability necessary to be both "a good citizen [and] a faithful subject." It is civil again because it is concerned with citizenship and with the unity and cohesion of the social body.

It should be stressed, once again, that Rousseau's objective is essentially political, not religious. He is aware that there can no longer be "any exclusive national religion" holding a monopoly of religious authority. In fact, he favours religious pluralism, or the official toleration of religious differences. However, his original question recurs: How can individuals be brought together in a secular and increasingly pluralistic society? How can the modern state be legitimized? These are two basic questions that dominate the whole of Rousseau's doctrine.

Noone (1980: 145) notes that Rousseau realized that religious divisions could be transcended only by shifting the focus of religious devotion. That is, by generating a deep fervour for an exclusively worldly goal: "a love of country independent of, but not necessarily contrary to, a love of God." He argues that Rousseau saw the need of strengthening the social tie between citizens and the state "by encouraging a type of emotional patriotism best exemplified by Sparta." In the process, Rousseau ended up investing the nation and the state with a religious aura, and elevating citizenship to quasi-sacred heights. This helps understand why Rousseau has been referred to as the "prophet of nationalism." As Sherover explains, Rousseau's notion of "citizenship entails that of patriotism." He has also been called the prophet of nationalism because of the central place he gives to the common national interest (Sherover, 1984: 212 n. 343).

In short, Rousseau's answer to the problem of legitimation and social solidarity in the modern world is the creation of a national civic religion, capable of binding all individuals to the state. Rousseau's intention was not to create a religion strictly analogous to traditional religions. Civil religion was not to be just another faith—it was to be a religion specifically designed to prop up the political order (i.e., the state). The civic profession of faith would serve both as religion prescribing "the true cult of the Divinity" and also as the "cult of the Legislator, the divine ordering force in human affairs" (Henry, 1979: 172). Noone is right in affirming that the pragmatic importance of this religion is "purely and simply secular." One may also add that is purely and simply political. The civil creed was not created for the sake of the individual. Rather, it was intended to solve questions of public order and discipline and to support and sustain the state.[9] Citizens are told, and to a large extent forced, to "love their duties." But the duties Rousseau has in mind are not religious. Had Rousseau's intention been "more religious than secular," Noone notes, he would have created a version more in tune with the pure and uncorrupted faith of the Gospels. Clearly this would have run counter to Rousseau's purposes, for the Gospels preach "the brotherhood of all men," encouraging a global and cosmopolitan loyalty. However, cosmopolitan brotherhood is incompatible with absolute commitment to a specific national polity (Noone, 1980: 149-51). In short, while there is little doubt that Rousseau's objective is essentially secular and political, he promotes it via a religiously enforced civic creed that, he believes, is required for social unity and true political health. In other words, he remains convinced that a religiously based source of legitimation is absolutely essential. Paradoxically, Rousseau ends up creating a twin version of the religion of the citizen that he had originally rejected.

This blunder represents an ironic lack of vision on the part of Rousseau. While he recognizes that the religion of the citizen places people in a "natural" state of warfare and may lead to "sacred" acts of killing, he does not foresee that his own version of civil religion may become as tyrannous and bloodthirsty as the religion of the citizen that he rejects. The sovereign, Rousseau claims, after fixing the articles of the civic faith, cannot "compel" anyone to believe them. Yet, he can banish from the state those who refuse to believe. Indeed, the state can extend its iron arm even further. Those who "behave" as if they do not believe the dogmas should be "punished by death" (Rousseau, [1762] 1973: 273, 276). While he is very tolerant with reference to spiritual issues, he becomes utterly intolerant concerning civic ones.

The most serious problem is that the dogmas of civil religion cannot be changed, for Rousseau refers to the civil creed as "though it were some sort of a priori condition of society itself" (Noone, 1980: 135). Citizens are forced to accept them for fear of banishment or death. Non-believers are automatically exiled. I will come back to this point later in my discussion of state-directed civil religions.

If my reading of Rousseau is correct, there is a high degree of similarity between the religion of the citizen and civil religion. They both lend themselves to political abuse and may lead to the "furies of fanaticism" (to use his own words) and widespread bloodshed. In the final analysis they are of the same nature, and come close to being one and the same religion. They may not be identical twins, but they are certainly political siblings. That this is so should come as no surprise. In the *Geneva Manuscript* (an earlier version of *The Social Contract*), Rousseau anticipates that the "advantages of the religion of man and the citizen will be combined" (cited in Beiner, 1993: 634). What is surprising, however, is the lack of attention that scholars have given to this point. As mentioned earlier, out of a massive literature on civil religion, only a few articles allude to the implications of Rousseau's doctrine (Casanova, 1994; Demerath and Williams, 1985; Gehrig, 1981b; Giner, 1993; Hammond, 1974; Wilson, 1979).

Rousseau's Ideal Citizen

In *The Social Contract* Rousseau conceives society as originating in, or being based on, an agreement between free individuals and the state. He believes that individuals entering into the social contract do not renounce their liberty. Rather, they entrust it to a "new moral person"—the Sovereign State (Cole, 1973: xxiv). The state becomes, in Rousseau's own words, a *"persona ficta"* (Rousseau, [1762] 1973: 177). Man loses his *natural liberty* in order to gain *civil liberties*. Natural liberty depends on the strength of each individual to attain what he wishes; civil liberty, by contrast, is "limited by the general will," not by force (178). Rousseau conceives the general will as the common interest or collective will of a free society. The general will is concerned with the good of the community as a whole, with social obligations and civic morality, not with purely selfish interests (Macfarlane, 1970: 65). So, civil liberty gives man "moral" freedom, and "makes him truly master of himself." When individuals fall prey to their own impulses or appetites they become mere slaves, while submission to the general will or the law is true liberty (Rousseau, [1762] 1973: 178). Rousseau assumes that when individuals submit themselves to the general will they are their own masters, for they obey nobody but themselves.

Rousseau makes a distinction between a "general will" and a "particular will." The former, as already noted, is oriented towards the good of the community, the latter towards its own good without reference to the interests and wishes of the collectivity. Once the general will becomes law, it is morally binding on all individuals. The pre-eminence of the general will is, according to Rousseau, the first public principle and the "fundamental rule of government." Rousseau concedes that "man's particular interest" may speak a different language from the "common interest."

This would happen when man's particular will (as a private individual) may be contrary to the general will he has as a public citizen. It would be unjust and damaging for the body politic, Rousseau warns, if an individual is allowed to "enjoy the rights of citizenship" without being willing to fulfill the "duties" he owes to the state (Rousseau, [1762] 1973: 123, 177).

Thus, in theoretical terms Rousseau's doctrine expresses the view that the state is based not on power, but on the will of its members. Power is in the hands of the "collective sovereign," that is, the people (Cole, 1973: xxv). But while the contract gives sovereignty to the people, it is the political community as a whole that is sovereign, not its individual members (Noone, 1980: 18). Recognizing that the idea attached to sovereignty has an "abstract and collective existence," Rousseau indicates in the *Geneva Manuscript,* that it falls in the hands of the state to execute what the "sovereign want[s] in the manner that he require[s]" (Rousseau, [1762] 1973: 281, 283). Later, in *The Social Contract,* he reiterates this idea by insisting that the social contract "gives the body politic absolute power over all its members" (Rousseau, [1762] 1973: 186).

As a member of a society based on a social contract, every individual is under the obligation to act and behave as a "good citizen," so as to serve the common good. A good citizen is a virtuous individual who is capable of overcoming his "selfish motives" or "sectional interest"and subordinate his particular will to the general will. A good citizen, in short, is morally obliged by the social contract. Rousseau, in fact, conceives the general will in strictly ethical terms—that is, as a "principle of moral conduct applied to political behaviour." In pragmatic terms, it means that "the General Will of the State is final in relation to its own citizens " (Cole, 1973: xxxiv-vi). In other words, Rousseau's perception of the ideal citizen is that of an individual "completely absorbed by the state" (Noone, 1980: 140).

How can citizens be forced to speak the same language of the general will and still remain free? How can social stability be maintained? This is the fundamental problem *The Social Contract* (particularly the chapter on civil religion) tries to address.

Rousseau's answer seems quite simple: instill in each citizen a profound love for his country and its laws, and make the knot of the social tie indestructible. For the social tie to be morally binding and legally upheld, laws are essential. They are the "unique motive force" of the body politic. Without them, the state "is only a body without a soul; it exists and cannot act " (Rousseau, [1762] 1973: 291). Simply put, Rousseau assumes that individuals sharing a common civic morality will willingly submit to the general will, seek the common interest, and be law-abiding citizens. Each individual, not "naturally" but through social agreement or convention, will wish the common good and avoid public harm. To attain this aim, however, the citizenry needs to be educated in the qualities of good citizenship. Good citizenship, in turn, has to be imposed and enforced through what Willaime (1993) has called *L'Etat éducateur*. Good citizenship, imposed from above, is the fundamental underlying principle of the civil creed, and one of the functions Rousseau assigns to civil religion in the modern world. In short, *The Social Contract* focuses on the political implications of public civility and morality. Its unifying thread is the need for a common ideology for a cohesive legitimate society. In the final analysis, civil religion in Rousseauan terms is nothing less than a historically specific state ideology, but of a particular variety—it has a transcendent focus and an element of sacredness built into it.[10]

As Noone (1980: 154) has written, there is something dramatically "sad" about the civil creed. In previous chapters, Rousseau presents a theory of political obligation, founded in the liberal idea of the "sovereignty of man." His main concern is to discover and clearly delineate the most fundamental principles of political rule that ought to underlie the organization of the state. Rules and obligations are based on social conventions, the most important one being the social contract. This special type of convention celebrates individual autonomy and freedom. The contract, in fact, "promises to reconcile freedom and obligation" (Noone, 1980: 5). Individuals voluntarily join together to form a political community. The resulting political community is not a natural phenomenon; it is an act of will on the part of each individual.

However, Rousseau's conception of the general will and the role he assigns to the state is essentially authoritarian. On the surface it would appear that the social contract coerces the individual "only to the extent that he voluntarily accepts this coercion" (Noone, 1980: 154). The problem is that Rousseau assumes that the general will is "always upright and always tends to the public advantage." While it may be "often deceived," it is "never corrupted" (Rousseau, [1762] 1973: 184-85). Add to this that the sovereign power is "absolute, sacred, and inviolable" (188), together with his argument that authority must remain undivided, and that the "Sovereign is sole judge of what is important" for the community (186), and it is not difficult to perceive the justification of authoritarianism and coercion. Moreover, Rousseau shatters the most basic principles of liberalism, for "consent once given is now irrevocable, and it is God, not man, that sanctifies the contract" (Noone, 1980: 154).

Rousseau's theory has a profound built in tension between his liberal ideas (the right of every individual against any restriction) and his antiliberal prescriptions (the total surrender of the individual to the general will and to the state). Indeed it is not difficult to discern in his writings a permanent conflict between the individual and the citizen, between the natural man and the social man, between natural freedom and civil freedom, and finally, between a particular egoistic will and a general unselfish will. This, of course, is neither a novel nor a surprising revelation. Several distinguished scholars have argued that Rousseau's intention of trying to harmonize the tension between the individual and the citizen remained, throughout his intellectual career, an "insurmountable antithesis," one that he was never able to resolve (Merquior, 1980: 46).

Durkheim on Civil Religion

More than a hundred years later, Durkheim also utilized the notion of civil religion, although he never mentioned the term itself. In *The Elementary Forms of Religious Life* he indicates that the purpose of his work is to study, analyze, and explain "the most primitive and simple religion which is actually known" ([1912] 1961: 13). In his view, the most primitive religious system is to be found in the totemism of the Arunta. He is particularly interested in investigating the beliefs and rites that compose it.

For Durkheim, it is impossible to separate totemism from a social order organized on the basis of clans. In fact, "totemism and the clan mutually imply each other" ([1912] 1961: 194-95).The totem serves a dual symbolic function: it expresses society and it has a religious character. The totem is not only a collective label but the symbol or "flag" of the clan. At the same time, it is the concrete, external expression of what he calls the "totemic principle or god" (236). The collective totem, Durkheim notes, represents the "civil status" of each individual, a status that is not acquired by conscious design, but by birthright (188). He traces the origins of the totemic filiation matrilineally (to the "uterine line") for, at the dawn of the human race, individuals "had no other totem than that of [their] mother" (289). While the totem constitutes the basis of "the moral life" of the clan, the totemic principle is "a moral power" (219).

Durkheim notes that because god and society "are only one," the clan simultaneously symbolizes both (236). This religious and civic unity is best observed during the periodic gatherings and assemblies of the Australian primitives. It is in the "midst of these effervescent" gatherings, and "out of this effervescence itself," that the idea of religion seems to emerge (250).This fundamentally social event, the assembly of the clan, not only inspires a religious feeling but also contributes to the maintenance of social integration. Its function is the preservation of the clan's self-identity and social cohesion. The clan's unity and cohesion is not the result of coercive forces; rather, it comes "solely from…having the same name and the same emblem" (194).

The major argument of *The Elementary Forms* is that religion— its origin, function and meaning—can be understood and explained only by reference to social forces. The origin of religion "is shown to be the 'effervescence' of the periodic assemblies of society; the function is seen as social integration; and the meaning is understood to be society's symbolic worship of itself" (Breytspraak, 1973: 76). Durkheim ([1912] 1961: 62) defines religion as a "unified system of beliefs and practices," relating to "sacred things," which integrates into "one single moral community called a Church, all those who adhere to them." Religion is the most important integrative force of society. It is indispensable in any social order, for it fosters the shared beliefs, sentiments, and values required to promote social cohesion, stability, and solidarity.

Thus, Durkheim identifies the heart of religion, any religion, with the experience of sociality itself (Cristi and Dawson, 1996: 322). Not surprisingly, he finds religion to be the origin of "all that is essential in society." But, more importantly, he believes that "the idea of society is the soul of religion" (Durkheim, [1912] 1961: 466). Durkheim claims that the very constitution of society is by definition a religious phenomenon. From his point of view, religious and civil society are "coterminous"—they both have the same or coincident boundaries. They both bind people together in a moral community, and they both represent a "collectivity that [is] nothing if not religious at its base" (Demerath and Williams 1985: 156). He is convinced that as long as individuals join together to form a group, there will always be some common religion or some common faith between them.

Durkheim claims that because "there is something eternal in religion," because religion is an inherent part of any social group, individuals have a "need" to profess their faith collectively. He thus argues that there "can be no society which does not feel the need of upholding and reaffirming at regular intervals the collective sentiments and collective ideas which make its unity and its personality" ([1912] 1961: 474-75). Indeed, Durkheim believes that the moral unity of a society can be achieved, and enhanced, through ceremonies and gatherings where individuals "reaffirm in common their common sentiments." Gatherings, in turn, should be revitalized through rites that are ways of behaving that spring to life only at the heart "of the assembled groups." These rites constitute the means by which the social bonding of the group is reasserted. They create, nourish, and re-create particular mental states within the group

(22). Hence, civic rituals arise that are, if not identical, very similar to religious ceremonies.

Sacred rites, Durkheim argues, are found in any society. They perform the same function today that they did in "lower" societies: they secure and preserve social and moral order by uniting the collectivity around some common values. They have the capacity to transport the individual into an extraordinary state of consciousness. It is under these "stimulating" influences that "society makes itself felt" (Durkheim, [1912] 1961: 241). This is the reason why Durkheim finds no essential difference between an assembly of Australian aborigines or an assembly of modern individuals. Their objectives are the same, and so are the results and the processes used to attain them. Hence, he sees no difference between festivities of Christians commemorating the birth of Christ, or of Jews recalling the Exodus, or of citizens honouring some great national event. It follows that the collective representations of the Arunta, their beliefs and rites, are no different from collective representations in modern societies stressing, for example, the glories of the past or the promulgation of a new "legal system" (Durkheim, [1912] 1961: 475).

In Durkheim's view, both religious ceremonies and mundane feasts produce a state of enthusiasm and excitement that are akin to "the religious state." Thus, the very idea of a religious ritual is often associated with the idea of a feast. At the same time, every feast, including those that have non-religious foundations, share certain qualities of the religious ritual (Durkheim, [1912] 1961: 427-28). For this reason, he believes that "all parties, political, economic or confessional," periodically hold meetings so that their followers can renovate their enthusiasm and their "common faith" (240).

If we cannot understand civic festivities in this light, Durkheim warns us, it is because we are going through a transitional phase, one of "moral mediocrity" ([1912] 1961: 475). By moral mediocrity he means that we have lost a sense of continuity with the past, and we have also lost the sense of community that characterized pre-modern societies. Durkheim, in fact, laments that modern individuals do not show enthusiasm for the "great things of the

past." He suggests that the "creative effervescence" of our pred-
ecessors is in the process of becoming extinct. What is even
worse, individuals have lost the need to keep alive the collective
memory. For Durkheim this represents a serious danger, and it is
in this context that he argues that festivals and celebrations are
essential to keep collective representations alive. They are necessary to rekindle the great principles, values, and ideas that have
guided humanity (475).

Durkheim is convinced that behind major historical turning
points there has always been an upsurge of "collective effervescence." Indeed, he attributes to collective effervescence events as
complex and diverse as the French Scholasticism of medieval
France, the Protestant Reformation, the French Revolution, and
even the socialist disturbances of the nineteenth century
(Hughey, 1983: 177 n. 14). In his view, during great revolutionary
or creative periods, social solidarity tends to be stronger. The
intense abnormal activity that results from revolutionary fervour
acts as a stimulus on the individual. When individuals find
themselves in the "midst of an assembly," breathing a "common
passion," they are capable of sentiments and actions that would
have been impossible for them to achieve on their own. They are
lifted out of their "normal level." Under the influence of collective upheavals, "men become different." In fact, Durkheim
locates at the root of collective effervescence acts ranging from
"superhuman heroism [to] bloodthirsty barbarism" (Durkheim,
[1912] 1961: 240-41).

Durkheim sees the totemic cult as a powerful moral and collective force. It is through this cult that individuals become
united, not only by kinship or ties of blood, but "by a community of interests and tradition." When they assemble to celebrate,
they become "conscious of their moral unity" ([1912] 1961: 432).
Modern individuals are not very different. To be sure, their sense
of the sacred is not the same: it might be attached to ideas, flags,
or heads of states rather than to rocks, springs, or ancestral ani-
mals (Wuthnow, 1994: 2). In other words, the religiously based
conscience collective fades away, but the sense of the sacred
remains. For human beings have an infinite capacity for "creat-

ing sacred things out of ordinary ones." As an example, Durkheim notes the sacred character that has been attributed to nobles and princes and the unique deference given to them (Durkheim, [1912] 1961: 243-44).

So, in modern society, moral beliefs, rituals, and public festivities still reinforce identification with and commitment to values, but of a different kind than in premodern societies. Collective effervescence may be experienced through values such as patriotism and national loyalty, but the sentiments felt in these circumstances, Durkheim would argue, are closely related to the religious sentiments experienced by Australian aborigines. In fact, Durkheim seems to suggest that the modern form of totemism is to be found in nationalism—a clearly new and distinct type of collective activity. As Purdy has noted (1982:309), from Durkheim's perspective patriotic feelings towards the nation are, to a certain extent, the modern equivalent of the moral solidarity experienced by the Arunta of Australia through loyalty to the clan.

While Durkheim emphasizes the importance of rites, assemblies, and festivities, he also stresses the significance of education. In several of his writings he examines the essence of a secular, national creed. In *Education and Sociology* ([1922] 1956: 107), he declares that the role of French public schools is to "interpret and express the French spirit." In Durkheim's view, teachers not only need a profound and exceptional sense of vocation, they should also understand that they have a moral duty to perform. The teacher is the "agent of a great moral person who surpasses him: it is society. Just as the priest is the interpreter of his god, the teacher is the interpreter of the great moral ideas of his time and of his country" (89). Three years later, in *Moral Education* ([1925] 1961: 260), he insists on the "need for [the] devotion and sacrifice that lies at the root of all moral life," and suggests that service to and sacrifice for one's country are values that should be transmitted to future generations. He maintains that French public schools must be "the guardians par excellence" of the French national character (3-4). As Wallace has noticed, Durkheim consistently reiterates the need for the love of the country, and he sees "the creation of patriotic citizens as the primary aim of the public schools." Wallace's article expresses eloquently Durkheim's contribution to a secular ethic of citizenship, and to the French spirit of nationalism. Durkheim's work was required reading in the normal schools of France. He had a profound influence on public schools and teachers' colleges, and his ideas on education were actively supported by the state (Wallace, 1973: 4-5; see also Richter, 1960).

Durkheim, along with other social thinkers at the beginning of the twentieth century, holds an evolutionary view of society. He shares with many of his contemporaries the certainty that society has progressed in a unilinear fashion, advancing from a "lower" type to the modern industrial form. Thinkers such as Herbert Spencer and the utilitarian economists were convinced that an unbridgeable distance separated the premodern and modern forms of society. They believed that the "natural" and "spontaneous" sense of moral community of traditional societies (*Gemeinschaft*) had been irrevocably replaced by the modern variant (*Gesellschaft*), "produced by 'the wholly external stimulus of the state' and based upon the egoistic, and hence nonmoral, pursuit of individual self-interest" (Hughey, 1983: 11-12). As Hughey observes, in the former type, the social order was perceived to be a natural phenomenon, while in the latter, it was "artificially" produced—that is, the result of a conscious effort. On this point, Durkheim takes a different stance, for he remains convinced that the true nature of society cannot and does not change. He observes that "the life of large social agglomerations is just as natural as that of smaller groupings. It is no less internal. Outside of these purely individual actions (egoistic activity) there is a collective activity in our contemporary societies which is just as natural as that of smaller societies of previous ages. It is certainly different; it constitutes a distinct type, but however different they may be, there is no difference in nature between these two varieties of the same genus." To this, he adds, "we have to choose: if society is originally a natural phenomenon, it stays such until the end of its life" (cited in Hughey, 1983: 12).

Although the true nature of society remains the same, Durkheim predicts a major restructuring of the sacred. The profound social and structural transformations that had taken place (i.e., social and religious differentiation, increasing moral density, and a highly differentiated division of labour) would also affect the way the sacred is experienced in modern society. While the ancient religious symbols had celebrated collective values that were of interest to the group as a whole, Durkheim envisions that the sacred would eventually be nested within the individual. He conceptualizes social solidarity and integration in the modern world less in terms of collective sentiments and more in terms of the bonds between increasingly autonomous yet "interdependent individuals." This type of integration would find its expression "in correspondingly individualized symbols of the sacred" (Beckford, 1989: 26).

Indeed, Durkheim comes to the conclusion that individualism represents the moral and religious expression of the *conscience collective* of the modern age. Moral individualism, which the great thinkers of the past had sought to achieve, and which eventually became embodied in the Declaration of the Rights of Man, is to become the basis of the "moral catechism" of modernity, the source of a new morality. Durkheim stresses that moral individualism is not to be confused with the "utilitarian egoism of Spencer and of the economists," for it involves a morality of cooperation and a profound respect for others. It is not the "glorification...of the self but of the individual in general" (Durkheim, [1898] 1973: 44-48). Because a sign of the modern age is that everyone attends to their own private affairs in order to satisfy personal demands, "we make our way, little by little, toward a state, nearly achieved as of now, where the members of a single social group will have nothing in common among themselves except their humanity, except the constitutive attributes of the human person (*personne humaine*) in general" (51). In Durkheim's *cult of the individual*, each person is the repository of the sacred, and the symbol and source of a new morality.

Durkheim knows (as Rousseau did a century earlier) that religion in modern society "tends to embrace a smaller and smaller portion of social life" (in Hughey, 1983: 17). He is aware that religious institutions have been gradually losing power, and he recognizes the critical role of industrialization in the accelerated rate of decline. However, he does not come to the conclusion that the *"functions* which had traditionally been fulfilled by religion [are] also in decline" (Beckford, 1989: 26). On the contrary, while he is convinced that religion's influence has diminished, he is no less certain that it will never completely wither away. Religion has for him a permanent existence. Religion, in fact, is an essential feature of any human society. He acknowledges, however, that its form is not static "that the religion of yesterday could not be that of tomorrow" (Durkheim, [1898] 1973: 51). Thus, he remains assured that no matter what form religion might take, societies will continue to possess a moral and religious foundation.

While Durkheim accepts the belief in the decline of religion and in the inevitable advance of secularization, he does not exclude the possibility of the reappearance of a universal religion, once the "moral mediocrity" of the modern age is overcome. He is hopeful, in fact, that local nationalism will eventually be replaced by internationalism, or by the "religion of humanity" (Giner, 1993: 32; Wallace, 1973: 9).

Just like Rousseau before him, Durkheim is confronted with a serious obstacle. If for Rousseau the pressing issue had been how to justify the need for religion in an increasingly secularized world, Durkheim's riddle is how can the individual, who is becoming more and more autonomous, "be at once more individual and more solidary?" (Durkheim, [1893] 1964: 37). How can social solidarity be maintained and revitalized in a world where everybody attends to their own personal business? Durkheim's answer is that the harmonizing functions that religion performed in premodern societies could be fulfilled by different agents in industrial societies. He expects that religious institutions will be replaced by educational institutions (Wallace, 1973: 3). Additionally, he believes that intermediary associations (including religious groups) will play a major function in overcoming the problem of "anomie."

Durkheim discusses anomie for the first time in the context of the "abnormal forms" of the division of labour brought about by the rapid development of industrialization and capitalism. In his view, both processes were characterized by a lack of moral discipline, and an absence of precise rules guiding "the relations...between social functions." Anomie was especially evident in periods of crisis, industrial or commercial, and in the chronic conflictual relations between labour and capital. Because of the drastic speed with which industrial transformations had taken place, "interests in conflict [had] not yet had time to achieve equilibrium" (in Lukes, 1973: 172-73). To ameliorate the ills of the modern industrial world, Durkheim proposes to restore the guild (occupational associations) in order to reintroduce morality into economic relations and bring "men a little peace, peace in their hearts and peace in their mutual relations" (in Lukes, 1973: 267).

From Durkheim's point of view, the state is first and foremost a moral agent, but it is too distant from the people. Durkheim, thus, is concerned with the danger that the state might be "closed in upon itself" and, as a result, be separated from the people. Professional and occupational associations would solve this problem. They would play a vital role acting as agents between the state and the individual and bridging the distance between them. Guilds would not only "facilitate communication," but, at the same time, they would provide a voice for the "less organized"sectors of society (Giddens, 1986: 7-8). In short, intermediary associations would solve the issue of the remoteness of the state as the source of morality for the masses (Beckford, 1989: 30). Durkheim also proposes to recreate the collective effervescence of the past by allowing individuals to relive the emotional experience of the sacred through periodic gatherings. In this form, the modern individual, interdependent yet isolated, would have an opportunity to renew and strengthen the bonds attaching him to society (Durkheim, [1912] 1961: 240).

Durkheim's premise is that civil religion is not something to be *imposed* on the individual. Rather it is a cultural and social force *acting* upon him. Citizens are not *expected* to endorse the creed (or the religious sentiments associated with collective gatherings); Durkheim assumes that they spontaneously or naturally do so. Civil religion springs from society itself and is carried on every time the group meets and celebrates together. Social representations, values, beliefs, ingrained in the collective mind, are carried from generation to generation. It is not the power of the sovereign (or the state), but the power of society that acts upon the individual.

The civic creed, in Durkheim's terms, has its own life; it is naturally diffused throughout the whole society. Loyalty to the group is spontaneously affirmed every time the group meets together and celebrates. The resulting social community is a natural phenomenon; it does not require an act of will on the part of each individual. Individuals join together to reaffirm common values. Civil religion presumably affirms values that are already widely shared.

Durkheim never asked himself the question of who control collective rites, what individuals are the most committed to them, how commitment is enforced, or who benefits by their continued existence. Neither did he question the idea that religion may serve not society in general, but particular groups or individuals (Hughey, 1983: 172). In other words, Durkheim's theory does not consider a range of phenomena such as conflict, exclusion of certain groups, coercion, or the imposition of dominant values and the power of dominant groups.

Durkheim's contribution to political sociology has not been very significant. As Giddens (1986: 1) has noted, in his private life he was only marginally concerned with politics, and during his intellectual career he did not produce any major work dealing exclusively with political theory. Yet, ever since Durkheim, sociologists have been intrigued with the idea, or the possibility, that civic or national symbol systems "represent a functional alternative to traditional religious systems as sacred legitimations of the social order" (Stauffer, 1973: 415).

Religion, Social Order, and the State

In the preceding discussion I have stressed the central ideas of Rousseau and Durkheim concerning civil religion. Any attempt at a critical analysis must be placed within a broader evaluation of their theories and their political consequences. But analysts have made little effort to confront the wall of separation that exists between Rousseau and Durkheim on the civil religion issue.[11] As a result, there have been even fewer efforts to recognize different varieties of civil religion.

It should be explicitly emphasized that both Rousseau and Durkheim are concerned with the so-called problem of order. An examination of their writings leaves no doubt that for both thinkers religion plays an important role in the solution of this problem: both conceive religion as necessary for social integration and societal harmony. Simple as it seems, this is a fact that has generally tended to be overlooked. Scholars refer to the integrative function of civil religion as if it were a Durkheimian design. Few seem to notice the radically divergent conceptions these thinkers have of religion and integration, and the role they assign to the state in accomplishing social order.

Durkheim is overwhelmingly concerned with the problem of morality. For him, a democratic state is, or ought to be, the main vehicle through which the values of moral individualism are implemented. He defines the state as the "organ of social thought," the "ego" of the collective consciousness. He emphasizes that the industrial division of labour must be imbued with "moral controls." These controls must be under the guidance and moral authority of the state (Giddens, 1986: 13, 28). The state is for him "the institutional form which replaces that of the church" in premodern societies. Giddens notes that Durkheim places "considerable emphasis upon the 'cognitive' as opposed to the 'active' significance of the State" (9). This means that, for Durkheim, the state is not founded on force. The state exists for the moral development of its individual members. As a moral agency, its role is to guarantee and advance the rights embodied in moral individualism. Moral individualism, in turn, has a significant role to play above and beyond the "changing torrent" or flux of particular opinions in the advancement of the religion of humanity, and, hence, in the advancement of national and international harmony (Durkheim, [1898] 1973: 52). Thus, the state is defined in terms of its ends, not the means at its disposal. It is far from being merely an association which "organizes domination" and violence, as Weber would argue (Weber, [1919] 1958: 82).

Not surprisingly, Durkheim focuses almost exclusively on the nature of moral ideas, moral conscience, and moral society. He concentrates primarily on the kind of moral authority conferred by the state and by religious systems and symbols. Obviously, the moral and religious values that emerge "naturally" support the political order, but his concern is moral authority, not political power. For him, any religion, "well[s] up naturally from the bottom, from the very depths of the social experience itself" (Demerath and Williams, 1985: 156). Simply put, religion is no more than the expression of a spontaneous civic order and societal processes. Religion, in Durkheim's terms, is inconceivable as a political resource.

From this Durkheimian proposition a series of problems arise. For example, one difficulty stemming directly from this assumption centres on the lack of attention scholars have given to the issue of whether civil religion (anywhere and anytime) is a spontaneous form of civic faith, or whether it can be conceived as a political phenomenon within a larger political frame of reference. In the former view, civil religion would "emerge as a function *of* societal processes; while in the second instance, civil religion might be viewed as functional *for* the civic order" (Garrett 1975, cited in Bourg, 1976: 142). This oversight is hardly surprising if we consider that Durkheim's ideas have provided the model for the analysis and interpretation of the civil religion phenomenon.

Had Rousseau's views been studied more closely or taken into consideration, a very different interpretation could be proposed. Strictly speaking, Rousseau is not concerned with the psychological or even collective needs that religion satisfies. Rousseau's main concern is the nature of legitimation and political power. In Rousseau's terms, civil religion has a political role to play. Being aware of religion's potential as an instrument of political stability and social cohesion, Rousseau advocates an imposed civic faith *for* the civic order. Civil religion is crucial for the promotion of political unity "without which no State or government will ever be rightly constituted" (Rousseau, [1762] 1973: 271). This civic unity is by no means a spontaneous process. Rather, it is the outcome of conscious political practice. Accordingly, Rousseau designs a blueprint for the creation of an authoritarian religion "of and for the state" (Demerath and Williams, 1985: 155). From his perspective, religion (including civil religion) is nothing more than the medium required to strengthen and support the state.

As mentioned earlier, Rousseau argues that while the sovereign "can compel no one to believe [the articles of civic faith], it can banish from the State whoever does not believe them" (1762/1973: 276). Banishment is necessary not to preserve piety but to avoid "antisocial" behaviour. Taking this idea a step further, Rousseau proposes that antisocial beings ought to be removed permanently from society. What would happen if an individual "after publicly recognizing these dogmas, behaves as if he does not believe them?" Rousseau's solution is simple, straightforward, and certainly frightening: "let him be punished by death" (276). Antisocial behaviour deserves to be punished because it disrupts the social order. This is a serious offence, for the social order is "a sacred right which is the basis of all other rights." This right, Rousseau knows, "does not come from nature." Rather, it must "be founded on conventions" (165-66). Civil religion, necessary to guarantee social order, is a central element of those conventions.

Rousseau's prescription has profound political consequences. He gives the state unlimited power to intervene, to punish, to put people to death, all in the name of preserving the common good. It is precisely this unlimited power of interference that may lead to despotism. In Vaughan's words, such "is the doctrine which brought a thousand troubles on Rousseau in his life, and has never ceased to weigh upon his memory in death. The moral objections which it provokes are glaring. They may be summed up in one word—Persecution" (1962: 89).

I am not arguing that Rousseau's entire philosophy is antiliberal and authoritarian. Rather, I maintain, and several authors agree, that his section on civil religion is an "embarrassment for those who otherwise admire Rousseau" (Noone, 1980: 6). Distinguished Rousseauan scholars, such as Charles E. Vaughan, and even "friendly critics" such as Alfred Cobban have not remained silent. They agree that the chapter on civil religion is not only "unfortunate" but it is also responsible for charges against Rousseau depicting him as "the apostle of tyranny and an enemy to liberty in the state" (Cobban, 1934, in Noone, 1980: 133). Merquior (1980: 37) admits that Rousseau's critics have accused him of advocating "state idolatry." While he himself does not agree with this claim, he notes that it is precisely this tendency towards state worship in Rousseau's work that not only separates Jean Jacques from the founding fathers of what he calls "qualified liberalism," but has "greatly contributed to...the portrayal of [him] as the originator of Jacobin fanaticism."

Civil religion, in Rousseau's view, is essential to integrate all individuals into a secular cult that will make them love their duties. Yet, in contrast to Durkheim, he realizes that the civic profession of faith is not the expression of common beliefs through collective rituals. The beliefs and practices of civil religion are imposed from above and are expected to be accepted by everyone. Rousseau's solution is quite paradoxical for he formulates an antiliberal prescription for the modern polity that stands diametrically opposed to the democratic and, to a certain extent, liberal tradition he represents. Rousseau solves the problem he faces by "affirming simultaneously and inconsistently" the inalienable liberal right of religious freedom and freedom of speech, "which no sovereign has the right to abridge or control," and the demand for a purely civic creed whose dogmas are left entirely for the sovereign to arrange (Casanova, 1994: 60).

We have already seen that in Rousseau's terms the "will of the people," embodied in the collective sovereign, speaks with one voice, and every citizen has an absolute duty to obey its dictates.

The political machinery requires that individuals, as citizens, agree with the general will. In order to avoid the social contract from becoming no more than "an empty formula," it should be implicitly understood that "whoever refuses to obey the general will shall be compelled to do so by the whole body." Once the will of the people becomes law, it is not possible for someone to disagree. This means nothing less that individuals will be forced to be good citizens, forced to acquire civic virtues, and even "forced to be free" (Rousseau, [1762] 1973: 177). Only as a man (not as a citizen) does Rousseau allow the individual to differ from the common interest. But once all wills are united into a single one, and the general will is declared, it becomes "an act of Sovereignty and constitutes law" (183). The government will make sure that all citizens abide by the rules of the social contract. "Sovereignty is the law-making will; government, the force that executes its commands" (Merquior, 1980: 22). In other words, freedom, for those who happen to disagree with the collective will, really "melts into air." Robert Nisbet, commenting on the authoritarianism of the Rousseauan doctrine, rightly notes that Rousseau proclaimed freedom, "but freedom *from society* never *from the state!*" (cited in Merquior, 1980: 63).

As Gehrig (1981b: 6) has noted, initiated "by and under a political ruler," civil religion in Rousseau's terms, is intended to legitimize the polity without introducing a rival religious force. As a religion of "good citizenship," directed by the state, its primary function is to provide political legitimacy and political stability. Rousseau envisions civil religion both as a *source for* social cohesion and as a *force of* social coercion and control. Good citizenship (civic consensus) is to Rousseau what value consensus is to Durkheim. What is fundamentally different is their consensual models and the means for achieving them. Hence, the pervasive tendency in the literature on this subject to overlook Rousseau and to link the integrationist thesis primarily to Durkheim is, in my view, inaccurate.

Summing up, Rousseau and Durkheim tackle the civic religious issue and the relationship between state and civil society in radically different ways. Whereas in Durkheim's work the problem is posed in the context of morality, in Rousseau's writings the issue is primarily political. While Durkheim suggests that every society *naturally possesses* a religious foundation, Rousseau simply claims that every society *needs* one. For Durkheim a religious foundation is *inevitable*—a natural phenomenon. For Rousseau it is only *indispensable*—the result of social conventions. As a logical consequence, civil religion in Durkheim's terms need not be carefully designed or premeditated. To a large extent, it just happens. As an inherent ingredient of the *conscience collective*, civil religion is shared by the society as a whole—there is no need to impose it. Largely unconscious mechanisms are at work to unite, cohere, and give solidarity to the group. Durkheim's main focus is on the cultural and religious aspect of civil religion. Its most important dimension is social, not political. In Rousseau's terms, by contrast, it is a premeditated religion, specifically intended to force individuals to respect and uphold the social contract and its laws. It is my contention that while Rousseau coined the term *civil religion*, he created, in fact, a *political religion* for the use and benefit of the state.

CHAPTER TWO

American Civil Religion and the American Debate[1]

Although the term *civil religion* has a long European heritage, the American sociologist Robert Bellah is responsible for bringing the concept to the forefront of the American sociological landscape. His famous essay, "Civil Religion in America" (1967), sparked a long and heated debate that held academic attention for nearly two decades, and reached its peak with the American bicentennial in 1976 (Mathisen, 1989: 137). In Bellah's own words, this is an article he has "never subsequently been allowed to forget" (1978: 16).

The context for the debate (and what gave it so much of its moral earnestness) was the legitimation crisis facing American institutions, touched off by the combination of the disturbances of the Nixon years, the civil rights movement, the Vietnam War, and the Watergate scandal. However, the debate was not "just a war of words or a bicentennial theme." Rather, it was a "potentially far reaching conflict of basic theoretical conceptions with a

---

Notes to Chapter 2 are on pp. 246-50.

capacity for reorienting the field as a whole" (Demerath and Roof, 1976: 29-30).

Since Bellah's conception of civil religion is important for understanding the ambiguities and deficiencies of the sociological literature on this subject, I shall examine his ideas and the major developments and articulation of the debate. It is my hope that by the kind of closer reading of the literature undertaken in this chapter, it will become clear why Durkheim's ideas, not Rousseau's, have been deeply influential in the work of American scholars. By discussing Bellah's understanding of civil religion, which I submit, is radically opposed to Rousseaus' original formulation, I also hope to expose the dubious conceptual basis of the Bellah tradition.

The Rebirth of Civil Religion

The religious identity of Americans had captured the imagination of scholars and students of American society long before Bellah alluded to the religious character of American life. What became known as civil religion was already "out there," and constituted a major theme in the writings of several prominent American scholars. Progenitors of the concept include Robin Williams's *American Society: A Sociological Interpretation* (1951) which posited the idea of a "common religion" in America; Lloyd Warner's ([1953] 1974) analysis of the Memorial Day celebrations in "Yankee City"; the "common faith" of John Dewey (1934); and Sidney Mead's "the religion of the Republic" (1967/1974). In a similar vein, Will Herberg (1960; 1974) spoke of "the American Way of Life," and, of course, G.K. Chesterton advanced the idea that the United States was "the only nation...founded on a creed" and coined the phrase "a nation with the soul of a church"(cited in Mead, 1974: 45). At the same time, several distinguished historians such as Ralph Gabriel, Yehoshua Arieli, and Daniel Boorstin "assessed the religious dimension of 'nationalism,' the 'American creed,' the 'democratic faith,' and 'culture religion'" (Jones and Richey, 1974: 4). Seymour Lipset referred to "Americanism" or the "American

Creed" to characterize a distinct set of values that American hold with a quasi-religious fervour (1963: 178). In other words, prior to Bellah's work the idea of a civic-religious "faith" in America had been discussed in academic circles, but there was no common conceptual term to describe, analyze, and interpret it (Jones and Richey, 1974: 4; see also Hammond, 1976: 169-70). These authors had noticed a religious framework in terms of which the values of American existence were expressed and understood.

The civic-religious dimension of the American experience is often traced back to a blend of ideas stemming from its Puritan tradition and from the Enlightenment. These two different traditions (Puritanism and self-seeking utilitarianism) have been present in American history since colonial times. America was founded on the belief that colonists had been entrusted with a special mission: to establish a new social and political order, "the kingdom of God, in the New World, far away from the disorders and corruptions of the Old World" (Henry, 1979: 23). The self-understanding of the original colonists was derived from Judeo-Christian symbols such as "God's New Israel," a "chosen people," and a "covenanted nation." Originating in the Puritan idea of a covenant between God and society, America was to be a community of God, for the glory of God, and subject to his judgment. It was to be a "City upon a Hill," a beacon of light and a powerful example to the world (Henry, 1979: 23; Hughey, 1992, 1984, 1983). From the American Enlightenment, the settlers adopted such ideas as equality, self-determination, and the right to "life, liberty, and the pursuit of happiness." Another fundamental idea that came from the Enlightenment was the emphasis placed on the necessity of "a *virtuous* citizenry" if a democratic social order was to function properly and be preserved (Hughes, 1980: 77; Stauffer, 1975: 392). For the colonists, a virtuous citizen was an individual imbued with a sense of moral responsibility who was morally obliged to work for the good of the community. Civic virtue was equated with political obligations, and political obligations with a duty to God. Simply put, civic responsibilities became infused with ethical significance.

The Mayflower Compact, for example, enacted in 1620, had no constitutional legitimacy—"it established no political institutions, nor did it enact any legislation," but it served, nonetheless, as an "enabling act for the necessary laws and institutions" required for the general well-being of the community. It provided the guidelines for a righteous and divinely approved social order (Henry, 1979: 61). The good of the commonwealth depended on the obligation "of all men in society, publicly, and at stated seasons, to worship the SUPREME BEING, the great Creator and Preserver of the universe." Piety and morality were to be the crux of the civic order, and were considered fundamental for the preservation of a civil society entrusted with a divine mission (Henry, 1979: 72). The Declaration of Independence merely crystalized and embodied the political ideals and convictions that the founding fathers of the American nation had inherited from the early settlers.

The earliest religious groups in America were "sects by definition." From the very beginning, the nonconformist, persecuted, and resettled churches of Europe shared a pluralistic religious environment where there was no established church (Rice, 1980: 57). Puritanism played a pivotal role in legitimizing religious pluralism. It offered a "theological rationale" for eliminating any sort of religious monopoly. But Puritanism did more than this. It "forced onto society's agenda...the question of 'religious liberty,' the separation of church and state" (Hammond, 1974: 124).

These ideas eventually became embodied in the Constitution. The first clause of the First Amendment reads, "Congress shall make no law respecting an establishment of religion." And its second clause states "or prohibiting the free exercise thereof." The Constitution, therefore, prohibits "a religious establishment, [but] protects the free practice of religion." This freedom *in* religion, which started early in the history of the American nation, was the real intention of the founders of the republic (Bellah, 1980b: 7). Under religious freedom the new nation assumed the traditional function of "the church." Because the ethical and moral values of the nation could not be monopolized by any specific church, a different religion emerged—a belief system independent of both church and state (Mead, 1974: 66).

This early civic religion was never intended to be a cult directed and controlled by the government. Rather, it was left to each individual to worship according to his or her own conscience and moral principles. But it was an "American conviction," Henry notes, "that the good Christian is the good citizen" (1979: 72). Hence, from its earliest beginnings as a nation, Americans did not have to have their loyalties divided (or so their ideology suggested). They did not have to suffer the conflict and tension between religious beliefs and civic responsibility that Rousseau feared. In the Puritan tradition, a "'God-fearing' person was by definition a law-abiding person as well" (Hughey, 1984: 119). Americans could be good Christians and good citizens at the same time, for ultimately, "'Christian' and 'citizen' were...two ways of saying the same thing" (Bellah, 1980b: 6; see also Demerath and Williams, 1989: 35). Early settlers were convinced that they possessed "the truth." There was also a religious necessity of making this truth known to the world. This conviction has been an important element of the religious self-understanding of Americans (Henry, 1979: 23).

To a certain extent, Bellah recaptured these old arguments, gave them a new and contemporary outlook (by referring not only to the founding fathers but to living presidents as well), and provided a common term for this national faith—*American civil religion*. Most important, perhaps, was his insistence that "this religion—or perhaps better, this religion dimension—has its own seriousness and integrity and requires the same care in understanding that any other religion does" (Bellah, 1967: 1).

Starting with a recognition that "the words and acts of the founding fathers...shaped the form and tone of the civil religion," Bellah argues that this tone, religious in nature, has continued to this day. Using evidence from inaugural addresses from Abraham Lincoln, George Washington, Thomas Jefferson, to more modern leaders such as John F. Kennedy and Lyndon Johnson, Bellah observes that civil religion in America provides a religious legitimation to political authority; gives the political system a "transcendent goal"; and gives Americans a "higher criterion" in terms of which the will of the people can be morally judged.

Bellah (1967: 3-8) notes that the words and actions of the founding fathers, and those of most American presidents, acknowledge, either implicitly or explicitly, a "higher criterion" for sovereignty than either people, state, or nation. Namely, a "non-sectarian" God that most Americans can accept and honour even if they do not necessarily agree on its meaning. The official speeches of American statesmen and political leaders have traditionally placed the political system under a God, both to ask for his guidance and to call upon the nation to uphold its most fundamental values (Demerath and Williams, 1985: 158). The God Americans invoke, Bellah notes, is "related to order, law, and right," and is "actively interested and involved" in American history (1967: 7). Bellah claims, in short, that the whole American political process, since the earliest days of the republic, has been rooted in biblical religious symbols and has been imbued with a transcendental quality.

Although Bellah is aware that what political officials say "need not be taken at face value," he nonetheless argues that those words often express "deep-seated values and commitments." So, while to the skeptical mind, a "semblance of piety" or the mentioning of God during inaugural addresses or presidential campaigns might be interpreted as no more than a strategy to win votes, Bellah insists that what people say on public and solemn occasions deserves serious attention and special analysis. Solemn public addresses express a sense of value and purpose not "explicit in the course of everyday life." They provide an indication of the essentially religious character of American political life. Bellah uses several examples to illustrate his point. Perhaps the most telling is the quote from Kennedy's inaugural address: "the rights of man come not from the generosity of the state but from the hand of God...let us go forth to lead the land we love, asking His blessing and His help, but knowing that here on earth God's work must truly be our own" (1967: 1-2).

Bellah rightly argues that due to the separation of church and state, religion in America is considered to be a strictly spiritual and private affair to be left to the conscience of each individual. But he further notes that this separation has not "denied the political realm a religious dimension." On the contrary, the American political tradition has historically been rooted in religious ideals. He argues that a religiously based belief and symbol system has played a crucial role in American institutional and political life. This public religious spirit "expressed in a set of beliefs, symbols and rituals" is what he calls the "American civil religion" (1967: 3-4).

In his analysis, Bellah assumes a generalized consensus regarding some religious and political principles concerning the nation's history and destiny. He claims that there are "certain common elements of religious orientation that the great majority of American share" (1967: 3). He also claims that biblical religion and utilitarian individualism have been the "most successful" interpreters of American reality, "providing meaning and generating loyalty" (1980c: 168). However, despite the fact that both traditions have been part of the American heritage since the dawn of the nation, Bellah believes that the original conception of America was fundamentally religious and moral, not liberal and utilitarian (1975: xiv). What shaped American national self-understanding in the earliest days was not the notion of each individual, working in his or her own interest and solely concerned with the maximization of personal happiness. Rather, it was the notion of American society as a community "under God" or as "God's new Israel."[2] The biblical tradition, "strongly social and collective," stressed communitarian ideals, charity, and private and civic virtue. Utilitarian individualism, while at odds with the biblical tradition, also became part of the American experience very early in its history. According to Bellah, it became accepted principally through the writings of John Locke, whose version of utilitarianism was "softer" and "deliberately designed to obscure the contrast with biblical religion." In the biblical tradition, the individual is assumed to be motivated by "conscience" (i.e., moral principles), while in the utilitarian tradition by self-interest. The contrast between these two antithetical traditions, Bellah notes, was "obscured" but not by any means "obliterated." He further claims that the marriage ("harmonization") of these two traditions was possible only after religion had been "corrupted" by utilitarian individualism. This happened when religion itself ceased to be an "effective link to virtue, charity or community" and became instead "a means for the maximization of self-interest" (Bellah, 1980c: 168-70).[3]

Noting that American civil religion "borrowed selectively" from both the Puritan and democratic Enlightenment traditions, Bellah argues that "the average American saw no conflict between the two. In this way, the civil religion was able to build up without any bitter struggle with the church powerful symbols of national solidarity and to mobilize deep levels of personal motivation for the attainment of national goals" (Bellah, 1967: 13).

Since the publication of Bellah's article, the concept of civil religion has become one of the most widely used ideas in the sociology of religion. It has also become part of the accepted vocabulary of social scientists and continues to be used by contemporary American scholars (see, for example, Beiner, 1993; Beyer, 1994; DeLue, 1997; Frohnen, 1996; Kessler, 1994; Novak, 1992, Rawls, 1996; Selznick, 1992, to mention just a few). It is often used in fields other than sociology of religion, such as political science, history, theology, and political philosophy. However, when Bellah's article first appeared, it hit academic circles like a bombshell. For more than a decade and a half, it generated an avalanche of articles and debates among scholars interested in the relationship between religion and politics in American society.[4] In fact, Bellah's essay, which roused both "passionate opposition" and "widespread acceptance" (Bellah, 1978: 16), was to become one of the most acclaimed and controversial publications in the history of the sociology of religion. Some authors have gone so far as to consider Bellah's civil religion thesis "one of the most prodigious ideas to come from the social sciences in many years" (Hadden, 1975: 386). While this may be an exaggeration, most scholars would agree that the notion of civil religion owes its rebirth to Bellah's article. However, discussions of American civil religion, particularly during the heyday of its discourse, have been largely shaped by a distinctive American focus. In fact, the original controversy, interest, and debate generated among sociologists was "essentially by Americans, about America, and for Americans" (Cristi and Dawson, 1996: 320).

Although the debate is wide-ranging, perhaps the most significant issues found in the controversy sparked by Bellah's views are: definitional disagreements, the functions, if any, played by civil religion, and questions concerning the empirical reality of civil religion in American society. The debate also centred on different types or models of civil religion, the structural differentiation of civil religion from other social institutions, and the relationship between civil religion and denominational religions (Gehrig, 1981b: 1). However, a review of the literature reveals that during the first phase of the civil religion debate (1967-73), Bellah had either steadfast supporters (for the most part sociologists of religion) or friendly critics. Disagreements among those discussing this topic were no more than amicable differences concerning "definition, description, and history" of American civil religion (Mathisen, 1989: 130-31). Possibly the most serious accusation at that time was that Bellah encouraged "an idolatrous worship" of American society (Bellah, 1970: 168). However, by the mid-1970s, while many scholars still supported him, several others began to take issue with his thesis.

The years 1983-88 mark the gradual waning of the American civil religion discussion. After two decades of disagreements and controversy, the debate tapered off but the concept itself did not disappear from the sociological scene. On the contrary, the civil religion notion which had initially provoked "more heat than light," eventually "mellowed into [a] dispassionate analysis." It became a serious issue of research, outliving "quarrels over its utility as a concept—even its existence as a phenomenon" to become a major topic of books and academic journals (Hammond, 1980e: 200). Today, more than thirty years after Bellah's publication, the debate over the definition and history of civil religion in America is over, but the notion of civil religion has not lost its theoretical significance in the social sciences. A neophyte to this subject would be surprised to find how many books on social and political theory and, of course, on the sociology of religion include in their indexes the concept of civil religion.[5]

In the next section I will examine the definitional disagreements and the conceptual clarifications attempted by various scholars, and give some examples of the wide range of social phenomena that are now included under the category of civil religion.

Setting the Ground Rules

The definitional debate commenced almost as soon as Bellah introduced the term "civil religion" into the sociological scene. As Gehrig has noted, the definitional problem is due, in part, to the coexistence of a variety of interconnected but different models of American civil religion. By this she means the different approaches taken by historians, theologians, political scientists, philosophers, or sociologists who define civil religion in quite different ways. Indeed the vast literature on civil religion indicates that the term not only has a variety of meanings, but also a multiplicity of names. Not surprisingly, this conceptual diversity made any agreement on the topic extremely difficult (Gehrig, 1981b: 17-18; see also West, 1980: 23, and Wilson, 1979: 148).

According to Bellah (1980a: vii), the essence of civil religion is the "religio-political problem"—that is, the relationship between religion and politics, or the religious nexus between citizens and the state. He defines civil religion as "that religious dimension found...in the life of every people, through which it interprets its historical experience in the light of transcendent reality" (1975: 3). In Bellah's words, American civil religion is a "genuine apprehension of universal and transcendent religious reality as seen in or,...as revealed through, the experience of the American people" (1967: 12). It represents an institutionalized set of "sacred beliefs" about the American nation, which provides Americans with a sense of cohesion and solidarity especially in times of profound national crises (1967: 8). In the context of American society, he mentions three such crises: the War of Independence, the Civil War, and the post-1945 period, especially the American involvement in Vietnam. He believes that American national self-understanding was so deeply shaken by each of these events "as to require expression in the civil religion." All three episodes provided the "tone" and themes of the civil religious discourse in America (1967: 9).

Bellah points out that, in the United States, the political order still has a solid "religious dimension." This religious dimension has neither displaced nor replaced denominational religions. It has become instead embodied in civil religion. Civil religion, thus, "runs parallel to, and sometimes finds expression through formal religion" (Toolin, 1983: 39). Bellah further argues that American civil religion is a "securely institutionalized" religion, with its own symbol system grounded in the Christian tradition (1980b: 12). Yet these symbols, though Christian in origin, do not stand for any God, any church, or any denomination in particular. Rather, they are "uniquely American, transcending denominational or religious differences" (Demerath and Williams, 1985: 157).

Civil religion narrowly understood "is the use of God language with reference to the nation" (Wuthnow, 1994: 130). Most scholars, however, make use of less minimalist definitions. One encounters a number of more broadly conceived definitions and typologies in the literature. Civil religion has been defined as a form of Protestant civic piety to be found in the fusion of American Protestantism and a highly utilitarian secular ideology (Wuthnow, 1988a: 244). Alternatively, it has been described as a "set of beliefs and rituals, related to the past, present and/or future of a people ('nation') which are understood in some transcendental fashion" (Hammond, 1976: 171).

Consistent with Bellah's thesis, John Coleman (1969: 69) defines American civil religion as "a special case of the religious symbol system, designed to perform a differentiated function which is the unique province of neither church nor state." He proposes what he thinks is a universal typology of civil religions, distinguishing three forms that would parallel the general evolution of religion itself: 1) undifferentiated civil religions, either church or state-sponsored, such as those found in all traditional cultures, and in Buddhism and Shinto Japan; 2) secular nationalism, of which the former Soviet Union would be an example; and 3) civil religion differentiated from both church and state.[6]

The American case represents, in his view, the most pristine example of the third type.

Martin Marty, following the Weberian tradition, notes two dimensions of American civil religion: priestly and prophetic. The former "comforts the afflicted," the latter "afflicts the comfortable" (Marty, 1974: 145). While the priestly form of civil religion[7] is usually "celebratory, affirmative and culture-binding, the prophetic mode is challenging and judgmental" (Ungar, 1991: 505). Ungar makes a distinction between ceremonial and dynamic models of civil religion. The ceremonial character of civil religion is to be found in presidential addresses and national celebrations, such as the Fourth of July or Memorial Day ceremonies. The dynamic model, by contrast, approaches the issue from an historical standpoint placing less emphasis on ritualistic behaviour or, what he calls, "documentary" evidence (Ungar, 1991: 504).

Other authors have argued that the civil religion model identified by Bellah in American society is more diversified and complex than he envisioned. Jones and Richey (1974), for example, distinguish five varieties of civil religion: folk religion, transcendent universal religion of the nation, religious nationalism, democratic faith, and Protestant civic piety.[8] Folk religion is a non-normative religion "emerging out of the life of the folk." The transcendent universal religion of the nation is a normative religion, "essentially prophetic," standing in judgement over the nation and its people. In religious nationalism the nation itself becomes sacralized, the object of veneration and celebration. Democratic faith basically means that humanistic values and ideals such as equality, freedom, and justice are "religionized," representing a sort of national creed, but without necessarily depending on a transcendent being or specific religious denomination. Finally, Protestant civic piety refers to the alliance between Protestantism and nationalism in America—that is, to the overall "Protestant coloring" of the American identity (Jones and Richey, 1974: 15-18). These authors note that, despite Bellah's apparent "monopoly in conceptualization," these other forms are important alternative conceptions with quite distinct assumptions and focus of analysis (6). They rightly argue that Bellah assumes only the transcendent universal model, and in so doing, he adopts a normative stance regarding the function and meaning of civil religion. Civil religion becomes a transcendental religion "rendering prophetic judgement on the nation" (16).

Perhaps one of the most eloquent opponents was the historian John Wilson (1971; 1974). He was one of the first scholar to stress the need to clarify the meaning of the term in order to identify and reduce the ambiguity inherent in Bellah's thesis. His criticism was based on "conceptual and historical differences" with Bellah's model of a structured civil religion (Mathisen, 1989:133). Wilson expressed concern that civil religion had become a "generic category" covering several different concepts and meanings (1974: 117). In his view, the problem stemmed from a basic inconsistency of assumptions, use, application, and models by different writers. Thus, with the intention of assessing their usefulness for historical research, he set out to examine three of the most common models implicit in the literature: theological, ceremonial and structural-functional.

The theological model is concerned with the kind of civil religion that has been variously called "American faith," "public piety," or the "religion of the Republic." It is best exemplified by Mead's classic article "The Nation with the Soul of a Church." It refers to an American faith based on universal Christian values, which would provide a transcendental meaning for national life. Wilson concludes that this model is so "highly theological" that it is of little or no use to historians (1974: 117-21). The ceremonial-ritual model, as its name implies, deals with the social role of cultic behaviour in society. It is concerned with how symbolic behaviour provides cultural unity regardless of ethnic, class, or religious differentiation. One example would be Warner's analysis of the Memorial Day celebrations and rites, which allegedly integrate diverse groups into a sacred unity—even though this unity may be short-lived. Wilson dismisses this model as well, noting that "it proves to be too fine a filter"—capturing virtually all kinds of ritual and cultic behaviour. It can be applied to an extensive range of phenomena, such as professional sports or the content of the media, "usually not associated with either civic order or religious concerns" (122-26). The third type, the structural-functional model, focuses on civil religion "as a particular religion within the American society." It is best exemplified by Bellah's analysis. Wilson considers this model to be the most "encompassing and sophisticated" version of civil religion. It has a "symbolic content" (the message of America's manifest destiny—a nation fulfilling God's will on earth), and it includes a series of "religious figures," such as Washington, Lincoln, Roosevelt, or Kennedy. Under this model, historical events are invested with a sacred reverence (e.g., the American revolution is seen as the triumph of American liberal democracy over the decadent and aristocratic forces of European nations). This model has also its own solemn rituals (e.g., celebrations such as the Fourth of July). Wilson maintains that the structural model is not only more "complex" and sophisticated than the other two, but "successfully" differentiates the "*particular kinds* of symbolic behavior and belief centered on the national polity." In strictly theoretical terms, he argues, this model represents an improvement over the others, and would best suit the historian interested in this issue (127-31). Yet, while Wilson praises Bellah's model as a highly stimulating and provocative analysis, he questions his observation that there is in America "an institutionalized, well-developed, and differentiated civil religion"(Wilson, 1974: 137). In his view, there is not enough evidence to support Bellah's claims. Instead, he argues that civil religion is a reality with an "episodic existence" (Jones and Richey, 1974: 9). It follows, then, that any model may be "partially or even episodically useful" (Wilson, 1974: 136).

In a later publication, Wilson proposes not three but four different constructions of what he calls "public religion" in America: social, cultural, political and theological. Wilson uses this time a "religious referent" to distinguish between the models. His emphasis is on the "manifest religious content" of civil religion rather than, for example, on "institutional or behavioral issues," which, according to him, "are more explicitly political" (Wilson, 1979: 149-50).[9] In other words, Wilson wants to analyze "religious modes of representations," or how "religiousness" is expressed in the different models proposed. His concern has little to do with the political significance of civil religion.

All four models proposed by Wilson try to identify how "sacredness" is used and understood. The social and cultural models are Durkheimian in orientation. The former points to the sacredness and symbolic unity of society (society itself is represented as sacred), while the latter to society's "ritual elements and symbol systems." In the cultural model, sacrality is not attributed to society per se, "for what counts as the object of religion is the culture" (Wilson, 1979: 151). The central elements of the social model are rituals and cultural beliefs and/or behaviours considered sacred by groups or even institutions concerned with civil society. In the cultural model, by contrast, explicit rituals and beliefs are not so important. They are interpreted less as the expression of social unity, and more as evidence of shared values. The political and theological models are concerned with the political order, although in slightly different terms. The political model neither sacralizes society nor endows culture with religious meaning. Instead, the political order itself is sacralized and is identified as requiring unconditional commitment and loyalty. The theological model refers to a transcendent authority or "norm acting upon the political order, the general culture, and even the society " (151-52). In my view, both the political and theological models represent political religions, insofar as their primary role is to strengthen the state or legitimize a particular political order. Such being the case, they are civil religions in Rousseau's meaning of the term, although Wilson calls them "public religion."

Undoubtedly, these conceptual differences, definitional disputes, and the growing diversity of the issues in question kept the debate alive. For a increasing number of scholars, however, the central issue ceased to be the conceptual clarification of the term. Many started to argue that more important than definitional discrepancies was the task of incorporating the discussion of American civil religion "into more broadly-based models and theoretical constructs" (Mathisen, 1989: 135). Fenn (1978), for example, linked civil religion with secularization theory, and

Markoff and Regan (1982) located it within theories of modernization, while Cole and Hammond (1974) and Hammond (1980c) placed it in the context of religious pluralism and societal complexity, and attempted to link it with the legal system. They stressed the need to identify different institutional sources of civil religiosity.

Cole and Hammond (1974: 177-78) believe that the legal system is an important structural carrier of civil religion. They suggest that, due to the lack of a "universally acceptable meaning system" such as that found in traditional religion, the legal system in the United States may eventually become a "universally acceptable substitute" or surrogate religion. In other words, they argue that the legal system is slowly being "elevated" to a civil religion status and will likely become the new "moral architecture" of the American nation. Hammond notes that from early in its history, the American Supreme Court has evoked a religious "breath of respect" in a way no single church has. Supreme Court judges have been called "the nine high priests." The law has played a significant role in the development of civil religion in America (1980a: 75; 1980c: 141). Hammond believes that the law is increasingly being entrusted with the task of articulating the collective morality of the nation, by establishing clear guidelines for what is considered proper or acceptable behaviour (Wilson, 1979: 130). Because the courts in America "interpret" the law, and identify "duties" and "aspirations," moral issues have the tendency to be transformed into legal issues, and vice versa. The "religious balloon strings," Hammond writes, "being no longer the property of the church only, [can] be grasped by anybody, including (perhaps especially) judges" (1980a: 75-76).[10]

Another arena where civil religion has been found is in popular collective rituals, such as competitive sports. Some discussions have thus centred upon what may be called the civil religion of the masses. For example, Rogers (1972) and Novak (1976) examine the theological or religious dimension of sports in American life. Wilson (1974: 125) notes that, at a deeper level of analysis, professional sports are "cultural rites" and collective gatherings of profound social significance. In his view, competitive sport, with its focus upon success, money, power, and technical expertise, captures in a direct and dramatic way "the content of the American culture" as it has developed in the twentieth century (1979: 135). Likewise, Novak (1992: 243) has argued that professional football is the most "accessible public liturgy of the nation's new self-consciousness."

Such studies indicate that the range of social phenomena labelled "civil religion" seems to have been constantly expanding and changing, especially during the earlier decades of the debate. Almost fifteen years after Bellah's seminal study, the authors of one study lamented that the issue seemed to be growing "more obscure with each new essay" (Markoff and Regan, 1982: 333).

Bellah seems to have been the most surprised and frustrated by the controversy, elaboration, and, perhaps, confusion of the concept that resulted from his 1967 article. In fact, he has spent a good deal of his intellectual career trying to clarify what he meant by civil religion. A year after its original publication, a reprint of his article appeared on *The World Year Book of Religion*, together with various comments and Bellah's response to them (Cutler, 1968). "It is clear," Bellah noted at the time, that what he meant by civil religion in America "is not exactly what most of the commentators mean, nor do they agree one with another" (Bellah, 1968: 388).

In 1974, Bellah delivered a talk at a conference on civil religion, at Drew University, that was published that same year as "American Civil Religion in the 1970's." In the aftermath of the conference some scholars speculated that even Bellah himself was, perhaps, calling into question the existence of civil religion in America. Bellah had remarked that "'civil religion' as an interpretive schema came into existence in 1967." This was taken to mean that he had doubts concerning the "objective existence of that which that schema set out to interpret." Bellah complained that he had been largely misunderstood and "misinterpreted." He responded to the panel on civil religion by "returning once more to the question of whether civil religion exists 'out there' so to speak." He assured his critics that he had never had the slightest doubt that what he "was describing and interpreting existed," even if "public opinion" surveys could not prove its existence (Bellah, 1976a: 153).[11] But, there were some scholars "out there" who rejected the existence of a civil religion in America as an objective social fact or empirical phenomena. Others recognized the concept's sociological utility, but did not agree on appropriate indicators or measurement procedures (Gehrig, 1981b: viii).[12]

More than a decade after the original publication, Bellah still seemed puzzled that opposition to his suggestion of a civil religion in America had shown "little unity," and even more baffled by the fact that those who supported his thesis were "in even greater disarray." He writes, "some of my opponents say there is no such thing, that I have invented something which does not exist; others say there is such a thing but there ought not to be; still others say there is such a thing but it should be called by another name, 'public piety,' for example, rather than civil religion" (1978: 16).

As for those who supported his idea, Bellah complained that they had stretched the term civil religion "far beyond any coherent concept, or at least far beyond anything [he] ever meant by it" (1978: 16). So, plagued by definitional problems and the "unnecessary reification" given to the term, Bellah sought to distance himself from civil religion. In the late 1980s he declared a moratorium on the use of the term: he had grown "tired" of debating and explaining that civil religion was not the "idolatrous worship of the state," and was also "weary" of the whole definitional debate. He was interested, he declared, "in the substantive issues, not in definitions" (1989: 147).[13]

In spite of the definitional problems and the proliferation of typologies, a survey of the literature reveals several common elements present in most discussions (Cristi and Dawson, 1996: 321). American civil religion is generally conceived as a belief system based on the Christian tradition. It is assumed to provide a frame of reference—or, to use Wilson's words (1979: 94), "frameworks of intelligibility"—through which Americans understand, interpret, and give meaning to their daily existence.

That is, it does function, or at least it did function for long periods of time, as a religious symbol system relating America and the historical experiences of the American people to the conditions of ultimate existence (Anthony and Robbins, 1982: 216; Toolin, 1983: 39). It is said to be structurally and functionally differentiated from both the political order and the religious order (Coleman, 1969; Gehrig, 1981b; Wimberley et al., 1976). Values such as freedom, democracy, justice, and charity are said to be imbued with a quasi-religious reverence. It is believed that these values have provided Americans, from colonial times to the present, with a sense of a common destiny and special mission (Gehrig, 1981a: 53). In fact, America's uniqueness is supposed to be based on a special set of values having a sacred quality. It is institutionally *"carried* by the public system of education, the judiciary, the presidency and other political institutions" (Cristi and Dawson, 1996: 321). The public school system, in particular, is seen as the most important institution "in and through which civil religion has continuous cultural presence in American life" (Wilson, 1974: 130; see also Hammond, 1968: 382-84). Schools play a key role in producing, transmitting, and maintaining American civil religion by "absorbing and then converting" each new wave of immigrants into "believers" of the American creed (Hammond, 1968: 383; see also Gamoran, 1990; Hammond, 1976: 177; 1980a: 72; 1980c: 161; Michaelson, 1970, 1971). As Bellah himself acknowledges, public schools provide a very important milieu "for the cultic celebration of the civil rituals" (1967: 11).

Bellah, in his original publication, marvels "why something so obvious" as the existence of civil religion in American society "should have escaped serious analytical attention." He considers this oversight, in itself, an "interesting problem," and offers two possible explanations. First, the Western conception of "religion" has always denoted membership in one, and only one type of collectivity or church. Second, Americans have never taken seriously the Durkheimian idea that every society "has a religious dimension" (a notion, he notes, that would have surprised no one in Asia). According to Bellah, these factors combined have impeded Americans' ability to recognize a religious dimension within their own society (1967: 19 n. 1). But, as mentioned before, the idea of a civic-religious phenomenon antedates Bellah's notion of civil religion. It had not really escaped the attention of the academic community of scholars.

Bellah's work seems to imply not only that every kind of group has a religious dimension, but that the existence of civil religion is inevitable at the national level, and inevitably part of the national consciousness. As Richardson notes (1974: 166), it is not difficult to accept that every group generates symbols and collective ceremonies that help forge group identity, guide the group, and hold it together. These symbols and rituals are "the 'religion' of the group." In Durkheimian terms, they constitute the collective ideals that religion expresses, and that make the "unity" and the "personality" of the group (Durkheim, [1912] 1961: 475). So, broadly speaking, one may say that any civil group will produce its own ceremonies and set of symbols, and, perhaps, its own civil religion.[14] What is less readily accepted and certainly more controversial is the idea that "every civil group will be the unity of both a nation and a state, or that every civil religion will be a *national civil religion*" (Richardson, 1974: 167). Richardson rightly differentiates the "nation" (a cultural element) from the "state" (a political unit). If nations and states have separate and distinct existence, or are "distinguishable social entities," it follows that they can produce "not simply different, but even opposed, religions" (1974: 167).

Richardson notes that, if one takes a Durkheimian stance, as Bellah does, there can be no major objection to Bellah's "sociological descriptions" of American civil religion. What becomes objectionable, in Richardson's view, is Bellah's conception of a "civic group" and his claim that American civil religion is "an inevitable social structure" that unites all Americans in one common faith (Richardson, 1974: 166). Indeed, Bellah's thesis implies that the "the group" is the American nation, which, in turn, is conceived as an homogeneous entity that, if not devoid of serious conflicts and tensions, at least is able to neutralize them through a civic faith. More strongly stated, Bellah's analysis of civil religion "implies the image of a national village, transcending all religious, racial, and class differences" (Hughey, 1983: 67). The history of this American village, as Bellah himself acknowledges, has often been presented by historians as a "success story," perhaps because Americans are "compulsively afraid of defeat" and have opted to remove "negative thinking" from their collective conscience (Bellah, 1975: 148).

Bellah fails to realize that he is also part of this legacy. He writes in the Preface to the *Broken Covenant* that American society is "a cruel and bitter one, very far, in fact, from its own highest aspirations" (1975: viii). The Covenant was broken "almost from the moment [the Pilgrims] touched American soil." He is aware that the history of America is a "somber one, filled with great achievements and great crimes" (1975: xv), and that American civil religion "has never been shared by all Americans." Lincoln uphill battle to summon the nation to its "ancient faith" is, according to him, an illustration of this difficulty (1976a: 154).

While it is true that similar statements can be found throughout Bellah's work, it is no less true that, in the last analysis, his thesis essentially ignores such evidence of conflict and exclusion. His vision of American civil religion is certainly the story of a people, sharing a common religious heritage and a common destiny and purpose. It implies a national religion uniting all American under a common faith.[15] Simply put, Bellah "looks for a set of values and symbols which nearly everyone holds in common and to which everyone responds similarly" (Hughey, 1983: 66). Thus, while he admits that the United States was built "upon the primal crimes of genocide and slavery," he also insists that "Americans have interpreted their history as having religious meaning. They saw themselves as being 'a people' in the classical and biblical sense of the word" (1974c: 107). This religious self-interpretation, he argues, is "central...to the American civil religion, and it is one [he takes] very seriously" (1974c: 116). But did African Americans, for example, share the same religious experience as the early pilgrims? Did they ever share the white interpretation of the American historical experience? Such are the questions that often remain unasked.

The history of American society is not the story of one America, but rather the story of different groups competing or even struggling to "define" the nation's self-understanding, what "morality should prevail," what groups should be excluded, and what symbols and rituals should be preserved and taught to future generations (Hughey, 1983: 69). American civil religion does not "speak with a single voice," but rather with many different tongues. It speaks "from different traditions" and offers conflicting views "of what America can and should be" (Wuthnow, 1988a: 244). What Bellah calls American "'ancient faith' was only one among several ideologies that competed at various times" (Hughey, 1983: 69).

In other words, Bellah does not distinguish between various groups, and has the tendency to lump together "'people,' 'nation,' the 'civil,' or 'political' order, and, implicitly, the national state" (Richardson, 1974: 167). According to Richardson, this produces a shift in his argument from a valid assumption to an invalid one: "from the valid assumption that every civil group inevitably generates a civil religion to the invalid assumption that a civil group is a nation state." What becomes problematic, then, is not Bellah's conception of civil religion, but the social cohesion he attributes to it, and his unduly broad understanding of a civic group (Richardson, 1974: 166-67). Several authors have expressed essentially the same idea. Schoffeleers' objection to Bellah's thesis, for example, is "its implicit identification of the state with the nation and its explicit identification of American civil religion with the religious self-definition of the American people as a whole" (1978: 13).

In short, Bellah conceives civil religion as essentially integrative, although he acknowledges that, in certain circumstances, it may fail to perform its proper role. It is a mark of Bellah's influence that this equation of civil religion with integration has tended to dominate most discussions of American civil religion.

Civil Religion as a Source of Integration

Because the American civil religion debate is clearly associated with the Durkheimian functionalist approach, most authors, particularly during the heyday of its popularity, were eager to identify the "functional" importance of civil religion. If we look at those functions that civil religion (or religion) allegedly performs for society, two claims are most commonly acknowledged, and accepted, in the literature: its integrative function and its legitimating function. Both functions are conceived as important indicators of civil religion's relevance to society (see Gehrig, 1981a: 56; Gehrig, 1981b: 31-32; Purdy, 1982: 307).

Clearly, the roots of the integrative force of civil religion can be traced back to the very genesis of the concept itself. The consensus model whereby civil religion is seen as fostering social integration, is linked to Durkheim's concern with societal order and harmony, especially to his ideas on religion as expressed in the *Elementary Forms of Religious Life* ([1912] 1961). Religion, in Durkheim's view, provides the basis for cultural integration. Religion is a cohesive force whose function is to uphold the moral order of society.

When dealing with the functions of civil religion, most authors fail to acknowledge that the Durkheimian model is only one way of conceptualizing social integration. Evidence suggests that there are other possible manifestations of integration. In fact, to understand this notion in all its complexity we must make some key distinctions regarding its meaning. First, one must be careful to distinguish between spontaneous integration (the Durkheimian approach) and forced integration (the Rousseauan one, which is more likely to produce conflict and division). In the latter case, an integrative national civic faith is to be decreed and promoted "from the top down as an artificial source of civic virtue" (Demerath and Williams, 1985: 156). It follows that integration may be functional for society, but quite dysfunctional for the individual (under military rule or a dictatorship, for example). Second, we may distinguish two distinct senses of the term integration. It may imply the resolution of disagreements through "persuasion" and "compromise," or it may entail coercion, manipulation, and even the use of force (Hamilton, 1995: 120). Third, we should also consider degrees and shades of integration. The question to be asked is, who is being integrated, and by what methods? For integration may work with only certain groups and not others. It may be very effective at the level of the power elites without necessarily uniting the masses or certain minority groups.[16] Finally, a basic problem common to most studies of civil religion is that too much emphasis is placed on religiously based beliefs and values as the basis for societal integration. It is important to recognize that there are a number of other processes through which social integration may be attained, including "economic interdependence, force, habit and pragmatic accommodation and acquiescence" (Hamilton, 1995: 120).

Even a superficial review of the literature reveals that whereas the definitional issue was the subject of heated polarization, a high degree of consensus has existed regarding civil religion's integrative role. Most authors share the idea that civil religion is an important factor in "nation building." It upholds the moral order of society, and allegedly provides Americans with a sense of national identity and national solidarity, uniting them in a moral community. Its essential function is to build, affirm, and celebrate a common national heritage (Bellah, 1967; Coleman, 1969; Kim, 1993; McGuire, 1987). Analysts also agree that civil religion is a kind of bridge between citizen and nation. As such, it is conceived as a mobilizing force towards the attainment of national aspirations (Bellah, 1967: 13). In short, American civil religion is said to promote national unity, sustain commitment towards national goals, and celebrate the American culture and way of life (Coleman, 1969: 76; Fairbanks, 1981: 216; Kim, 1993: 259; McGuire, 1987: 161; Toolin, 1983: 47).

Simply put, there is a widespread belief that a civil religion, *Americanism*, imparts a moral and religious significance to the entire matrix of American experience. Novak writes: "Americans treat America as a religion." So, being an American "is a state of soul" (1992: xxix, 45). In a similar vein, Leon Samson, claims that Americanism is to the American people "not a tradition or a territory...but a doctrine" (cited in Huntington, 1981: 25). This doctrine, this American "creed"—*American civil religion*—it is claimed, is the glue that keeps Americans together.

While one is often struck by the high degree of consensus found on this issue, in some ways this should come as no surprise. Given Durkheim's enormous influence on students of civil religion, a significant number of scholars have taken as a matter of faith the alleged integrative function of civil religion. Authors such as Coleman (1969: 76), for example, claim that, "by definition," civil religion acts as an integrative force in society. Demerath and Hammond (1969: 205) note that civil religion may be one of several "structural arrangements" available for the moral integration of modern, differentiated, and religiously plural society. Due to theological and denominational disagreements, religious organizations in America have proven unable to provide moral integration. This has had, perhaps, the unintended consequence of strengthening the potentially integrative force of civil religion (Gehrigh, 1981b: 33). Still others have argued that religious pluralism, by not allowing any particular religion to monopolize the religious symbol system, has generated a need for some universal meaning system. This need is seen as the true source of the civil religion phenomenon (Cole and Hammond 1974: 177; Hammond, 1980b: 122). In other words, civil religion has come to fill the void, providing the type of "overarching moral glue which fragmented religious symbolism" has been unable to offer (Markoff and Regan, 1982: 343). Bellah's own analysis is in keeping with the Durkheimian premise that integration is based upon a "common moral understanding." It is this common understanding, assumed to be grounded on a religious symbol system, which helps to explain, give meaning to, and ultimately legitimize American society (Gehrig, 1981a: 57-58).

Perhaps because integration is at the heart of Bellah's thought, in some of his writings he takes a prophetic role and sounds an alarm bell against the forces of disruption. In *The Broken Covenant* (1975: 163, 142) he warns that the integrative role of American civil religion may not always be fulfilled.

Disillusioned, he writes, "today, the American civil religion is an empty and broken shell." He also acknowledges that not only in the present but possibly throughout American history, civil religion has not always led to integration. Referring to the American Revolution and the Civil War, he admits that allegiance to the dogmas of civil religion "led not to 'social integration' but to war and the near destruction of the nation" (Bellah, 1976a: 154). He voices a similar concern regarding the Vietnam War, which shattered the tenets of faith of the American people, creating civil disharmony and promoting cultural confusion rather than social cohesion. It is interesting to note that these comments were, for the most part, written some eight years after the original article was published. It appears plausible to argue that as years went by and more critics and negative reactions emerged, he was forced to shift his position from a model rooted in consensus and equilibrium to one characterized by conflict. Nonetheless, while on occasions Bellah takes a critical stance and recognizes civil religion's capacity for both integration and separation, harmony and conflict, his study and interpretation of American civil religion essentially imply integration and social cohesion.

Gehrig argues that, on the issue of integration, Bellah takes a middle position, leaving the question of the integrative power of civil religion "empirically open" (1981a: 57; 1981b: 35). Mathisen (1989: 139) argues more explicitly that Bellah has gone through a transition in his work from a consensual position toward one that includes conflict, critique, and strife. Bellah himself insists that he does not endorse the "functional" integrative interpretation of civil religion, and that there has been no "change over time on the consensus/conflict axis" in his examination of civil religion (Bellah, 1976a: 154; 1989: 147). In any case, the civil religion envisioned for America by Bellah is "a common civic faith born, in large measure, of the need to sustain a pluralistic culture by transcending its divergent and particularist religious perspective" (Cristi and Dawson, 1996: 323). So, despite some qualifications, there is little doubt that Bellah conceives civil religion as a powerful integrative force transcending society and politics, and most other accounts of civil religion fall in line. Indeed, the general tendency has been to assume that civil religion, at least in America, "both stems from and shores up a cultural consensus and moral unity that society requires for its very existence" (Demerath and Williams, 1985: 163).

Durkheim's theory of religion has been understood to mean that religion unites people, maintains group cohesion, and sustains social integration. However, as Hammond rightly notes, Durkheim argued not only that religion engenders cohesiveness, but that the "phenomenon of cohesion" has a religious dimension. For Hammond, the starting point of Durkheim's theory in *The Elementary Forms* is the "unity" factor more than the "religion" factor. In this sense, religion "is more the *expression* of an integrated society than it is the *source* of a society's integration" (Hammond, 1980c: 139; 1974: 116).

Durkheim's thesis implies a cohesive "moral community" that is not artificially created or manipulated. It implies, therefore, a cultural phenomenon that tends to be "naturally" engendered. The quasi-religious feelings and sentiments that it elicits are believed to be widely shared by members of the community. These structural components (spontaneity and overall consensus) are the basic elements of the Durkheimian model. This model, where civil religion emerges out of culture rather than being consciously created, has provided American scholars with the blueprint for the interpretation and explanation of civil religion in America and elsewhere (e.g., in Canada, see Kim, 1993; Cheal, 1978). Even a quick review of the literature suggests that the assumptions of a national "moral community" or the "moral consensus" implicit in the notion of civil religion, together with its capacity to unite diverse sectors of the American population, are seldom made problematic. Scholars have not even considered the possibility that civil religion may itself be a factor promoting disintegration. Neither have they explored the idea that civil religion may be an explicit ideology rather than an implicit cultural phenomenon. In fact, the Rousseauan viewpoint, in which political leaders consciously exploit and/or manipulate traditional religious symbols to achieve political goals has seldom been explored.

Other Voices of Dissent

Richard Fenn, perhaps the most vocal opponent of the integrationist thesis, questions the very existence of American civil religion. He is especially skeptical of Bellah's transcendent model and of its functions (Gehrig, 1981b: 15). Fenn rejects the assumption that any religion, civil religion included, can provide a basis for social cohesion or solidarity in modern societies. The pluralistic and secular nature of advanced societies makes the question of integration, based on religious symbolism, a "present and future impossibility" (Fenn, 1972: 31). No religion can offer the moral integration necessary for a universal meaning system or a national creed. The reason is simple: modern societies no longer require a religiously based cultural consensus. Cultural integration now depends more on "techniques" of socialization than on "religious training" (17). So, religion in advanced societies has no major social functions for the "total social system." Fenn also rejects the idea, or the possibility, of the integration of modern societies "into moral communities." This, in his opinion, is again a practical impossibility (31). But he does not reject the possibility that religion may still retain expressive role for particular individuals or groups, or may even help delineate "boundaries," or legitimize the needs of different groups (17).

Fenn notes that in modern (and pluralistic) societies, the individual is faced with a variety of sources from which to select group affiliations. Moreover, the process of differentiation and secularization, characteristic of modernity, has produced a situation where only "partial" rather than "total" ideologies can exist. Partial ideologies may unite people around separate issues and interests, but it is unlikely that a total ideology could emerge that "could mobilize the passion and the intelligence of an entire population" (16). Under these circumstances, no religious system can offer an overall normative basis of integration, and no religious symbol system can monopolize moral authority within society (17). Fenn, in fact, warns sociologists to be more cautious in claiming to have found "functional alternatives" to religion for the society as a whole (e.g., Bellah's civil religion, pop culture, science, or even aesthetics). So he concludes that cultural integration may be possible "only on the level of pragmatic interests and utilitarian norms" (18). Contrary to Bellah's views, Fenn argues that consensus in modern society is not so much based on "values" (religious or otherwise) but rather on the "requirements of efficiency." In a Weberian sense, these requirements refer to the "rule of the experts" and their ability to satisfy popular demands; in a Marxist sense, to efficiency in satisfying the demands of the market or the needs of the "cash nexus" (28).

Total cultural integration, one may agree with Fenn, seems an unlikely possibility in the modern world. However, partial ideologies do generate partial cultural integration. Only certain segments of the population share specific values, beliefs, or norms, and only certain societal groups have the power to try to enforce them. Lukes has aptly referred to this as the "mobilization of bias," which he defines as that "set of predominant values, beliefs, rituals and constitutional procedures that operate systematically and consistently to the benefit of certain persons and groups at the expense of others" (cited in Purdy, 1982: 311). Fenn fails to consider the cultural integration (moral community) of dominant groups or, in Stevens's words (1975: 364), the "programmatic consensus" of political elites. In addition, Fenn also fails to consider the possibility that civil religion itself may be a part the socialization techniques of modern societies, a point to which I will return in chapter 3.

In sum, despite the persuasiveness of their views, the dissenting voices are few. The general tendency continues to be to define civil religion as a phenomenon that naturally promotes social cohesion. Scant attention has been given to the ideological divide that is likely to develop when values are construed by different groups in terms of their own political interests and particular agendas. This helps to explain why students of civil religion in general, and American scholars in particular, have paid even less attention to cases of forced or imposed civil religion, or to cases of civil religion used as a political resource, whether in the context of American society or internationally.

The state appropriation of civil religion is more apparent in times of profound political crises. Indeed, when the swaying edifice of democracy is on the brink of collapsing, or when it has already collapsed, political leaders seem to turn their attention to civil religion (see Cristi and Dawson, 1996; Purdy, 1982; Regan, 1976). This would suggest that, while some generalized form of a national self-sacralization may be a constant of any society, we may also expect episodic manifestations of specific civil religions. In other words, the transcendent reality identified by Bellah (civil religion and its politico-religious symbol system) may not be a permanent feature of society, so much as something that varies with particular historical or national circumstances. Consequently, civil religious themes would tend to emerge or become more visible in periods of national or international crises (Purdy, 1982: 313). It follows that a specific model of civil religion "may prove to 'fit' one era but not others" (Wilson, 1974: 136).

Marty was one of the first scholars to argue that civil religion is episodic and can be used to answer "different needs at different times." In his view, civil religion is a "cluster of episodes which come and go, recede back to invisibility after making their appearance; only gradually are they institutionalized and articulated in organizational form" (Marty, 1974: 141-42). This view has been reiterated by other authors. Regan notes that, during stable political periods, civil religious themes, although present, "appear as a minor motif of institutional life." Only when the political environment is shaken or disrupted, due to internal or external conditions, does the development of civil religion becomes an urgent undertaking (Regan, 1976: 104; see also Wilson, 1979: 21).[17] Under these circumstances, civil religion may be seen as a phenomenon arising in response to "episodic crises of legitimation," uniting and integrating those in power, rather than as a permanent "legitimator of power and authority in the polity" (Purdy, 1982: 314).

The comparative literature tends to confirm the episodic nature, or episodic use, of civil religion (see Adams, 1987; Brasswell, 1979; Cristi and Dawson, 1996; Markoff and Regan, 1982; Purdy, 1982; Regan, 1976; Stevens, 1975; Takayama, 1988).

These studies suggest that political leaders, in periods of significant political transition or extreme social turmoil, use the religious symbol system both as a tool of social control and as a vehicle for the legitimization of their political actions. This is not to say that a more visible civil religion is necessarily an essential or even effective solution to political crises.

Seminal as these comparative studies are, they point to the need to revise Durkheim's notion of civil religion and pay more attention to Rousseau. Even in the context of American society, the assumption that civil religion is a widely shared, spontaneous phenomenon uniting most Americans under its sacred canopy does not hold true. Only in extraordinary cases (perhaps in Islamic countries, in Israel, or in periods of great natural disasters or grave social crises) may spontaneous integration occur.[18] In exceptional circumstances one may find a whole group, community, or society temporarily united under a common cause requiring service to the nation over the satisfaction of individual needs.

Again, by taking the Durkheimian approach, scholars have been forced to equate civil religion with a national civic faith. If civil religion performs a role for society as a whole, then by logical necessity it has to be a national religion. Liebman and Don-Yehiya (1983), for example, accept the belief that the existence of civil religion depends on the extent to which a *nation-state* views itself as a "moral community." By moral community they mean a group united by common values and a common cause, which requires sacrifices for the benefit of the whole nation. Their equation of "moral community" with only a nation-state is problematic. Groups such as the Michigan Militia in the United States constitute a group united under common cause and common values. They make up a "moral community," not in the sense of being ethical or honourable, but in the sense of uniting a group of people under a common goal and a common banner, but they do not represent the nation as a whole. Groups as diverse as those formed by political elites, guerrillas, or terrorists may feel united, as Durkheim would say, by a "community of interests" that makes them conscious of their "moral unity" (Durkheim,

[1912] 1961: 432). Obviously, they do not constitute a moral community in a national sense. Moodie's (1975) analysis of civil religion in South Africa is another case in point. It clearly suggests that South African civil religion, far from being a national civic faith, was the religion of a white Afrikaner minority. The case of Chile under Pinochet, discussed in chapter 5, is yet another illustration. These examples suggest that the "nation" in some cases may be just a small group such as the political elite, military rulers, or even fanatics who by no means represent the entire country.

Those who oppose the idea of cohesive moral communities charge that the notion of civil religion may be no more than a "social construction of reality"—the creation of an intellectual or academic elite (Marty, 1974: 141). Garrett adopts this position, confining civil religion to "a small cortege of intellectual and cultural elites" (cited in Bellah, 1976a: 154). Novak speaks of a "high-church" civil religion sustained by what he refers to as the "Northeastern élites" and locates Bellah's analysis in this tradition (Novak, 1992: 137-38). Others have argued that civil religion's language of cohesion and integration has become an inauthentic rhetoric, a "rhetoric without a reality," or a "socially constructed myth" (Demerath and Williams, 1985: 164; Gehrig, 1981a: 56). Not surprisingly, Demerath and Williams have observed that the civil religion of America is "losing both emotional depth and historical continuity" (1985: 163).

The claim that civil religion may not act as a stable integrative force in society should not obscure the fact that civil religion, as a response to political crises, may be used to justify and legitimize a political integration decreed by ruling elites, as the cases of Spain, Chile, Malaysia, and China testify (see Cristi and Dawson, 1996; Regan, 1976; Stevens, 1975; Zuo, 1991). In such cases, Rousseau's view of an imposed political religion, specifically devised to manipulate "public loyalties" may be more viable than Durkheim's "culturally grounded" civic faith based on widely shared set of values and moral bonds (Demerath and Williams, 1985: 165).

Civil Religion as a Source of Legitimation

Chapter 3 will survey some of the major theoretical issues raised by the notion of legitimation. The present section provides only a brief discussion of civil religion as a source of legitimation in the context of American society.

Peter Berger (1967: 29) defines legitimation as a "socially objectified 'knowledge' that serves to explain and justify the social order." Religion performs a legitimating function by providing "an ultimate system of meaning" that helps to interpret and explain social existence in a way that justifies the socio-political order. Berger notes that while there are many forms of legitimation, religion has historically been the most important and effective instrument of legitimation (1967: 32).

In a similar vein, De Azevedo (1979: 9) notes that all political regimes, democratic or not, "ont besoin d'une mystique propre, d'une sorte de métaphysique qui les explique et les justifie et, en outre, les rende légitimes devant le pays et le reste du monde." In his view, this *mystique* has usually been provided by religion. Because societies customarily have sought to legitimize their social institutions in transcendental terms, or in terms of an "ultimate set of values," the starting point for the study of legitimation has often been religion (Gehrig, 1981b: 35).

The idea that religion acts as a source of legitimation goes back, perhaps, to the dawn of social reflection, but for our purposes we need go back no further than Durkheim. As discussed in chapter 1, Durkheim considers religion to be an essential and permanent feature of any society (Durkheim, [1912] 1961: 13). He defines religion as a system of beliefs and practices that separates the sacred from the profane, but also, as a "system of ideas with which the individuals represent to themselves the society of which they are members" ([1912] 1961: 257). For Durkheim, religion, integration, and legitimation are hardly separable. Religion legitimates the social order by providing an ultimate system of beliefs and values essential for social behaviour.

Bellah, following the Durkheimian tradition and, in his view, "one of the oldest sociological generalizations," notes that any stable and cohesive society rests on a "common set of moral understandings" about what is collectively accepted as right or wrong. In turn, these moral understanding "must rest upon a common set of religious understandings." It is through these common religious understandings that people are able to have "a picture of the universe in terms of which the moral understandings make sense" (Bellah, 1975: ix). Bellah argues that such moral and religious meaning systems provide both a "cultural legitimation" and a basic "standard of judgement" from which society can be criticized and perfected. He claims that there has always been (and perhaps will always be), a certain tension between religion, legitimation, morality, and civic responsibility. Every society has to confront this tension or, put in another way, every society has to confront the religio-political problem. It is in this confrontation or dialectical tension between religion and politics that Bellah locates the essence of civil religion (1980a: ix-xv).

As already noted, Bellah argues that, from the beginnings of the American republic, moral understandings, rooted in a conception of divine order under God, have performed legitimating functions in American society. These moral understandings are historically contingent and subject to change. Consequently, the possibility for renewal, rebirth, and even erosion, of civil religious values is always present. In fact, Bellah recognizes that the legitimating strength of American values has declined, and that values themselves have undergone a transformation. In early America, he argues, "personal virtue" was seen as the essential basis of a good society, and freedom was "almost equivalent to virtue." A virtuous individual was one who had the freedom to work for the betterment of his community, or the freedom to "do good." As a chosen people Americans had certain moral obligations. The values of freedom, justice, and charity provided the basis of their religious self-understanding. To be sure, under the influence of utilitarianism, freedom to "do good" slowly came to signify freedom "to pursue self-interest," which, as Bellah points out, has now come to be understood as "freedom to do your own thing" (1975: xii). Thus, what virtue, freedom or justice means for the twentieth-century American bears little resemblance to what it did for the eighteenth-century Puritan. Nonetheless, Bellah believes that the religious symbols of American civil religion still have the power to legitimate American social arrangements and experience (Gehrig, 1981b: 36).

Indeed, Bellah is convinced that a common denominator can be found between the present-day United States and early American society: a "religious dimension" or a religious self-understanding of the American way of life. He suggests that despite the profound potential for transformation of values and moral understandings, there is, at least in America, some timeless element in civil religion. While there may be some evidence of "corruption," there is also evidence of an ever present pressure for "higher standards" of morality. Americans in the past tolerated slavery, violence, ethnic, racial, and gender discrimination; today they do not (1975: xi-xii). While religio-political notions may have a different connotation for Americans today, they are at still the heart of the American political heritage. In short, Bellah remains convinced that American civil religion, its symbols, and the "mythological structure that supports it" help every new generation of Americans interpret, understand, and legitimate their social existence "in the light of [a] transcendent reality" (Bellah, 1975: 3).

Commentators agree with Bellah's idea that religious values (such as a nation under God) and political values (democratic ideals) have always marched hand in hand in America, for religion and politics have always been intimately interwoven. Religion was (and perhaps still is) an important source of legitimation for the political order in the United States. De Tocqueville, during his visit to America in 1831, was perhaps one of the first to note the peculiar religious nature of American social existence. He observed that from the very genesis of the republic "politics and religion contracted an alliance which has never been dissolved" (in Hammond, 1976: 174, 176). At the same time, he referred to American church religion as "a political institution" that had made a significant contribution to the preservation of the democratic process by providing moral unity in the midst of religious diversity and political change (Bellah, 1967: 12).

De Tocqueville was particularly impressed by the marriage in American society of religious and democratic values. This was a novel experiment, since in America there was no state church (as in England) and no politically imposed belief system. De Tocqueville reflected that the "symbiotic relationship" between the religious and the political system was the result of the "innovative American feature of legal non-establishment" (Gehrig, 1981b: 6). Hammond echoes de Tocqueville's views and argues that the non-problematic union of politics and religion in the United States lies in the "pluralistic, religious libertarian, disestablishment pattern" that developed early in the life of the republic (1976: 176).

De Tocqueville never used the term civil religion. Instead he presented a model of a new religion, which he called "republican religion," whereby Christian values (cleansed of papal authority) and democratic political values (cleansed of aristocratic forces) were intimately linked. His study was the first analysis of a "generalized democratic belief system" based upon the moral and socio-historical traditions of American society. De Tocqueville differentiated this belief system, as Bellah did more than a century later, both structurally and functionally, from religious denominations and political society. What de Tocqueville described as a "republican religion" or "republican virtue" was a synthesis of democratic and religious values and a belief in a supreme being. This mixture, in his view, was the basis of good citizenship and social cohesion in America. As Gehrig has observed, while Rousseau "developed" the notion of civil religion, theoretically, when formulating the requirements for a modern polity, de Tocqueville "discovered" republican religion empirically when he crossed the Atlantic and visited North America. His notion of a republican religion has been instrumental for students of American civil religion (both for sociologists and social scientists in general), and has had a great impact on American political thought (Gehrig, 1981b: 6-7). Indeed, de Tocqueville's conception of republican religion is undoubtedly a forerunner to Mead's religion of the republic and to Bellah's classical analysis of civil religion.[19]

Ever since the publication of *Democracy in America*, key figures in American political thought have been influenced by de Tocqueville's ideas. Bellah's debt to de Tocqueville is quite evident. He is convinced that religion has been the basis of civic morality in America. In his view, religion has been the central foundation of a "republican political order" and "a constant theme from Washington's Farewell Address to the present" (Bellah, 1976a: 156). Following de Tocqueville, Bellah assigns primary importance to the power of religious symbols to integrate American society.

Obviously, there is wide disagreement over the question of the functional dimension of religion, especially its legitimating function. The idea of the demise of religion, which has come via the Enlightenment and particularly via nineteenth-century writers, is still very much alive today. Thinkers such as Marx, Tylor, and Frazer were convinced that each new advance in science, would be followed by a corresponding decline in religion. Today, while many writers reject the idea of the disappearance of religion, others insist that religion has lost is political and social significance. Thus, at one end of the pole we find authors such as Fenn who reject the idea of religion as a legitimating factor in modern society. At the other end are those who believe that, despite the long-term trend of secularization in western societies, religion still functions to legitimate the social order. Bellah is a prime representative of this view. He believes that religion will never cease to have cultural and social resonance (Hamilton, 1995: 165). Those occupying the middle ground believe that while religion in advanced societies has no "*direct* control" over the legitimation of the political order, it still exerts an "indirect influence" (Fenn, 1974: 144).

We have already seen that Fenn doubts that a post-industrial, technocratic society can be held together by religious beliefs—the process of secularization makes religious legitimation unnecessary (1974: 143). Fenn distinguishes five stages in the secularization process: 1) separation of religious roles from other social institutions; 2) differentiation or "clarification" of boundaries between religious issues and secular ones; 3) emergence of overarching religious symbols that transcend group interests in society (it is at this stage that he sees the emergence of civil religions); 4) dispersal of the sacred as different minority groups seek to legitimate their own claims on religious grounds; and 5) differentiation between individual and corporate value systems. Each stage involves both conflict and negotiation between secular and religious authority (Hamilton, 1995: 179-80). It is interesting to note that Fenn sees the development of civil religions as a stage in the process of secularization, but also as a de-secularizing force. Commenting on this dual tendency, Hamilton notes: "in attempting to determine definitions of the situation the state may seek to curb religious autonomy and restrict the scope of religion, especially sectarian forms, yet at the same time seek to borrow the authority of sacred themes and principles in order to legitimate itself" (1995: 180).

According to Fenn (1974: 143), the process of secularization has resulted in religion losing both social control and social significance, handing over its traditional legitimating functions to other social institutions, such as the educational, political, economic, or legal systems.[20] Secularization, however, does not eradicate religion from modern society. Rather, "it fosters a type of religion which has no major functions for the *entire* society" (Fenn, 1972: 31). Fenn proposes that the religious situation most suitable to modern society is that which grants a limited sphere to the sacred and clearly differentiates between corporate and individual value systems (Hamilton, 1995: 180).

Fenn dismisses the legitimating function of civil religion by presenting an argument very similar to the one he uses to reject its integrative function: legitimacy in modern societies depends not on the "manipulation of religious symbols," but rather on the ability of those in power to meet the demands of the public, such as, for example, high levels of consumption (1972: 17). A religiously based source of legitimation necessarily fades away because policies and programs are guided by criteria of technical rationality (Gehrig, 1981a: 58). Fenn concludes that legitimacy will increasingly depend less on "notions of what is right," and more likely be addressed in terms of the leaders' effectiveness in addressing and fulfilling "basic human needs," or even artificial wants. What really counts are not the basic values of society itself, but rather the ability to set up priorities for public policies and the capacity to read the needs of the public (Fenn, 1972: 27).

Scholars such as Stauffer, by contrast, do not reject religion altogether. Stauffer seems convinced that even highly advanced, functionally oriented, and technocratic political systems still need some sort of cultural legitimation. In his article "Civil Religion, Technocracy, and the Private Sphere" (1973), he rejects the position taken by "privatists," such as Luckman and Fenn, who deny the need for cultural legitimation in modern societies. He also rejects their suggestion that institutions are guided by and accepted for their functional rationality rather than in terms of overarching ideological systems. In his view, the privatists, "and the 'end of ideology' school they represent, " ignore the cultural consensus that exists, or may exist, at least among the powerful or dominant groups. Moreover, cultural legitimation may also be required in periods of social and political strain when "dissensus" is likely to escalate—a fact that is also overlooked by privatists. It is in this context that Stauffer argues that the analysis of civil religion remains essential for students of religion and for those interested in systems of legitimation. Despite some dubious claims—for example, that the civil creed can be prophetic and justificatory of national purposes—"he finds the concept of civil religion useful for the identification of modern legitimating systems" (Gehrig, 1981a: 58; 1981b: 36-37).

One scholar has observed that religious freedom and voluntarism in America (i.e., the fact that churches have had to "compete" as voluntary associations) has led to a peculiar conception of the separation of church and state whereby the religious and political organizations are kept separate, "but the symbols are not" (Hammond, 1980a: 67). Hammond argues that in exchange for the right to believe according to their own moral principles and private conscience, Americans surrendered the "church's monopoly on religious symbols and shared them with government." This has meant that politicians and government officials have not had to "compete politically" with churches. On the contrary, churches in the United States have had to compete with one another rather than with the state. This has allowed political leaders in America to be both "favorable" to religion and "free" to use religious symbolism. Not surprisingly, Hammond notes, we find in America a civil government with a profound "religious flavor" or, in Chesterton's terms, "a nation with a soul of a church," a nation where the civil and the religious seem to coalesce in perfect harmony. This religious flavour, this churchly soul, is particularly evident in the rhetoric of presidential inaugural addresses (Hammond, 1980a: 67-71; see also Bellah, 1976; Bennett, 1975; Donahue, 1975; Wilson, 1979).

The preceding discussion suggests that the relationship between religion and politics in postindustrial America is still alive and well. Demerath and Williams (1985: 162) have observed what they consider to be the "great incongruity" of American existence. Americans have "long prided [themselves] on the *paradox* of great religious freedom combined with strong religious observance." Perhaps this should not come as a surprise or be considered so paradoxical after all. The words of Philip Schaff from more than a century ago may help to remind us of this. He noted that religious freedom in the United States is "an orderly exercise of religious duty and enjoyment of all its privileges. It is freedom *in* religion, not freedom *from* religion" (cited in Wilson, 1986: 114).

Despite the voices of Fenn and others disclaiming the efficacy of religion for legitimating the political order, American politicians have not lost sight of the politico-religious link. This alliance of religion and politics in America is well established and well documented. The old idea of the public utility of religion seems to be well learned by every new generation of leaders holding political power (Donahue, 1975: 65). Even today when political figures seem to be judged in terms of secular criteria, such as economic stability or prosperity, religion in America is not easily dismissed. Indeed, of all the modern industrialized nations in the world, the United States appears to be the least secularized, if secularization is measured in terms of church attendance (Hamilton, 1995: 169). Commentators have also noted that American political leaders continue to give a prominent role to religious symbols both when shaping their political agendas and when trying to define themselves politically (Demerath and Williams, 1985: 160; Donahue 1975: 49).[21] In other words, American politicians continue to borrow the authority of religion to legitimate their political ends.

Donahue, for example, has identified several politico-religious symbol "clusters" that American political officials adopt, consciously or not, "with manipulative intent or not," in their attempt to win over the electorate. These clusters include explicit biblical references, messages of political and religious integrity, political campaigns equated with religious crusades, images of political leaders as priests comforting the afflicted, or as prophets pleading redemption or "imploring a divine mandate" (Donahue, 1975: 49-53). This is not a one-way relationship, however, for the "religious rhetoric" of politicians parallels, at the same time, the "political rhetoric" of church officials. Hammond claims that as a result of the politico-religious alliance, or of the "ambiguous line" of demarcation between church and state, the pulpit in the United States has been politicized, and such politics often find their expression in American civil religion (Hammond, 1976: 177; see also Regan, 1976: 101). One could add that the nation, likewise, has been sacralized and such sacredness also finds its expression in American civil religion.

I have already pointed out that civil religion implies a meaning system and entails the use of religious language and metaphors to sacralize civic life. As noted at the beginning of the chapter, one of the key elements embodied in the meaning system of American civil religion is a "messianic conception" of America as an agent of God and an "exemplary utopia." America sees itself as a "redeemer nation and Americans as chosen people," entrusted with the preservation of democracy and freedom in the world (Anthony and Robbins, 1982: 230, 216).[22] Coleman reminds us that it is the nation, not the national government itself, that is believed to be imbued with churchly characteristics and virtues. He further notes that the nation that is "sanctified is the *ideal* America as the land of freedom, justice, and mercy" (Coleman, 1969: 74, 75; emphasis added).

Fenn has rightly argued that a society would collapse, or at least could not long survive, if the majority of its citizens assume it to be transitory, illusory, morally wrong, or otherwise of no value in itself. In his view, every society relies for its survival "on the tendency of most individuals to 'take it for granted' most of the time" (1974 :145). Despite Fenn's criticism of the functionalist account of religion, he has accepted, to some degree, Durkheim's theory that every relatively stable society will possess a set of shared beliefs that express the highest aspirations of the collectivity. This set of common beliefs, Durkheim would have agreed, is what individuals take for granted. While for Durkheim, Bellah, and their intellectual heirs, values are elevated to a level of transcendence, Fenn believes that technical rationality, not religious symbols, contribute to this taken-for-granted knowledge. This would confirm Hamilton's claim that Fenn's roots lie in the Durkheimian/functionalist approach, and that he has not entirely detached himself from this tradition (Hamilton 1995: 181).

In sum, despite some disagreement on this issue, several scholars agree that modern societies still seek to legitimize the socio-political order in terms of an ultimate set of values (Gehrig, 1981b: 35). This is what De Azevedo (1979) has called a religious mystique (or a system of meaning), which every society needs to explain and justify itself. The problem of legitimacy includes the question of whether an "existing political authority is moral and right or whether it violates higher religious duties" (Bellah, 1980a: viii). Generally speaking, then, legitimation falls within the realm of religion. But legitimation "always involves the justification of power" (Kokosalakis, 1985: 371).

But students of civil religion have not really explored, or perhaps even understood, the historical legacy of civil religion in its ideological (political) form, and the link between power and religion (politics and ideology). Given the fact that political figures are, to a large extent, the official interpreters of civil religion, any civil religion may be used for political ends. As a political tool, civil religion may be invoked (to a greater or lesser degree) to legitimate and justify political power. Hughey has convincingly argued that Durkheim was, to a large extent, "unable to see the ideological implications of his own intellectual effort, or for that matter, to recognize the significance of intellectuals, prophets, and individuals generally in the formulation and rationalization of religious and moral ideas" (1983: 26). Hughey's criticism of Durkheim is also a criticism that can easily be applied to Bellah and his followers. This, and related issues, will be discussed in the next chapter.

CHAPTER THREE

The "Problem" of Legitimacy, Power, and Politics

I n the United States, Bellah tells us, the "will of the people is not itself the criterion for right and wrong [for] there is a higher criterion in terms of which this will can be judged" (1967: 4). Thus, in Bellah's terms, the fundamental legitimacy of the nation is located in a supreme being or a higher law—the nation is said to stand "under higher judgement" (17). In essence, the political process has a transcendental purpose and an authority derived from God, to whom Americans are ultimately answerable. It is here that Bellah locates the heart of the civil religion phenomenon and its legitimating function. Agreeing with Bellah, major contributors in this field perceive legitimation to be a crucial component of civil religion. But, by linking legitimation with a being in the other world, they often fail to consider those who hold the reins of power in this world. Most authors discuss civil religion as if it were divorced from political society, or as if it were outside the competence of the

Notes to Chapter 3 are on pp. 250-54.

state. In other words, while the issue of the legitimacy conferred by civil religion to the social and political order is, undoubtedly, linked to religion and power, the power factor has been consistently obscured by scholars interested in this field.

The Intellectual Roots of the Problem

One has to go far back in the history of social thought, to find the origins of the problem of legitimacy—a problem that is closely linked to the relationship between church and state. Simply put, the classical problem refers to the question of how some individuals come to have the right to rule over others or how a political authority comes to be accepted, by the majority of those governed, as morally entitled to demand obedience.

Under the Christian tradition, rulers derived their claim to authority directly from God. However, when religion and political life became separated, when legitimation ceased to be linked to traditional theologies, a latent tension developed between religious and political authority. This tension has been reconciled or institutionalized in a variety of ways in different societies. "Whether we wish to call such forms of institutionalization civil religions," Bella tell us, "or confine that term to only some of such forms, it is here that we must locate the problem of civil religion" (Bellah, 1980a: viii).

In theocratic forms of polity, characteristic of most ancient and primitive societies, there was no distinction between religious and political institutions or between religious and political authority. Divinity, society, and the individual constituted a single cosmological whole. Originally, Rousseau writes, "men had no kings save the gods, and no government save theocracy" ([1762] 1973: 268). The world was regulated by a religion of "functional deities." Gods of "locality, tribe, polity," the gods of war, and those who guaranteed the social and political order, were in charge of defending their own particular interests, fighting other gods, or taking care of everyday routines (Weber, [1915] 1958: 333). The political process was no more than an expression of the sacred kingdom—a microcosm of the divinely instituted cosmic order that permeated all human experience (Berger, 1967: 34). Politically powerful individuals were perceived of as gods, or as intermediaries of an absolute power (Gehrig, 1981b: 35). In everyday life, obedience to the ruler was synonymous with obeying the gods. Political conformity and political opposition were identified with either admission into a perfect cosmic order or alliance with chaotic and malevolent forces (Bellah 1980a: viii; Takayama, 1988: 330). This meant that beyond the boundaries of "cosmic harmony" was nothing but "outer darkness" (Bellah, 1980a: viii). The earthly kingdom was unquestionably the kingdom of god. Hence, in undifferentiated societies, legitimation, as we understand it today, was not really necessary—everything worked according to a divine plan or a natural-divine cosmos. All human action—social, political, even personal—was filtered through religion. Indeed, every aspect of society "was the 'field of religion'" (Berger, 1973: 314). The problem arose when the boundaries of "locality, tribe, and polity" were shattered by the emergence of universalist religions proclaiming a "God for the entire world" (Weber, [1915] 1958: 333).

Bellah observes that with the emergence of historic religions, a drastic "reorientation" of divine kingship and its symbol system occurred. New "structures of religious authority" developed that were, in principle, autonomous or separate from the state, as in the case of the Christian church, for example. The relation to the divine was "unmediated by political authority." Ordinary people could relate to a god without the direct mediation of the divine king. On the other hand, this separation also meant that political authority did not have to share power with the authority of the gods. There were instances, however, such as Confucianism, Judaism, and Islam, where a sharp division between religious and political institutions did not take place. In such circumstances, political authority was considered illegitimate when it did not "conform to transcendent ethical norms" held by society. To these two scenarios, and jumping to modern times, Bellah adds a third possibility: when "a distinct set of religious symbols and practices" emerges dealing with issues of "political legitimacy and political ethics" that are not connected with either religious or political organizations. That is, a set of religious symbols arises that is independent of both church and state. This is the solution to the religio-political problem that characterizes, in Bellah's view, the American case (Bellah, 1980a: viii-xi).

Christianity, the process of modernization, the growth of rationalism, trends towards secularization, are some of the factors accounting for the end of theocratic forms of polity and for the eventual separation of church and state. It was a "Christian innovation," Apter writes, to divorce the sacred and the secular universe "by challenging the state religion of Rome" (1963: 68). The death of theocracy, however, did not entail the disappearance of religion from public life. On the contrary, through most of the history of the Western world, Christianity (or some form of it) has been the official religion and has provided a religious framework for the legitimation of the state (Bellah, 1978: 16). Winfred E. Garrison rightly observes that,

> for more than fourteen hundred years...it was a universal assumption that the stability of the social order and the safety of the state demanded the religious solidarity of all the people in one church. Every responsible thinker, every ecclesiastic, every ruler and statesman who gave the matter any attention, held to this as an axiom. There was no political or social philosophy which did not build upon this assumption...all...believed firmly that religious solidarity in the one recognized church was essential to social and political stability. (cited in Mead, 1963: 60)

It is no surprise that the notion of political legitimacy, as a theoretical issue, explicitly emerged only in late Antiquity or the High Middle Ages—the Greeks, for example, made no distinction between legitimacy and lawfulness. Its genesis is said to have coincided with the emergence of representative government. As Merquior notes, when the "'direct' democracy of the polis" gradually faded away and new forms of rule appeared, a problem arose: "the problem of how to justify the legitimacy of *representatives*" (Merquior, 1980: 25).

Ever since that need originated, the problem of legitimation has been at the very heart of social scientists' concern with the nature of modern society. Indeed, as Garrison's remark makes clear, the relation between legitimacy and religion, and the idea of the political utility of religion, is part of a long tradition of Western political thought. In the 1500s, Machiavelli observed that it was fundamental to the ruler's success that he "appear to be religious," for religion was a useful instrument of social control. The prince, Machiavelli advised, should encourage a religion that teaches "that he who best serves the State best serves the gods" (cited in Donahue, 1975: 64-65). It was also critical that the prince should appear to "whoever sees and hears him, all mercy, all faith, all integrity, all humanity, and all religion." He warned that the last quality was the most necessary. If the prince did not have it, he should at least make a show of possessing it (Machiavelli, [1513] 1985: 70).

Machiavelli is one of the first thinkers to openly discuss the idea of the political importance of religion. Perhaps the first proto-theory of civil religion *à la Rousseau* is to be found in his writings. Machiavelli understood Roman civic religion as a powerful political religion, the true pillar of civic solidarity and republican virtue. Roman religion was, in his view, both a source of political legitimation and the guarantor of the political virtue of Roman citizens. Larrain notes (1979: 17, 18) that Machiavelli is also one of the first to deal with issues clearly associated with "ideological phenomena," and to link "religion to power and domination."

Classical thinkers from Hobbes, Locke, and Rousseau to more modern thinkers such as Durkheim and Weber and even to recent writers such as Bellah have addressed, in one form or another, the issue of the relevance of religion to the legitimation of the political order.[1] Hobbes, for example, believes that ignorance and fear are the "natural seed" of any religion. Men, he notes, make "little, or no inquiry into the natural causes of things, yet from the fear that proceeds from the ignorance itself, of what is that has the power to do them much good or harm, are inclined to suppose...several kinds of Power Invisible....And this fear of things invisible, is the natural seed of that, which everyone in himself calls religion" (cited in Larraín, 1979: 23). Despite his conviction that religion is the birthplace of false ideas and narrow-mindedness, Hobbes still sustains its political significance for the common good—that is, for the harmony and stability of society. His entire moral philosophy and the central place he gives to religion is, in fact, politically oriented (Larraín, 1979: 24).

Hobbes's main concern is political control. He wants, above all, to persuade people to obey political authorities, but he also wishes to avoid sedition, rebellion, or anything that can spark or provide a fertile ground for insubordination. In his concern with averting the perpetual "war of all against all," Hobbes postulates the need for religion and autocratic monarchs. Both are essential for the common good. Both are needed to maintain order and avoid civil war (Larraín, 1979: 23).

Hobbes explicitly advocates a state or political religion in order to facilitate political stability. He proposes the subordination of the church to the state, what Rousseau calls "the reunion of the two heads of the eagle." As Leo Strauss notes, Hobbes's attitude is direct and leaves no room for different interpretations: religion is to be regulated by the state and always be in accordance with the state. In fact "religion must serve the State and is to be esteemed or despised according to the services or disservices rendered to the State." At the same time, the sovereign's power must be unrestricted if he is to protect the lives of the subjects and secure political submission and conformity (Strauss, 1973: 74).

Hobbes believes that people can be kept in obedience by instilling in them a religious reverence for the law. This devotion to the law should be complemented with education. Citizens need to be educated about their political obligations, or their duties to the state. It is essential, Hobbes advises, to make them both aware and fearful of the personal and social costs of civil disobedience, rebellion, and dissent. If individuals are taught the Machiavellian idea that political principles "proceed from the gods," those who break the law would learn that they do not only offend their rulers but also anger their gods (Larraín, 1979: 23). As Larraín notes (1979: 25), Hobbes justifies religion for the sake of the sovereign, just as Machiavelli before him, "had justi-fied it for the sake of the prince."

Rousseau's debt to Machiavelli's ideas on the utility of religion and its effects upon civic behaviour has already been noted. Going against the prevailing view of his time, which conceived of religion as the greatest source of superstition, Rousseau declares that religion is necessary both as an integrating and legitimating force. Rousseau begins chapter 1 of the *Social Contract* with his now famous sentence "man is born free; and everywhere he is in chains" ([1762] 1973: 165). But his main concern is not how this has happened. As one author rightly contends, Rousseau is not even concerned with questions such as "'how can we escape this misery?' or 'why does such evil persist?'" Rather, the question that the *Social Contract* attempts to answer is "what can render it legitimate?" (Wuthnow, 1988a: 242).

At the time Rousseau was writing, several approaches were used to explain the origin of the social order, and hence of polit-ical obedience. Political legitimacy was generally conceived as an outgrowth of parental authority, as the right of the strongest or wealthiest, or as the outcome of conquest. Rousseau considers all of these explanations false. The justification of a political order cannot be based on natural predispositions, economic strength, or brute force. None of these factors can engender a legitimate right or warrant political obedience. By natural rights man is born free and equal. The source of legitimate authority, Rousseau speculates, is to be found in a social contract, ordained not by fear or force, but by a commonality of interest (Merquior, 1980: 20).

Since there is no "natural authority," and "force creates no right," Rousseau reasons that conventions form the basis of, or are at the heart of, all legitimate authority ([1762] 1973: 169). Practical political principles arise to help meet the social needs of a society and the need for political obligations of citizens. Rousseau himself, as we have seen, discusses the need for a com-mon ideology in a cohesive legitimate society (i.e., civil religion).

He argues that, just as the body politic needs religion to legitimate the social order, the administration of public affairs requires, in turn, that each citizen should have a religion that will make them love their duties as well as their country and its law. Good citizenship, which is to be secured and strengthened by civil religion, is essential. "Without civic virtue...the general will risks inertia, usurpation of sovereignty becomes inevitable, and illegitimacy reigns unopposed" (Merquior, 1980: 23).

As societies become more internally complex and institutionally differentiated, the need for legitimation increases, and legitimating the social order becomes, in turn, more complicated. Gehrig observes that sophisticated systems of legitimation arise in cases where "interpretations of reality" are disputed by alternative meaning systems. The separation of church and state, gods and government, creates intense competition between religious and political systems. Modern pluralistic societies, in fact, have to deal not only with the "erosion of traditional meaning systems," but with different sources of competition: the competition of religious and political institutions, and the competition of different religious systems of legitimation (Gehrig, 1981b: 36).

In much of Christian history, church and state, or religion and politics, have been intimately interwoven. This relationship, however, has often been plagued by deep tensions, compromises, and unhappy alliances. The pendulum has swung either to the side of the state or to the side of the church. That is, either the state has succeeded in making the church an "engine to further national policy," or the church has gotten the upper hand by utilizing the state "to further religious interests" (Krinsky, 1968: 13; see also Bellah, 1980b: 5; 1978: 17).

Broadly speaking, once the separation of church and state occurred, the division of spheres has always remained problematic. The state has tried to dominate or exploit a "restless church...but never removed its refusal of final allegiance." While the church has never accepted it loss of authority, it has used the state, whenever possible, for its own benefit (Bellah, 1978: 17). Apter has noted that when the distinction between the sacred and the secular authority emerged, the church was forced, so to speak, to create the "ideal of temporal rule," as a means to compensate for its loss of power to the state. The religious system and the political system have become two competing ideologies, "each representing powerful institutional forces" (Apter, 1963: 68). All this has occurred despite some "great periodic yearnings in Western history" to fashion a social order "where there would be no split in the soul between Christian and citizen" (Bellah, 1978: 17).[2]

The modern state has not escaped this tension. Political authority, by claiming the right to adjudicate matters of life and death, both with respect to "internal deviants and external enemies," obviously deals with questions of ultimate concern (Bellah, 1980a: vii). Weber reminds us that force is a "means specific to the state." In fact, he defines the state both as "a compulsory association which organizes domination" and as an association which monopolizes "the legitimate use of physical force within a given territory." The modern state, Weber argues, is "a relation of men dominating men...by means of...'legitimate violence'" (Weber, [1919] 1958: 78, 82; see also Weber, [1915] 1958: 334). Religion, in contrast, alleges an authority that transcends any kind of secular power (Bellah, 1980a: vii). It claims to reveal the meaning and mysteries of this world, and offers an ultimate and transcendental reality. It offers, in other words, "an ultimate stand toward the world by virtue of a direct grasp of the world's 'meaning'" (Weber, [1915] 1958: 352). A world that is apparently irrational, chaotic, and unjust appears, through religion, to acquire meaning and order (Hamilton, 1995: 138).

Although the relationship between church and state is no longer the critical problem it once was, religion is still a "friction point" in contemporary democratic societies (Krinsky, 1968: 3). To be sure, the tension between religion and the state, or faith and politics, almost always comes to the fore when legitimation is considered.[3] Bellah (1980a: vii) observes that "in no society can religion and politics ignore each other. Faith and power must always, however uneasily, take a stance toward one another." Obviously, the political answers given to this tension are many and varied. Each society has tried to harmonize the relationship between religion and the state in its own way, as required by its particular institutional arrangements and historical circumstances (Krinsky, 1968: 15). Yet, apparently no solution has ever brought to a vanishing point the tension that Rousseau discussed and tried to resolve (Bellah, 1980b: 6). As several commentators have noted, the history of the Western world has often been wracked with hostility and confrontations between religious authority and secular interests (Krinsky, 1968: 1).

Legitimacy in Sociological Theory

Whereas the question of legitimacy is part of a long tradition of Western political thought, the emergence of legitimacy as an important sociological issue coincided with the development of classical sociology. Its clearest and most comprehensive expression is to be found in the work of Max Weber (Merquior, 1980: 9). However, the notion of legitimation that is derived from classical sociological theory has proven to be somewhat in unsatisfactory for the analysis of political power in modern society (Kokosalakis, 1985: 370).

There are two basic ways of looking at the phenomenon of legitimacy: that which views legitimate domination in terms of *belief*, and that which views it in terms of *values*. In the former case, referred to as the "subjectivist" approach, the emphasis is placed on the political, specifically, on the relations between rulers and the ruled. Weber would be a prime example. In the latter, the "objectivist" approach, the emphasis is transferred from "the political to the *socio-cultural*." What is important here is societal values, "not the experience of rule" (Merquior, 1980: 5). Durkheim, Parsons, and their followers fall in line with this point of view.

From the subjectivist standpoint, the problem of legitimacy is explained in terms of whether or not most individuals subject to a specific political authority "believe" that this authority is morally right. The subjectivist approach equates legitimacy with the "conviction" on the part of individuals or citizens that it is "right and proper" to conform to a specific political authority.

However, legitimacy has little to do with feelings. As Merquior argues, identifying legitimacy with the "feelings of the ruled says next to nothing about the *criteria* of legitimacy." The objectivist approach, as its name indicates, assumes the existence of objective standards, "external to the mere floating 'conviction' of the majority" (1980: 5). A government is legitimate only if official policies, programs, or governmental actions are congruent with, or reflect the basic principles and values of, the majority of those governed. The objective approach stresses shared values, but it also refers to the capacity of a regime to find solutions to the basic problems facing any political system. It allows, at least in theory, for "the possibility of a lack of overall legitimacy" whenever the society's values collide (for example, in a civil war), or as a result of political, ideological, or social antagonisms arising from social unrest (4-5).

Merquior suggests that the conceptualization and treatment of legitimacy in social theory is inadequate. As he notes, both approaches are flawed: the one is faced with the dilemma of how to ascribe values to social collectivities on a "reasonable empirical basis"; the other, with the equally difficult puzzle of how to ascribe beliefs. But Merquior's concern is not only with the problem of opinion instability in survey research. He also notes the fallacy of basing legitimacy on a set of dubious assumptions about value consensus in society (4-5). Both approaches, he observes, start with the "assumption of belief," stressing either the "psychological" component (the personal conviction that it is right and proper to obey), or its "social aspect" (societal values "external to the ruled's consciousness"). In other words, both make legitimacy dependent upon "*believing* in the ruler's claim to power." In so doing, neither of them confronts the problem from the "actual political experience of legitimacy (or illegitimacy)." These weaknesses, Merquior suggests, could be overcome by conceiving legitimacy in terms of power (5-7).

But in social theory power has rarely been accorded a central place (Kokosalakis, 1985: 368). The general tendency in all sociological theories has been "to reduce power to a secondary characteristic of social life" (Giddens, 1981: 49). Even in Marxism, where power is a first-order concept, political power is merely the organized power of the propertied class for oppressing others. In *The Manifesto of the Communist Party*, Marx lists several measures that, once in place, will make public power lose its political character—the most important ones being abolition of property, introduction of a graduated income tax, abolition of rights of inheritance, confiscation of property of emigrants and rebels, centralization of credit, and state control of the means of communication and transportation ([1848] 1978: 490). To the extent that economic and material interests are considered to be the prime determinants of the polity, power is treated as a "secondary concept" (Kokosalakis, 1985: 368). In Marxist terms, once the revolution swept away the old conditions of production, the existence of class antagonisms would disappear, and so would political power. However, it could be argued that the elimination of an exploitative mode of production may not eliminate all sources of power. Simply stated, a socialist society does not put an end to political hierarchy and political power. Ideas of any sort, whether religious, moral, political or even aesthetic, Geertz reminds us, "must be carried by powerful social groups to have powerful social effects." Ideas have to be somehow institutionalized to have an intellectual and concrete existence. "Someone must revere them, celebrate them, defend them, [and ultimately] impose them" (Geertz, 1973: 314).

In view of the central role of power in Weber's theory of legitimate domination, the claim that in all sociological theories power has not received the attention it deserves might seem unjustified. This is not the case for despite the centrality given by Weber to the notion of power, his theory of legitimate domination is derived from his theory of bureaucracy and is "rather one-dimensional" (Kokosalakis, 1985: 368). Weber's work can be characterized as a comparative historical sociology centred on an attempt to explain modernity and modern man.[4] He is deeply interested in the study of religious and social change. He uses the concepts of rationalization and bureaucratization to explain the process of modernization. In his view, these processes have had profound implications for social, political, and religious systems. The *Protestant Ethic and the Spirit of Capitalism* ([1905] 1930) represents Weber's effort to understand the effects of rationalization in the context of modern Protestantism.

For Weber, bureaucratization—the establishment of an impersonal social order that functions according to abstract and rational rules and regulations—is domination objectified. Weber sees bureaucratization intimately linked with the process of rationalization of the modern world. "Bureaucracy has a 'rational' character: rules, means, ends, and matter-of factness dominate its bearing" (Weber, [1921] 1958: 244). He notes that the modern world is gradually losing its sacred character to rational and efficiency-oriented explanations of reality. Functional rationality and rationalization imply a world defined, organized, and ruled by total calculation—that is, by "calculable rules" and by "calculability of results" (Weber, [1921] 1958: 215).[5] In the process of rationalization, the social order, originally ethically motivated and embedded in a magico-religious world, becomes detached from all ethical considerations. It becomes a dehumanized world where goal attainment is based on "purely objective considerations" and utilitarian principles. In a successful bureaucratic organization, for example, there is no place for love, hate, or any other "irrational, and emotional elements which escape calculation" (Weber, [1921] 1958: 216). In the end, impersonal forces come to rule over individuals. For this reason, Weber sees in bureaucratization the modern chains of man.

Weber argues that all processes of development (including economic development) are conflicts for power. At the same time, he believes that the most fundamental "yardstick of values" in any process of development is the "reasons of state" (cited in Gerth and Mills, 1958: 35). As already noted, Weber defines the state as an association that manages domination. In his political writings, concepts such as "national power," "national greatness," or the state's political interests surface over and over again. National greatness, or the success of a nation in achieving world domination, is postulated by Weber as a desirable political goal. Yet, it cannot be achieved without strong political leadership. Politics requires a "passionate devotion," and an ethic of decisive action (Weber, [1919] 1958: 115). To counterbalance the domination of politics by bureaucratic mentality, Weber resorts to the idea of a powerful state to protect the nation, and powerful and strong leaders to protect the interests of the state. It is against this framework that he discusses his theory of legitimate domination.

Weber was deeply affected by the political crisis in Germany during his time. After the defeat of Germany in the First World War, the nation had become isolated, and the most important authority and symbol of the nation, the kaiser, had become the target of international scorn (Gerth and Mills, 1958: 37). This Weber found clearly harmful and certainly hard to accept. In his view, "a nation forgives if its interests have been damaged, but no nation forgives if its honor has been offended" (Weber, [1919] 1958: 118). If the symbol of the nation was humiliated, so was the entire nation's honour damaged.

Weber attributes Germany's internal and external difficulties to a bureaucratized social structure that has prevented the rise and "efficient selection" of true political leaders (Gerth and Mills, 1958: 37). What Germany needs, he declares, are responsible and competent leaders willing to act in politics according to the "ethic of responsibility."[6] In Weber's view, to do this a politician must be both a leader and a hero. In the political order, Weber's solution to the dilemma of modernity is an authoritarian leader who has no personal ambition, only a passionate commitment to an impersonal cause (Weber, [1919] 1958: 127-28). Weber has been seen by many as "an imperialist, defending the power-interest of the national state as the ultimate value" (Gerth and Mills, 1958: 35).

Weber is convinced that to the degree that "magical elements of thoughts" are displaced, the march of rationalization will move forward. However, modernity is also pushing us backward. Indeed, the malaise of modernity is associated with the depersonalization and "disenchantment" of the world brought about precisely by the rationalization and bureaucratization of every aspect of our lives. Weber dislikes the modern man that is emerging: the "narrowed professional," administrative official, or political official with no heart and little brain. He believes modernity is creating an army of docile and obedient bureaucrats. This type of individual is "a petty routine creature, lacking in heroism, human spontaneity and inventiveness" (Gerth and Mills, 1958: 50-51).

To his rather pessimistic view of modernization and rationalization, and his fear of "leaderless democracy," Weber brings the concept of charisma or "gift of grace." People with charisma are "self-appointed leaders" whom individuals follow and obey because they "believe" in their exceptional qualities. Heroism, valour, and success are idiosyncratic attributes of charismatic leaders (Gerth and Mills, 1958: 52). The heroic charismatic leader is emotionally (not rationally) driven and is endowed with spontaneity, courage, and personal charm. He breaks with all institutional routines—"those of tradition and those subject to rational management" (Gerth and Mills, 1958: 52). He is, so to speak, beyond the power struggle, for the power that he embodies, and takes, is not acquired for his own glory but for the glory of the nation or cause. Charismatic leadership is only one form in which legitimate domination might occur. A second form of legitimate domination in the modern world is by virtue of legality. That is, "by virtue of the belief in the validity of legal statute and functional 'competence' based on rationally created *rules*." The third and final justification for legitimation is the "authority of the 'eternal yesterday'"—that is, traditional domination (Weber, [1919] 1958: 79). Here the leader's critical test for legitimacy "depends upon his doing what others have done before him" (Demerath and Hammond, 1969: 60). In sum, for Weber, legitimation of political authority and political obedience is to be found in three pure types: charismatic, legal, and traditional domination.

Weber defines all three types of legitimate domination "by *voluntary submission* to power systems in whose validity the subject *believes*." Thus, legitimate domination may be based on devotion to the exceptional character of charismatic leaders, on respect for the law, or on the respect for the sanctity of traditions (Merquior, 1980: 97-98). While Weber was well aware that traditionalism in modern societies was either dead or dying, he rejected the evolutionary view that saw the world advancing in a straight, irreversible line. Instead, he subscribed to a "'pendulum' pattern based on a recurrent oscillation between charismatic irruptions and bureaucratic expansion" (Merquior, 1980: 100). However, despite Weber's claim that European culture has not followed a "unilinear development," Gerth and Mills (1958: 51) hold that a unilinear organization is clearly assumed in Weber's view of the bureaucratization of the world.

Weber's conception of legitimate domination, as Kokosalakis suggests, prevents "in principle" any analysis of the uses or abuses of power. This means that in Weber's theory of legitimacy there is "no room for illegitimate forms of domination." Quoting Mommsen, he notes that even in his acclaimed concept of charisma as a political solution, it is difficult to distinguish between "the genuine charisma of responsible democratic leaders, as for instance Gladstone or Roosevelt and the pernicious charisma of personalities like Kurt Eisner or Adolf Hitler" (Mommsen, 1974: 83, 91; cited in Kokosalakis, 1985: 370). Gerth and Mills have also observed that the concept of charisma is indeed "free of all evaluations."[7] The only element common to all charismatic leaders is that individuals follow and obey them because of trust ("faith") in their personal qualities, heroism, or exceptional achievements (1958: 52). In short, Weber's sociology of legitimacy is overtly centred on the relationship of the ruler and ruled. Domination is conceived as operating mainly in terms of beliefs. The criticism that his theory of legitimate authority relies too heavily on "systems of *beliefs*,"seems entirely justified (Selznick, 1992: 271).

When legitimacy is viewed as grounded on belief, claims to legitimate domination may rest either in the beliefs of the rulers in their own legitimate right to demand obedience ("as embodied in ideologies of rulership"), or in the beliefs of the ruled in their leaders extraordinary qualities or gift of grace (Merquior, 1980: 6). However, authority may not always rest with consent based on belief. On this issue, Selznick (1992: 272) writes: "a legitimate ruler may be a tyrant, whose claim to rule rests on principles that encourage uncritical acquiescence on the part of subjects and supine obedience on the part of officials." This would suggest that Weber's premise that authority invariably depends on a "legitimazing belief" on the part of the ruled does not hold ground. Authority may also be based "in interest, coercion, or both." Here there is no need for an "inner acceptance of the ruler's claim to rule" (Merquior, 1980: 208). To be sure, in such cases, we are in the realm of what Weber called power, which is inherently less stable a means of social control than authority which, in Weber's terms, is legitimated domination. However, several political regimes during the course of the twentieth century have enjoyed legitimacy on the basis of such power. In any case, Weber's main concern is not so much the "wielding of authority," but rather "its acceptance and legitimation in the eyes of the followers" (Demerath and Hammond, 1969: 60).

Kokosalakis (1985: 370) observes that it is not just the Weberian sociology that shows little sensitivity in the area of power relations. Parsons's conceptualization of legitimation and power is also "one-dimensional." For Parsons the social order is primarily ruled by a set of core values that filters through society. He conceives of power as a "generalized capacity" to accept "binding obligations," which "are legitimized with reference to their bearing on collective goals" (Parsons, 1963: 237). Power is not a personal attribute; rather, it is a system resource. Parsons sees power operative only in terms of social values and social systems, not as a relationship among social actors. As a result, he sees power as a "'symbolic medium' running throughout a 'social system' rather than [as] a potentially coercive relation" (Merquior, 1980: 193). Values, however, are supported by power dynamics, and socio-political institutions are often the "foci of power at the service of distinct values and interests" (Merquior, 1980: 7). Parsons does not seem to consider the relationship between values and the particular social groups that are the carriers of those values. From his standpoint, those in positions of power always conform to the general values of society and always attempt to achieve the objectives "preestablished by the 'total system.'" The possibility that the structures of power may be used "routinely and systematically" to advance personal and/or particular group interests that have little to do with the common good, or that may even be in opposition to it, is not given much consideration. On the contrary, the assumption is that powerful individuals are relatively "benevolent, civic-minded" citizens primarily concerned with the well-being of the society. Parsons, in short, tends to consider power as "neutral" and those in power as merely using authority collectively entrusted to them (Hughey, 1983: 152). This would explain why Giddens has suggested that in "Parsons' theory of power human beings appear only as 'cultural dopes'" (in Kokosalakis, 1985: 371).

Finally, Kokosalakis notes that even scholars who belong to the conflict tradition, such as R. Dahrendorf and C. Wright Mills, are guilty of the same problem. The central focus of their discussions of power is the economic or political capacity of some groups or individuals to exploit others. This is misleading because it implies that the dynamics of power "operate outside" any ideological, religious, or even ethical framework (Kokosalakis, 1985: 370, 367).

Kokosalakis's discussion suggests that, despite a wide range of variation in modern theories of legitimate domination, all share a basic theme: the conception of legitimation as a wholly "desacralized" and "demystified" social phenomenon. The question of whether power "has lost entirely its age old mystifying character" is often left unanswered or never made problematic. In other words, legitimation is conceived as "a matter of abstract, rationalized and technocratic, administrative procedures" (Kokosalakis, 1985: 370, 372).

Kokosalakis stands with Merquior in finding the sociological theories of legitimation inadequate to explain the uses of power, but for slightly different reasons. He argues that Marxists, conflict theorists, and structural functionalists alike can all be challenged because they accept the idea that the bases of legitimation in advanced societies are entirely secular, rationalist, and based primarily on technical efficiency. By viewing the dynamics of modern legitimation and modern culture in entirely secular terms, they all fail to pay attention to the role religion still plays in the modern polity. Many other theorists have come to similar conclusions. Some have specifically criticized political science research on power, arguing that scholars in this field have almost nothing to say about the symbolic and cultural role religion plays in shaping political debate and political praxis (Demerath and Williams, 1989: 33).

The issue raised above, while largely true, needs some qualification. Marxist theorists have acknowledged the role religion plays in modern society as a source of false consciousness. In essence, Marx's ideas concerning religion and politics can be reduced to three basic themes: religion as an illusion (compensation for human suffering caused by imperfect social and political relations), religion as a symptom of alienation, and religion as an opiate. At the same time, however, Marx was well aware that religion, its illusions and narcotizing effects, had to be unmasked before political action could proceed. In this sense, religion had a profound political significance. Religious consciousness was simply a reflection of material and social realities; religion was an *inverted world-consciousness*. Once these social realities were transformed, religious consciousness would fade away. Individuals would then realize that God was the projection of an idealized human nature (Marx, [1844] 1978: 53-54).

Marx believed that in Germany the critique of religion was "in the main complete." Feuerbach and others had already established that the criticism of religion was "the premise of all criticism." But, to a certain extent, Marx regarded the Young Hegelians' criticism of religion, especially Feuerbach's, as superfluous, for it addressed symptoms rather than the disease itself. For Marx, religion was not the product of certain universal features of the human condition (as it was for Durkheim and, to a certain extent, for Weber). Rather, religion was the product of specifically contingent social arrangements. In order to give up illusions, what was required was to "abandon a condition which require[d] illusions" (Marx, [1844] 1978: 54). Political emancipation demanded the *"emancipation* of the state from Judaism,

Christianity, and *religion* in general" (Marx, [1843] 1978: 32). In other words, Marx dismisses religion, and one can only speculate that he would have dismissed civil religion as well. This may explain why most Marxist scholars have not participated in the civil religion debate.

Neither Marx nor Engels attached much importance to the issue of political legitimacy.[8] Legitimate authority presumes consent and the rightful claim to obedience or agreement. But, insofar as the bourgeoisie had usurped power and privileges, a legitimate agreement could never be possible. Bourgeois society, in fact, precluded a free, independent state with its own ethical basis. The state was nothing "but a machine for the oppression of one class by another." The state was merely an "executive committee" for managing the affairs of the bourgeoisie. This is the reason why under new, free social conditions, "the entire lumber of the state" would be thrown "on the scrap heap" (Engels, [1891] 1978: 629). Marx's critique of the state parallels his critique of religion: claims of autonomy and independence by the sovereign state are as illusory as religious claims of divine sovereignty.

Religion and Legitimation Today

Scholars have argued, for quite some time, that religion is losing ground in the modern world. Theories of secularization and modernization have helped to reinforce this idea, for they have tended to downplay the significance of religion in political legitimation. Some authors portray religion as playing no part in the legitimation of modern societies (Fenn, 1978), or as having a minimal legitimizing influence (Roof and McKinney, 1987), or as playing only an indirect role (Parsons, 1964). Others, however, contend that something of a religious rebirth is happening, not only in the United States, but around the world (Billings and Scott, 1994; Casanova, 1994; Hamilton, 1995; Hunter, 1991).

Starting perhaps a few decades ago, new developments in the sociology of religion have called into question the assumptions of secularization theories (Finke and Stark, 1992; see also

Hamilton, 1995, esp. ch. 15). In the process several sociologists of religion have also reconsidered the importance of religion in contemporary life and have recognized the dual function religion still plays "in the legitimation of power and privilege and in protest and opposition" of all kinds, despite its alleged decline in public life (Billings and Scott, 1994: 173). Studies have shown the importance of religion as a "political resource," either as an emancipatory force or as an aid to the maintenance of the status quo (Williams, 1996: 368). Berger (1967) sees religion as capable of legitimating or challenging the socio-political order. In this sense, religion can be either a "world-maintaining" or a "world-shaking" force (Billings and Scott, 1994: 173). He seems convinced, however, that the process of privatization is inexorably displacing religion from public life. Religious beliefs have become subjective—that is, the quest for "meaning" and "salvation" has been transferred to the inner corner of the self. Since this quest is a strictly private affair, a matter of "choice" or "preference," a common world view is no longer possible (Berger, 1967: 133-34). Luckman refers to this personal search for identity and self-realization as the "invisible religion" of modern times. This means that the sacred sense formerly given by religion to all aspects of social life "is now only a patchwork of largely privatized experiences" (Beckford, 1989: 106).

Despite the allegedly growing privatization of religion, social scientists are once again paying more attention to religion's involvement in political life. As has been suggested, due to basic developments (both in theory and in praxis), traditional conceptions of legitimation based on beliefs or value consensus have also been called into question. Legitimation is conceptualized more in terms of "bitterly contested struggles where religion still plays a vital role," rather than in terms of societal values and beliefs. Individuals and groups have become the primary agents in these struggles (Billings and Scott, 1994: 174). Religion is not only involved in highly controversial issues and popular struggles, but it seems to be itself "embroiled in controversy." From debates about issues such as privacy rights, abortion, prayer in public schools, or America's military and economic stance in the world, "religion seems to be in the thick of it." But religious groups do not always take the same position in the battlefield. On the contrary, they seem quite polarized. "Scarcely a statement is uttered by one religious group...without another faction of the religious community taking umbrage" (Wuthnow, 1988a: 6). At the same time that religion is becoming political, politics is being "reinfused with religious symbols and claims" (Billings and Scott, 1994: 174). This has led some observers to note that as a result of the complex relationship between religion and politics, it is no longer easy to determine "whether one is witnessing political movements which don religious garb or religious movements which assume political forms" (Casanova, 1994: 41).

Clearly, at the root of many of the issues in which religious groups have become embroiled in recent years lies the increasingly delicate boundary between church authority and state authority. Due to the institutional separation between the state and church, and the tendency towards the secularization of the political order that goes with modernity, the churches can no longer rely on the state to enforce their moral claims. This tension finds its expression, at least in America, in debates over such questions as whether or not the government has the right to keep religion out of the public school system, or whether religious groups have the right to challenge the Supreme Court's decision on moral issues (like the legalization of abortion). These struggles, often bitterly fought out "in church basements," in the streets, in the media corridors, or in courtrooms, are mere "flash points," indicative of deeper changes in the relationship between religion, government, and society in the United States (Wuthnow, 1988a: 7).

Trends towards the politicization of religion and the religionizing of politics, together with the prominence attained by special purpose religious groups on the political scene, indicate a shift away from conceptualizations of religion as either playing no role at all, or being an "indirect legitimator" of the political order, to one that stresses a radical and active presence "vis-à-vis both secular legitimations and religiously based but competing moral visions of the good society" (Billings and Scott, 1994: 175). Wuthnow holds the state responsible for the growth of special groups in American religion. He argues that, as the arm of the state has extended in key areas of people's lives, and as government rules and policies are affecting the daily lives of ordinary citizens, there has been a corresponding proliferation of special interest groups. These groups have turned to politico-religious activism for the "express purpose of combating, restraining, or promoting certain types of government activity" (1988a: 114).

The religious mobilization of moral crusaders, either on the right or on the left of the politico-religious spectrum, and their efforts to legitimize or delegitimize those in positions of authority, challenge the idea that modern society is legitimized entirely in terms of functional rationality or technical expertise. Religious groups, especially but not exclusively in the United States, are no longer content to play an ancillary role regarding what they consider fundamental moral issues. Some religious groups not only want to influence values or individuals' consciences, they seem determined to change them—even if this requires violent activism (Billings and Scott, 1994: 174-76; Jelen, 1995: 280). To accomplish their politico-religious goal and mobilize political influence, special interest groups with religious concerns are increasingly playing "more by political rules rather than by religious rules" (Wuthnow, 1988a: 207).[9] It follows that religion, politics, and morality, "once seemingly far removed," have come to be once more closely intertwined (Billings and Scott, 1994: 174).

Hence, even though there is some truth to the claim that political authority is justified nowadays primarily in secular terms, there seems to be evidence indicating that religiously informed activism has an influence on the "legitimacy of certain policies, the shape of constituencies and coalitions, levels of participation, cultural climates, and the social definitions of public and private spheres in the United States" (Billings and Scott, 1994: 178). Commentators have observed a similar blurring of boundaries between religion and politics in other parts of the world.

Wuthnow (1988a) notes that changes in both religious and political life have produced a profound restructuring or realignment of religion. Elsewhere he notes that the sacred, which is "deeply conditioned" by the social location in which it appears, is "produced" or socially constructed. He contends that if the sacred is produced, so is its public manifestation (i.e., "public religion"). As a cultural product, public religion "does not simply happen." A variety of organizational vehicles concerned with the production of culture are actively involved seeking to influence the beliefs and values of society (Wuthnow, 1994: 2-6).[10] Both issues, restructuring and production, are very important to understanding the role of civil religion in modern society.

In sum, even in our post-industrial, postmodern age, a completely secular politics operating outside any religio-ideological context seems to be more illusion than reality. The legitimation of power in the modern state, as Kokosalakis rightly notes, while largely a matter of rational and efficient procedures, "is also a question of meaning, values and political purpose" (1985: 375). Because power is always embedded in a meaningful symbolic context, it "must always be legitimized within a symbolic cultural and value laden frame of reference" (368). Symbolic power, in turn, implies action, interests, moral fulfilment, and authority (Novak, 1992: 30). Legitimation, thus, has a moral and ideological component that cannot be reduced to formal rationality (Kokosalakis, 1985: 372).

The Invisibility of Power

In the preceding discussion I mentioned that in sociological theories the linkage between power and religion has not received sufficient attention. The sociology of religion, by following the mainstream sociological tendency, has also not come "to grips with the full theoretical significance of the dialectical relationship between power, authority and religion" (Kokosalakis, 1985: 368). Power, although an "*implicit* theme" in the sociology of religion literature, has hardly ever been addressed "directly and precisely" (McGuire, 1983: 1).[11] It should come as no surprise, therefore, that the notion of power in the literature on civil religion also shines through by its absence.[12] By not paying attention to the Rousseauan view of civil religion, experts on this issue have made virtually no attempt to see power as an essential element, perhaps the leading force of the civil religion concept. Only a small number of cross-cultural studies, often in non-Western settings, have dealt with this issue, particularly when civil religion has emerged as a temporary alternative to a political crisis.[13]

Bellah interprets civil religion as setting a standard by which the nation is called to be moral, righteous, and just. The nation has value only to the extent that individuals recognize, even if only in an imperfect and fragmented way, a "higher law" (Bellah, 1974b: 255). There may be some occasional distortions, or even corruption, but Bellah seems to think that civil religion is generally upright.[14] The American nation, after all, "stands under transcendent judgement" (Bellah, 1974b: 255). It follows that in Bellah's analysis political power can be effectively limited and criticized on moral and religious grounds, for the nation is subject to God and his judgment (Bellah, 1975: ix). In other words, he assumes that civil religion has the capacity, or at least the potential, to question the authority of political leaders and political institutions (Gehrig, 1981b: 38). Following Bellah, the general trend of students of American civil religion has been to support the idea that "civil power stands under the sovereignty of God and that the nation must judge its own acts in the light of divine righteousness" (Richardson, 1974: 164).

When Bellah (1967: 4) points out that civil religion "provides a transcendent goal for the political process," he is thinking about the political machinery in theological terms. Politics is approached as if ultimate moral and religious issues are at stake. Marty (1974: 145) and others have called this the "prophetic" dimension of civil religion—a dimension that has a "predisposition toward the judgmental." In Bellah's terms, it is this aspect of civil religion "that makes possible renewal, national self-criticism, and the ability and openness to learn" (Jones and Richey, 1974: 14). The problem is that America is construed "not as striving to understand and follow God's will, but as the very embodiment of that will" (Demerath and Williams, 1985: 160).

The question to be asked is, who (apart from God) sets the standards by which the nation is called to be just and righteous? Who decides if the nation is honouring its covenant or not? Moreover, analysts seldom consider that the allegedly prophetic capacity of civil religion may be liberating for some groups but repressive for others. It may be either "innovative or supportive of the *status quo*," benefiting some and excluding others, depending largely on which side of the fence one stands. One should be careful to distinguish between what Gehrig calls prophetic "attempts" and prophetic "successes." But more than this, one should be able to ascertain who are the beneficiaries of the so-called successes, and what conditions or power dynamics are at work either "facilitating or resisting prophecy" (Gehrig, 1981b: 37). When scholars discuss the prophetic capacity of civil religion, they pay little attention to the actual disparity that may exist between "prophecy *attempted* and influence *gained*" (Demerath and Hammond, 1969: 212). In other words, civil religion's prophetic dimension would seem to provide a rather weak and unreliable indicator for national self-criticism, or for understanding the shape and course of American self-judgment. It would also appear that self-criticism in American politics may easily get embroiled in a kind of vicious circle. Bennett writes: "the state, through its leaders, calls upon deity and dogma to bless actions, while the actions, in turn, are offered as proof that the state has chosen the best and most profound grounds for action" (1975: 88). Bennett illustrates this point by quoting from a speech by Lyndon Johnson: "Above the pyramid on the great seal of the United States it says in Latin, 'God has favored our undertaking.' God will not favor everything that we do. It is rather our duty to divine His will. I cannot help but believe that He truly understands and that He really favors the undertaking that we begin here tonight." Implicit in Johnson's address is the message that Americans are answerable to God, but their actions are agreeable to Him.

Richardson (1974: 161) has suggested that linking religion or civil religion with the nation-state, or with any dimension of humanity, has important consequences. First, actors or groups assigning an ultimate meaning to the nation, are expressing, in a sense, "what concerns them ultimately." Second, there is a tendency to conceive "ultimate reality" as resembling human reality and experience. Jones and Richey (1974: 10) have expressed this idea as follows: when human life is taken as a model for ultimate reality "ultimacy is conferred on that human aspect and the ultimate is reconceived to resemble it."

Richardson (1974: 162) suggests that linking religion with any social dimension has both sociological and theological implications. In sociological terms, it means creating, by means of symbols and rituals, an "ultimate meaning" for social and political life. In theological terms, it is "a way of 'modeling' or picturing what God is and our relation to him." Simply put, it is a way of linking worldly affairs with ultimate and transcendental reality, and vice versa. He writes, "a person who identifies with a political group and its civil religion not only...affirms that this group has a transcendent goal and some ultimate value (the sociological aspect), but he will also tend to think that the categories of politics—sovereignty, law, justice, the state—are especially appropriate for describing ultimate reality (the theological aspect)." But to assign a transcendental dimension to something, is also to assert "that it is, in some way, 'true'" (162). This becomes a serious and pressing problem, if one considers civil religion to be located "in the instrumentalities of government exercising real power" (Rice, 1980: 65).

To be sure, civil religion uses theological symbols, language, and rituals to describe, conceive, and/or legitimize politics and the political process.[15] But theological judgments do not operate in a vacuum; they have social and political resonance (Richardson, 1974: 162). A nation "under God" means somehow that a transcendent reality is the "pusher" or "puller" of the social and political order (Marty, 1974: 144). It means "a higher criterion for sovereignty than either state or people" (Rice, 1980: 60). Civil religion, thus, becomes normative.

What confounds the problem even more is that sacred/theological symbols can promote civic corruption as well as civic virtue. In fact, in particular circumstances, civil religion may even involve a nation in an ideology that gives religious sanction to very harmful aspects of social life. The latter would happen when civil religion and its sacred symbols are consciously manipulated by politicians to facilitate or mask actions, including immoral ones, with "moralistic rhetoric" (Bennett, 1979: 106). There is always the potential danger that religious beliefs used by political authorities may exploit civil religious symbols, rituals, and ceremonies to enhance, legitimize, or justify political rule. Needless to say, this is a danger not only of civil religion, but of religion proper, or of any secular ideology for that matter.

American scholars have been too much concerned with the religious dimension of civil religion, and not concerned enough with its political implications. This may be explained, perhaps, in terms of Americans' strong anti-government ethic. Mead, for example, believes that persuasion, not coercion, is part of the American political mentality. He argues that church-state relations have traditionally rested on two assumptions: the conviction that any society depends upon a set of shared beliefs concerning individuals and their place in the cosmos; and the equally strong conviction that the only way these beliefs will be preserved "is to put the coercive power of the state behind the institution responsible for their definition, articulation, and inculcation." Mead argues that Americans, from the very beginning, adopted the first assumption, but strongly rejected the second one. He suggests that the gist of the American Revolution, and the intention of the founding fathers, was to give up coercion and embrace persuasion (cited in Rice, 1980: 66, n. 50). Huntington, on the other hand, seems to hold a less romanticized view. Americans, he claims, "have gloried in the conspicuous consumption of wealth," but have never had a "gospel of power." This means that American power-holders "must create a force that can be felt but not seen"(1981: 75). What is at issue here is the extent to which the American political tradition has rejected the power of the state.

Distrust of government and opposition to centralized power are (or at least were) at the heart of the American political creed. The impact of the American Revolution, the influence of a laissez-faire Lockean tradition, and the impact of the Protestant tradition fostering the idea of an individual relationship with God helped strengthen the American "ideological commitment to a weak state," and to an anti-collectivist and anti-authoritarian political order (Lipset, 1986: 114-15). The genesis of the American nation and the genesis of its anti-state ethic are, in fact, inseparable. The religious values and beliefs of the American creed, which constitute the core of American national identity, are "liberal, individualistic, democratic, egalitarian, and hence basically anti-government and anti-authority in character." The essence of constitutionalism, individualism, liberalism, and egalitarianism can be reduced to one thing: "freedom from government control" (Huntington, 1981: 4, 33). The creed of American political existence has stressed individualism, "local autonomy, and limitation of executive power" (Clark, 1962: 214). It is reasonable to argue that this aversion or opposition to state power has remained a characteristic of the American way of life well into the twentieth century. Having said this, it is also reasonable to note that the power and faculties of the American government have significantly increased in the second half of the twentieth century. However, the illusion or the reality of an anti-statist ethic has obscured the possibility that civil religion may become linked to state ideology and state power.[16] The desire to keep the state at arm's length does not necessarily mean that the state has indeed remained uninvolved in the production of civil religion.

A further criticism that can be made is that Bellah and his followers have seldom considered the intensity with which Americans accept the basic ideals of the American creed, and the fact that these ideals may vary over time and from one group to another. Huntington notes that changes in the basic set of ideals reflect mutations in the allocation of power in American society and in the "intensity of commitments that Americans have to those ideals." He argues that American society has gone through times of "creedal passion" and periods of "creedal passivity" that are strongly connected with developments in American politics (Huntington, 1981: 4).

In short, the pervasive hostility that Americans have towards centralized power combined with the moralistic component of American civil religion may help explain why the notion of power (or the idea that civil religion may be a powerful tool) has seldom been part of the debate over civil religion in America. American scholars have opted to render invisible the linkage between state power and civil religion.[17]

"Americans are eminently prophets," Santayana is said to have commented, "they apply morals to public affairs" (cited in Huntington, 1981: 67). Bellah and his followers are not the exception that confirms this rule. In keeping with Santayana's observation, they too have donned the mantle of prophecy in their writings on civil religion. They have stressed the moral elements, the consensual aspect, and the religious ethos of the American creed, not its political ramifications. But Kokosalakis's (1985) analysis of the relation between religion, power, and legitimation in modern society is a reminder of the way civil religion may operate in the modern world. Civil religion, like religion proper, does not stand outside power struggles. Rather, power relations operate inside the religious, political, and ideological context of civil religion.

Just as the link between political power and civil religion has been shucked off in most discussions, so has the notion that civil religion may be an ideological phenomenon closely linked to a dominant group or class. Indeed, the direct political content of the belief system of civil religion (as much in the United States as anywhere else in the world) has received little notice in the theories or models of civil religion. The religious rhetoric and message of the civil religious discourse have been quite carefully analyzed, but the political ideology behind those messages has been submerged in the literature. Political ideology, however, can never be entirely divorced either from the structures of civil religion or from an analysis of the dynamics and distribution of power in society. I should clarify that I use the notion of ideology as a set of ideas or principles intended to reorder collective experience, to regulate political understandings, and to mobilize support and collective action (Williams, 1996: 371, 374). In this sense, ideology is as a generalized belief system or "more or less formal systems of thought that benefit a particular group or class of people, but where the ideas themselves are presented as universally true or valid" (Williams, 1996: 374). Implicit in this definition is the view that ideologies may be developed by, or benefit different groups; they are not the prerogative of a particular class.

Bellah, of course, is partly to blame for the lack of attention given to the ideological aspect of civil religion. He targets culture rather than ideology. He seems unwilling to consider the possibility that civil religious beliefs are ideologies, or may be used as such by some groups to legitimize their control over others. Instead, he insists that American civil religion is not and "has never been primarily an ideology intended to reinforce the authority of the state or to cast a halo over institutions" (Bellah, 1976b: 167). In this sense, he is no different than Durkheim. As Giddens (1978: 105) has rightly noted, unlike Max Weber's sociology of religion, which specifically advances the notion that religious beliefs help legitimize group interests, in the "whole of Durkheim's writings, he nowhere confronts the possibility that religious beliefs are ideologies, which help legitimate the domination of some groups over others."

While most authors have opted to follow Bellah's lead, a few have made a passing reference to the ideological aspect of civil religion. Hammond (1980a: 77) uses the notion of ideology in the context of Rousseau's model of civil religion. He argues that Rousseau intended civil religion to be an "ideology at once transcendent but focused on the nation-state" to legitimize, in a functional sense, the political order. Hammond is not referring to civil religions in general, but to civil religions in Rousseau's meaning of the term, which, he insists, "have not routinely developed" and are "probably quite rare" (1988a: 77). Hammond's study is one of the few to clearly distinguish between a Durkheimian and a Rousseauan approach to civil religion. He acknowledges that once civil religion is conceived as a transcendental ideology its analysis "shifts some distance out of the Durkheim camp, where it has generally been" (1980a: 44).

Bennett believes that when a civil religion is "functioning normally" it is a model of "defensible public morality." By this he means that civil religion becomes, or at least has the potential to become, a "moral basis of state action." Under its normal functioning, civil religion cannot be conceived as a forum for political indoctrination or as a "factional ideology within a sate." Bennett does recognize, however, that many obstacles, such as political lies, political propaganda, intimidation, and diverse and competing moral claims, prevent the normal functioning of civil religion. Under such circumstances, the rhetoric of "self-righteousness" and public integrity may become ideological and lead to the justification of destructive and even immoral political measures (Bennett, 1979: 122-23). Fenn has also noted in passing that civil religion is often reduced to an ideology at the service "of political cynics" (cited in Bourg, 1976: 146). For Stauffer et al. (1975: 392), America's "myth of origin," deprived of its transcendental relevance, has become little more than a "justificatory ideology" for political power-holders and for "racial and ethnic prejudice."

Civil religion, like any other cultural phenomenon, is "produced." Children learn about it in the school. They are exposed to it in direct and indirect ways through civic rituals. "Resources, planning, time and effort, money, lobbying, legislation, and professional expertise are all required to maintain it" (Wuthnow, 1994: 132). Civil religion as *culture* is internalized through socialization and education. Civil religion as an *ideological* political phenomenon, like religion proper, is an "organizing principle...for mobilizing collective action...clothed in the universalist language of God's will and transcendent justice" (Williams, 1996: 374). It is directly linked to the state and to political officials. At the level of power dynamics, civil religious ideology is used or may be used to support and legitimize the "uses, the structures and the relations" of political power (Kokosalakis, 1985: 371). Observers such as Williams and Alexander, for example, have found that religion of the "prophetic" type uses its moral authority "to connect Populist principles and policies to righteousness and God's will" (in Williams, 1996: 376).

Needless to say, civil religion is neither the only nor the most important ideological instrument of rule. The state may justify the uses of power in terms of economic relations (laissez-faire ideology), or legitimize it by reference to the will of the people (the social contract, liberal ideology), or it may simply revert to an ideology of might makes right (totalitarian or fascist ideology). What I have tried to argue in this section is the ideological side of civil religion, its inherent political nature, and its profound political significance. Civil religion thus conceived is far from being a cultural given at all times. It follows that the role played by those in power in its creation, dissemination, and diffusion should also be taken into consideration.

The Consensus Legacy and Its Problems

To understand the question of the relationship between civil religion and politics it is necessary to understand the sociocultural, moral, and religious frameworks within which political power operates in the modern world. The linkage of religion and politics, faith and power, is essential for an understanding of the religio-political problem—a fact that Bellah himself has recognized (1980a: vii). Likewise, Williams and Demerath have noted that church-state relationships "quickly bleed into broader structural and cultural questions of religion and power" (in Demerath, 1994: 107).[18]

As indicated above, the role of religion in the United States has been examined quite carefully and covers an extensive literature. Empirical studies of religion's involvement in American political life are also numerous (Billings and Scott, 1994; Burns, 1996; Demerath and Williams, 1992; Evans, 1996; Hunter, 1991; Jelen, 1993; Morris, 1984). Scholarly interest in the New Christian Right, in recent years, indicates that the relationship between religion and politics is still a "contentious issue" in America. As Jelen notes (1995: 271), religious beliefs have always been "essential underpinning[s] of the American political culture." However, the role of civil religion in American politics has not received a parallel attention. On the contrary, studies of civil religion as a political resource are practically non-existent.

To be sure, the relationship between religion and politics is at the heart of Bellah's thesis on civil religion. In his view, the essence of civil religion is the "religio-political problem" (1980a: vii). The political problem, however, has been minimized and obscured by the adoption of Durkheim's integrationist theory. The classic structural-functionalist tradition delineated by Durkheim, and adopted by Bellah and others, views the question of social and political order (legitimation and integration) in terms of consensus. As a logical consequence, civil religion appears to be operating in a cultural environment where conflict and strife are minimized. But, clearly, civil religion is a far more complex phenomenon than the integrationist approach supposes. While civil religion may justify and support the sentiments that give cohesion to a given society, it may also be the expression of those values that predominate because they are supported by the most powerful and influential groups in that society. By taking only a partial insight into the nature of civil religion, consensus theorists have been unable, or unwilling, to conceptualize civil religion as a phenomenon subject to political manipulation and control.

In any case, the harmony generated by civil religion in America is less solid than most authors are willing to accept or even recognize. This is not to say that the main theorists of civil religion naively believe in the American dream, or naively assume that all Americans speak with one voice. Civil religion is postulated to exist and, perhaps, be needed, because the United States does experience internal differences and tensions. It is, nonetheless, supposed to help bond people together despite their differences.

Bellah has recognized that American civil religion has a "different relationship" to republican and liberal traditions, both of which are part and parcel of American political heritage (Mathisen, 1989: 140). Yet, he still insists that although republicans and liberals "may differ in their social programs...they do not necessarily differ in their civil religions" (1976a: 155). A few scholars have acknowledged that American civil religion, as a historical fact, has been "resilient, episodic, and dualistic" (Mathisen, 1989: 140). Wuthnow points to the existence of religiously based conservative and liberal visions of America that provide conflicting senses of its destiny and mission. Indeed, he claims that these two visions are so frequently at odds that they "appear to have become differentiated along a fracture line." Each side sees itself as the repository and defender of higher moral principles (Wuthnow, 1988a: 254). These two visions are "theological opposites and parallel those of priest and prophet, or republican and liberal" (Mathisen, 1989: 140). Again, Bellah disagrees. In his view, there may be "several public theologies, but only one civil religion" (1976a: 155).

Americans certainly have different understandings of reality. Confrontations over moral issues are being increasingly interpreted in terms of a "culture war" currently emerging in American society (Evans, 1996: 15). Disagreements over issues such as homosexuality, abortion, or pornography are more than mere cultural conflicts about opposing values. Rather, they are struggles "to achieve or maintain the power to define reality" (Hunter, 1991: 52). Culture war theorists depict the American nation as drifting towards two polarized groups—orthodox and progressive—with radically different conceptions of their society and its morality (Evans, 1996: 15). These two world views have so little in common, that some scholars believe they are "incommensurable." Hunter suggests that the struggle between orthodoxy and progressivism in the United States is creating a new kind of societal coalition that is bringing together different people, regardless of their religion, social class, or ethnic background (Jelen, 1995: 276; see also Evans, 1996: 21). But since conflicting world views imply profound and incompatible differences that seem to be non-negotiable through normal democratic procedures, culture war theorists believe that this warfare is also "non-resolvable" (Evans, 1996: 16). Jelen notes (1995: 276) that one of the "first casualties of the culture war is likely to be political civility." We have seen examples of such loss of civility in the United States particularly among protesters in front of abortion clinics.

Mathisen (1989: 140) confirms the dualistic nature of American civil religion, and suggests that Americans may never perceive their history and experience "with a single eye." Marty takes a more radical view and argues that there may be "as many civil religions as there are citizens" (1974: 143). Elsewhere, he would appear to agree with those critics for whom civil religion is the "faith of only some citizens...it merely adds one more 'denomination' to an already crowded religious map" (Marty, 1976: 195).

Vincent Harding, an African-American scholar, claims that "civil religion is a repressive WASP construct, used to locate the black outside the approved realm" (cited in Marty, 1974: 143). Likewise, Thompson, while claiming that civil religion can be cleansed of its "perversions" and "distortions" and led back to its original republican ideals, admits nonetheless that it has often been in alliance with racial prejudice and discrimination. He writes:

> the religion of the Republic has been idolatrous, substituting homage to the god of racial supremacy for loyalty to the one true God. Believing in a humane creed, white Americans have systematically oppressed and brutalized black Americans. Professing an inclusive creed, whites have carefully excluded blacks from full and equal participation in our society. Confessing a just creed, whites have rarely extended equal justice to blacks. Honoring a tolerant creed, whites have denied blacks the decision-making power that could affect the character of our institutions and better their competitive position in society. (1971: 270)

Thompson laments that Americans have confined civil religion "solely to their own kind" and have converted it "into an arrogant white Americanism" (1971: 270). This view has been echoed by others scholars who have pointed out that civil religion, "at least the current academic version of it, is not so neutral as its designators would have it; it is a reflection of a WASP apprehension of a world" (Marty, 1974: 143-44).

By emphasizing one overarching unity binding all Americans to the American way of life, scant attention has been given to groups not fully in tune with civil religion, such as African Americans, Aboriginal people, Mexican-Americans, Appalachians, new immigrants, and so on, who may have their own self-consciousness and may not be part of the dominant tradition or the dominant class (Novak, 1992: 129). Novak is right when he argues that in the United States there are cultural traditions that have never been fully integrated into the national experience, and many regions that have been inadequately represented in "national consciousness and national symbolism" (307). It may be more instructive, he adds, to identify several civil religions, rather than one overarching belief system to which all Americans subscribe. Civil religion can then be viewed as a well-institutionalized belief system, but also as a potpourri of different "cultural traditions and resources that have not yet been fully integrated into the national way of life." To recognize these two aspects, Novak writes, is to understand American civil religion as "still in process and in tension, to view it as a national self-understanding not yet adequate to the nation's full experience" (1992: 129). Novak's remarks seem to suggest that the tension is produced because new and excluded groups have not yet been socialized or have not yet accepted the American way of life. Such being the case, civil religion will always be in process and tension as new and permanent waves of immigrants enter the United States, and as different cultural groups struggle to define their social and political reality.

This aspect of American life has either been downplayed or simply ignored. This is not really surprising. Samuel Huntington has made a distinction between different visions of American self-understanding. In his book *American Politics: The Promise of Disharmony* (1981), he argues that the gap ("cognitive dissonance") between the ideal America and political reality has received little attention in the traditional theories of American political thought. In a section entitled "The One, the Two, and the Many," he discusses the structural paradigms of American politics. Theories of "the One" are based on the belief that a broad consensus has always existed in the United States on basic political and cultural values and belief. Hence, the values embedded in the American creed, since the earliest days of the nation, have "served as a distinctive source of American national identity." "The Two" paradigm refers to class-conflict theories—the tension between the haves and have-nots, between the powerful and the powerless, between entrepreneurs and the proletariat. In such a model, the key to understanding American identity is the conflict between classes. Finally, theories of "the Many" hold that the central feature of American politics and self-understanding is competition among different interest groups. Theorists of civil religion have tended to take the first vision and have not given enough consideration to other models of American identity.

Despite its popularity, the idea of a broad universal consensus seems to be an ideal without reality. Individualism, liberalism, and utilitarianism have, to a certain extent, diminished if not destroyed the basis of a common life and consensus. In fact, as Demerath and Williams have noted, and as I have tried to demonstrate, "it is doubtful whether America ever existed as an ideological whole." Although Puritan New England may have been socially integrated (and even this may be questioned), it is clear, particularly after the Second World War, that as America grew in social, political, religious, and economic complexity, it also grew in terms of "dissensus and conflict." What we find in America now is an "uneasy coexistence of splintered groups differing as to race, ethnicity, economic position, and, of course, religion" (Demerath and Williams, 1985: 163-64).

Indeed, journalistic accounts portray American society as so polarized, so fragmented, so full of tension that one gets the impression that America is cursed with a quasi-civil war rather than blessed with a common civil religion. American society has become "too 'loosely bounded' to support a coherent canopy of meaning." Rather, the "American mosaic" has come to look more like the "fractured vision of cubist art" (Demerath and Williams, 1985: 164). Perhaps what Bellah and others take to be American civil religion is a compelling force for only a small though powerful group in society (Markoff and Regan, 1982: 333).

John Wilson suggests that the era of the American way of life has come to and end or reached its final port, for there is no longer a "recognizable spiritual ethos" in American culture. He notes that, from mid-twentieth century there has been a "decisive departure" from the long tradition of American society anchored in a "common religion" based on the Judeo-Christian tradition. This tradition, or perhaps this common religion, he argues, no longer exists (1986: 118).

It follows that the cohesiveness attributed to civil religion is not as profound as we have been led to believe. The image of civil religion in America as a canopy of shared values, operating exclusively in terms of consensus and social cohesion, turns attention away from the role that civil religion plays in defining (or obscuring) national self-understanding; stabilizing (or upsetting) social and national expectations, and its sense of destiny and mission; maintaining (or undermining) social values and beliefs; strengthening (or weakening) social harmony; relieving (or exacerbating) social conflicts.[19] Reducing civil religion to only one tradition also means reducing its capacity as an analytical tool, "reducing the intellectual compass" (to use Geertz's phrase) within which studies of the civil religion phenomena may be carried out, both in the United States and in comparative or cross-cultural frameworks.

Civil Religion: Its Agents and Structural Support

The reader should be reminded that Bellah and his followers insist that civil religion, at least in America, is totally independent of both church institutions and state institutions, but serves nonetheless to legitimize the political order. This section challenges this claim.

We have already seen that, as an idea system, the American creed has dominated the political process and shaped American political life. Even Bellah recognizes (1978: 23) that politicians have "carried the burden" of American self-interpretation. I have also noted that ideas neither exist independently nor operate in a vacuum—they are produced, and used, to promote and legitimate particular social or political vision. The fact that civil religion can be perceived as a cultural phenomenon does not preclude its use as an important ideological tool of the political machinery. But one has to look elsewhere—history, philosophy, theology, political science, or to publications outside the United States—to find the linkage between civil religion and its political uses.

Sheldon Ungar, a Canadian scholar, has explicitly shown the interaction between civil religion and politics in the United States. He eloquently examines the relationship between civil religion and politics in the context of the nuclear arms race before the collapse of the communist bloc (Ungar, 1991). His study suggests that the United States generated a clearly defined civil religious ideology to justify American nuclear monopoly and policies. Military superiority, Ungar notes, came to be viewed as a "sacred trust," the outcome of the "uniqueness" and exceptional "destiny" of the United States. His study also shows how elements of civil religion were employed to legitimate the American arms race, and how the civil religious rhetoric was particularly evident after the American faith in their technological superiority was shattered by the Soviet launching of the *Sputnik* on 4 October, 1957. The American "humiliation" and "moral panic" that followed, Ungar suggests, were somehow mitigated by a state ideology promoting public support "for almost anything in the name of national security." State-financed and state-controlled research and development, standing in direct contradiction to the American tenets of a liberal economy, were justified in the name of technocratic superiority. Ungar persuasively demonstrates how this state ideology was presented in "metaphysical" terms, promising to restore the unique "moral and historical" mission of the United States—to defend, and dictate, the values of democracy and the free market to nations around the world. Ungar concludes that a complex of civil religion ideology, political power, and legitimation informed the stance of the American state against Soviet communism. Civil religion, in his view, operated as a "mediating factor in political behaviour." In short, he explicitly demonstrates that civil religion was used during this period as a political resource.

Likewise, Bennett reminds us that the United States opened its arms to the twentieth century with the annexation of the Phillippines. In this exercise, "the military extermination of Filipino independence fighters was, for many in America, almost a holy obligation." He goes on to quote a speech delivered on the floor of the U.S. Senate at the time of the invasion. The senator in question claimed that "God has not been preparing the English-speaking and Teutonic peoples for a thousand years for nothing but vain and idle self-contemplation and self-admiration. No. He has made us master organizers of the world....And of all our race He has marked the American people as His chosen nation to finally lead in the redemption of the world." Civil religion, Bennett suggests, became a powerful source for the justification of the war (1979: 123n. 30).[20] The political use of civil religion has also been noticed by Novak (1992) with reference to the breakdown of American political legitimacy during the Vietnam era and the Watergate crisis. As Bennett tells us, and as Novak's analysis of American foreign policy indicates, during crises of legitimacy the state "adopts through its leaders a perverse form of self-legitimation in which all state actions are virtuous since the state is seen as the source of virtue" (Bennett, 1979: 129). Under such circumstances, dissent regarding government policies is often interpreted as questioning the very essence of the nation.

Novak blames the "moral self-righteousness" of government institutions and political officials on their easy access to the symbolic "trappings" of civil religion. Especially in times of stress and crisis, national self-definition in America tends to be expressed in terms of a religiously based language. Insofar as the president has the greatest access to the symbols of government, and since he gains power by the manipulation of those symbols, the president has "power over reality." He has what Novak calls "symbolic power." This view has been echoed by a few other scholars who acknowledge that American political leaders and political officials have enormous access to the symbols of office and mythologies of the nation, thus influencing the construction of civil religion (Novak, 1992: 259; Edelman, 1964: 73; see also

Wilson [1979], esp. chap. 3). Hammond (1980d: 193) would argue that when the "trappings" and not the "principles" of civil religion are treated as sacred, civil religion runs the danger of becoming trivialized.

The public school system provides yet another basis for questioning the idea that an independent and highly differentiated belief system exists in America. It is interesting to note that the same scholars who claim that civil religion in America is completely separated from the state also stress the importance of schools as providers of a context for the "cultic celebration of civic rituals" (Bellah, 1967: 11). Bellah and others, however, have tended to see the public school system as neutral in its effort to promulgate national unity and a non-sectarian morality. But the role of public schools as a powerful instrument for the indoctrination of American civil religion cannot easily be dismissed. The public school system not only provides structural support to preserve the culture, but, to a large extent, functions as a "direct institutionalization" of American civil religion. Indeed, public schools in the United States have been recognized "as the Durkheimian church of the public religion in America" (Wilson, 1979: 126-27). Hammond, who agrees with the idea that American civil religion is fully independent from church and regime, claims at the same time that civil religion in the United States is "both parent and child to the public school." He also reiterates the idea that schools are its major source of "structural support" (Hammond, 1980a: 75; 1968: 383).

But the state is not entirely detached when it comes to public education. Rather, "it is active and even coercive" in enforcing a national, unitary American way of life, "often in its most chauvinistic and benighted form" (Novak 1992: 303). The public education complex is, in fact, directly linked to government, and it is essential to the socialization of each new generation (Wilson, 1979: 120). A religiously consensual political culture does not just happens; it needs to be implemented and cultivated. This means that the state uses (or at least may use) civil religion to socialize students to the dominant norms and values of American society, and to foster or speed the integration of students into the wider society (Gamoran, 1990: 247). However, as far as I can tell, only Gamoran's article "Civil Religion in American Schools" (1990) deals specifically and directly with the role today's public schools play in producing and transmitting American civil religion. Gehrig (1981b) has given a brief analysis of the relationship between public education and American civil religion, and Robert Michaelson, in *Piety in the Public Schools* (1970), has offered an historical examination of the school's religious and civic functions. The lack of attention to the way civil religion is produced through the public school system constitutes yet another serious flaw in civil religion theorizing.

Finally, American civil religion resides not only in the educational system, but in the legal system as well—both institutions being its "major civil agents" (Hammond, 1980a; 1980b; and 1980c). As already noted in chapter 2, the law explicitly indicates the range of life styles and ethical norms that are deemed to be socially acceptable in American culture. While in other societies, particularly those having a weak institutional differentiation, the boundary-setting task might be taken by religion, in the United States this is a role played by the law. The American legal tradition, in turn, is closely connected with the political machinery or the "political matrix" of American society. As such, it has been "conventionally identified as a branch of the government" (Wilson, 1979: 130-32).

In short, several institutions associated with the government would seem to provide structural support, and serve as carriers, for the maintenance of civil religion in America. Civil religion has found a niche "in such 'civic' arenas as schools, public buildings, national holidays, and other regime symbols" (Jelen, 1995: 274). In other words, civil religion is deeply bound up with the educational, political, and legal interests of the American experience. If this is the case, how can we consider it completely separated from the state?

This should not be taken to mean that civil religion is always manipulated. I am not necessarily arguing that the legitimizing ideology of state institutions is inevitably based on lies and errors (to borrow Rousseau's words). It is not civil religion per se that produces false consciousness. Rather, it is the use—specifically, the political use—of civil religion that may produce distortion or false information, especially when certain political agendas are presented as universally true but do not constitute what Parsons calls "a balanced account of the available truth" (cited in Geertz, 1973: 199). Civil religion has both cultural and political influence. It may be at times "a noble religion, celebrating some very noble civic virtues" (Herberg, 1974: 86). However, while it is true that its influence may be morally neutral, it is no less true that in some circumstances it may also be morally corrupt. I will return to this issue in chapter 5.

Summing up, the preceding discussion calls into question the belief that there is a highly independent civil religion in America. The central argument has been to demonstrate that not even in the United States is civil religion totally separate from the state. This means that civil religion in America does not fit the model of a "fully differentiated" civil religion, as Bellah (1967) Coleman (1969) and others have claimed. Wilson has rightly argued that a structural analysis of American society appears to provide no evidence to support this claim. I also agree with his comment that the lack of attention students of civil religion have given to this issue is surprising (Wilson, 1979: 132, 140). Civil religion in the United States, as much as anywhere else in the world, may be used (and has been used) by political institutions for purely political ends. As an expression of a particular ideology, a particular regime, or a particular group, civil religion may have varying political goals. In the next chapter I examine how it has been used as a conscious tool of political manipulation—for legitimation purposes to facilitate national policies, political programs, or even political propaganda—outside the United States.

CHAPTER FOUR

State-Directed Civil Religions in Comparative Perspective

Although Bellah's original article referred specifically to the United States, he has not limited the applicability of the term civil religion solely to American society.[1] Yet, as mentioned elsewhere, the concept has had a distinctively American flavour, and has been analyzed, discussed, and debated almost exclusively in American terms (Cristi and Dawson, 1996: 320; Markoff and Regan, 1982: 334). Also, the argument presented in previous chapters clearly suggests that American civil religion has been portrayed as a cohesive force, which helps achieve national goals, reaffirms common moral values, and fosters social and cultural integration. However, the cultural cohesion it allegedly reflects has been exaggerated, for it is neither as solid nor functioning as well as its "more idealistic" advocates have described it (Demerath and Williams, 1985: 154-55).

Notes to Chapter 4 are on pp. 254-55.

The brief comparative survey of state-directed civil religion that I present in this chapter challenges some of the most basic assumption underlying the American usage of the term, and demonstrates that civil religion is not always a cohesive force in society. Indeed, what follows supports my contention that civil religion, rather than being the spontaneous cultural phenomenon characteristic of Bellah's portrayal, may be the product of deliberate invention, planning, and manipulation. A discussion of sacred and secular civil religions à la Rousseau, in different societies and at different times will illustrate this point.

Civil Religion as Political Religion

In his article "The Conditions for Civil Religion: A Comparison of the United States and Mexico," Phillip E. Hammond (1980a), a prominent figure in the literature on civil religion, and, as mentioned earlier, one of the few scholars who makes a clear distinction between the Durkheimian and Rousseauan traditions, takes the position that civil religion, in Rousseau's meaning of the term, is independent of both church and state. Hammond's otherwise excellent article reveals an inadequate understanding of Rousseau's theory, for he does not consider Rousseau's civil religion as an ideology whose essential function is to serve as the "handmaiden" of the state. Recognizing Hammond's fallacy is fundamental to understanding why Rousseau's ideas concerning civil religion may be easily distorted, and used or abused by politicians or authoritarian political systems.

Hammond claims that Rousseau *"seems to suggest* the most fully developed civil religion relies exclusively on neither the church nor the state but to a significant degree at least counts on independent vehicles for its support" (1980a: 44; emphasis added). Hammond thus argues that Rousseau's civil religion, in order to survive, needs "independent organizational vehicles to 'carry' it" (58). This means that civil religions, of the Rousseauan variety, depend upon certain social and political conditions to develop. Neither church nor state but an independent belief system has to succeed in monopolizing "God talk," in adopting a theological rhetoric, and in providing an ideology "by which ultimate meaning is bestowed upon national life." In other words, development of a Rousseau-type civil religion depends upon the existence of a belief system capable of merging both civil and religious ideological forces and able to succeed in holding the "balloon strings" of civil religion. Hammond insists that this form of civil religion is "quite rare" (77). He notes that the types of "political religions" found in some developing nations have "little in the way of any 'theology' *independent of the state* [so], they are not fully civil religions in Rousseau's meaning of that term" (43-44; emphasis added). Hammond claims that when Rousseau coined the term *civil religion* his intention was to "harmonize" religion and politics and find a solution to the problem of religious decline. His answer was the creation of a transcendent ideology that was to be "the handmaiden of neither the church nor the state" (77).

There appears to be a basic contradiction between Hammond's interpretation of Rousseau's theory on civil religion, and his own writings on the subject. It is not always clear whether he is referring to a civil religion that is closely linked to the state or a phenomenon that is totally independent of it. For example, in a different article published the same year, he asserts that, contrary to Durkheim's theory—in which civil religion emerges spontaneously out of "social life itself"—Rousseau believed that "civil religion is a sensible thing for leaders to create and encourage" (Hammond 1980c: 138). But if Rousseau's version of civil religion is, as Hammond insists, independent of the state, one is tempted to ask, who are these leaders? Clearly, the "balloon strings" of civil religion—to use his metaphor—are held by political leaders. Political leaders frequently use solemn occasions and public forums for the transmission of civil religion themes. Political institutions and public rituals become, at times, "agencies for public indoctrination rather than means of exploring principled public sentiment" (Bennett, 1979: 129). Leaders, in fact, have official access to political and religious symbols and to the "structural conveyances" of the political platform. This simply means that leaders can transmit, activate, and manipulate religious symbols to produce certain political ends (Bennett, 1975: 88). Moreover, Hammond himself acknowledges that Rousseau in *The Social Contract* "discusses several means for 'strengthening the constitution of the State,' and it is in this context that he introduces the notion of civil religion, an aid in governing" (1980a: 43). If Rousseau's intention is to strengthen the constitution of the state, how can civil religion, as he devised it, be independent of it?

The problem is exacerbated by Hammond's claim that the United States has a civil religion "of the sort Rousseau urged"— that is, a transcendental ideology independent of both church and state. "All the necessary conditions" for the emergence an independent civic faith were present from the very genesis of the American nation (republican morality, Protestant faith, liberalism, and religious pluralism). This amalgam provided a fertile soil for the development of civil religion in its highest form—a fully differentiated civil religion. Hammond, then, suggests that this "enabled the church in America to relinquish its monopoly on holding the string of the religion balloon and...enabled government officials to grab it" (1980a: 66). It seems quite puzzling to me to argue that American civil religion is an idea system totally independent of both church and regime, and simultaneously affirm that government officials have grabbed the balloon strings of civil religion. It is the responsibility of political leaders, Hammond notes, to "create and encourage" the civil religious ideology. If civil religion is the construction and expression of political leaders, how can it be independent of the political system?

In my view, Hammond betrays a profound misunderstanding of Rousseau, for in a full Rousseauan sense, civil religion is a state-imposed religion.[2] Rousseau's civil religion cannot be conceived independently of the nation-state. In fact, insofar as there is a civil religion of a Rousseauan type, it cannot but be established by the state. Civil religion as understood by Rousseau is a *political religion* to be fixed and dictated by the state, for the state. Rousseau not only suggests this, but clearly advocates it. Indeed, for Rousseau, civil religion was to be *imposed* upon the citizens of the state. Such being the case, civil religions of the type Rousseau recommended are not so rare; they are routinely found in authoritarian regimes, and may be found in democratic systems as well.

The idea that the most fully developed civil religions rely on neither church nor state was suggested by Bellah's in his initial formulation, and advanced by Hammond (1980a) and Coleman (1969), but not by Rousseau. After several careful readings of Rousseau's chapter on civil religion, one is hard pressed to find any such suggestion. Rousseau does not even suggest "independent vehicles" to carry it.

Hammond may be right in arguing that any ideology requires "institutionalization" and independent carriers to promote it. He is not alone in this. Hughey (1983: 103) also claims that no ideology can survive without "institutional supports and a carrying stratum." Likewise, Demerath and Williams (1985: 160), consider an "institutional base" essential for the organization and "ritualized reinforcement" of ideologies. For Rousseau, the carrier was to be embodied in the state. The state "would become the church" (Novak, 1992: 123), and the tenets of faith would be nothing less than a "statist orthodoxy" (Neuhaus, 1986: 99). Civil religion, as a political device, was specifically designed to guarantee citizens' loyalty "to a contingent social order" (Wilson, 1971: 17). What Rousseau named civil religion was, in fact, nothing more than a theory of a political religion necessary for the support of the state, or, as Hammond recognizes, at least one needed to strengthen its constitution. Its purpose was the enforcement of civic responsibility, essential for the maintenance of social stability and the common good (Wilson, 1971: 14)

This understood, the danger of coercion looms large in Rousseau's account of civil religion. The task of the legislator, Rousseau writes, is to change human nature, to transform each individual "into part of a greater whole." Rousseau is quite specific about this: the legislator must "take away from man his own resources" and offer new ones that are "alien to him" so as to give him a "moral existence" and make him subordinate and accountable to the community as a whole. The more "these natural resources are annihilated," the more likely he is to be a good citizen and embrace the general will. Thus, "if each Citizen is nothing and do nothing without the rest...it may be said that legislation its at the highest possible point of perfection" (Rousseau, [1762] 1973: 194-95).

In essence, Rousseau entrusts the legislator with a potentially coercive task—that of transforming human nature, moulding the morals of the people, making them virtuous citizens, and orienting them towards the good of society. The sovereign is to determine those "social sentiments" that are essential for being both a "faithful subject" and a "good citizen" (Rousseau, [1762] 1973: 276). From this point of view, the highest point of perfection of civil religion and its most powerful contribution to the modern nation-state, is the creation of a specific "pattern of social relations" and political obligations that every citizen is forced to embrace. Its practical contribution is to "civic behaviour" (Wilson, 1971: 14; see also Bennett, 1979: 111). Rousseau's concern is civic responsibility, and respect for the contract and its law.

Civil religions of the type Rousseau encouraged are intended to introduce normative changes to force individuals to alter their civic and moral nature. By and large, it is a fundamental requirement of some political religions to produce new citizens. Another essential requirement is to convince individuals that the "ultimate ends of the state and [its] moral aims are one" (Apter, 1963: 90). So much is this the case that often political slogans or doctrines are transformed into political beliefs. States with monolithic structures and autocratic government are prime candidates for political religions.

As discussed in chapter 1, Rousseau allows citizens the right to private opinions as long as such opinions and beliefs have no political implications. Thus, it is solely with "reference to morality and duties to others that the dogmas of religion concern the state" (Wilson, 1979: 160). Such a statement illustrates the tension between the individual and the citizen and the danger of repression that are present in Rousseau's work. Religion is a private and acceptable thing as long as it does not impinge on the security and the stability of the state. Civic behaviour is the "social location" in which the tenets of civic faith will manifest themselves (Wilson, 1979: 161). Non-acceptance of the purely civil profession of faith could mean, as I have already noted, exile or even death.

Rousseau's interest is essentially instrumental: how can religion be used for the benefit of the community? In his scheme, the state may invade the private and religious realm to lay down rules or prescribe beliefs as long as they will benefit the community, as long as social cohesion is maintained. The relationship between politics and religion is conceived in terms of "political behavior as derived from beliefs" rather than in terms of "functions or values." It should be stressed, as Wilson reminds us, that civil religion thus conceptualized does not "preclude understanding society as sacred or cultural values as the means to deeper social cohesion" (1979: 160-61).

This understanding of civil religion is not unique to Rousseau. Rather, it is part of an ancient tradition. It is often traced back to imperial Rome, where a variety of religious ideologies were tolerated, "with the critical test or proof being expression of allegiance to the imperial cult." Rousseau's civil religion, like the Roman cult, was created and directed towards the attainment of political ends (Wilson, 1979: 161). As an established doctrine, its "test of orthodoxy" is not so much faith but civic behaviour, so no "delinquent under its reign will be punished for being impious, but just for being unsociable" (Merquior, 1980: 37).

It is not difficult to understand why a civil religion of this type may be laden with danger or with what Hughes (1980: 78) calls "demonic potential," particularly if it emerges in non-democratic societies. In this context, serious consideration should be given to Rousseau's dreadful suggestion that someone should be exiled or eliminated for showing antisocial behaviour (or a lack of civic faith). Such attention becomes even more important when we consider the tragic consequences of several twentieth-century political regimes that seem to have put into practice Rousseau's maxim (Giner, 1993: 31). History chronicles many places where the deadly horrors of such political religions have been found. Political dissidents declared mentally ill, assassinated or simply "disappeared" have been common in modern totalitarian regimes all over the world. Dissidents' antisocial behaviour has often been no more than a refusal to accept the demands of the civil religion of their day.[3]

Hence, contrary to Hammond's claim, civil religions of the type Rousseau encouraged are not so difficult to find. Civil religions are means of making religiously based beliefs, values, and ideas "operative in a secular society" (Rouner, 1986: 1). But they are also means of making the polity acquire a sacred character. Thus, civil religions à la Rousseau may appear under different forms and varieties, such as theocracies, political messianism, sacred authoritarianism, totalitarianism, and secular or religious nationalism. Indeed, cases of Rousseauan civil religions are to be found in revolutionary regimes, such as revolutionary France, Fascist Italy, Nazi Germany, Franco's Spain, Pinochet's Chile, Brazil during the revolutions of 1930 and particularly of 1964, China, State Shinto in Japan from 1868 to 1945, and in former Marxist-Leninist regimes.[4] Nonetheless, tendencies to use civil religion, as Rousseau understood it, are also found in democratic societies.[5]

Sacred and Secular Civil Religions

A distinction is often drawn between totalitarian and authoritarian political systems. Linz (1964: 293-97) has formulated some of the main characteristics of these types of regimes. The totalitarian political organization involves unlimited domination, and no respect for laws or codes. It is anti-pluralistic and tends to be highly mobilized and organized around a single leader and political party. It includes an official ideology, often extremely nationalistic, with sacred "chiliastic elements." Brutal and complete political repression is ensured by control of the mass media, armed forces, and police. The goal is "systematic neutralization of the opposition," that is, of anti-social elements and enemies of the nation. Nazi Germany immediately comes to mind as a prime modern example, and a tragic reminder of the consequences of a totalitarian regime.

The main characteristics of authoritarian regimes, on the other hand, are "limited" political pluralism, lack of an elaborated and well-articulated ideology, the presence of a typical "authoritarian mentality" (that is, modes of thought that are "more emotional" and "less codified" than ideologies), and weak political mobilization (Linz, 1964: 297). According to Linz, authoritarian regimes are "imperfect forms of either totalitarian or democratic polities, tending…in one or the other direction" (293).[6] Because Mussolini never achieved absolute control over Italian society as Hitler did over Germany, Italian Fascism has been described as a "failed totalitarian experiment" (Pasquino, 1986: 46).

Although Linz and others see the lack of an articulated ideology as a characteristic of authoritarian regimes, Evelyn Stevens (1975) argues that claims to legitimacy in authoritarian political systems often rest on a set of beliefs that are ideologically and rhetorically used as an explanation and justification for the government's actions. Stevens suggests a taxonomy of authoritarian regimes in terms of "secular" and "sacred" versions of authoritarianism. The taxonomic criterion involves the "mental processes" by which the exercise of power and decision-making procedures are justified (Coleman and Davis, 1978: 56). An authoritarian regime can be either sacred or secular depending on whether legitimating claims are based on religious or nonreligious beliefs and values. Thus, contrary to Linz's claim, Stevens suggests that there is a religiously based ideology sustaining sacred authoritarianism.

What Stevens calls sacred authoritarianism, others have termed "political messianism" (Apter, 1963: 63; Moltmann, 1986: 55). Here political solutions tend to take the form of theocracies, and policy-makers try to demonstrate that their policies and actions are in harmony with religious values and principles (Coleman and Davis, 1978: 56). This type of regime presumes a pre-ordained and coherent program of action and recognizes only "one plane of existence, the political" (Apter, 1963: 63). Its political structure is based on a "mystique" involving some higher principle or force, above the individual, that conceives the political machinery (i.e., the state) as a medium through which it may work out its ultimate ends and moral obligations. This mystique may be as varied as "the dialectical laws of history and social development for the Marxists, the destiny of the nation and race for the Hitlerians, or the ideal of the true Christian society for Franco" (Inkeles, 1964: 91). This contradicts Bellah's and Coleman's evolutionary model, whereby civil religion in its fully differentiated expression (as a totally independent system of beliefs) would appear only in the "modern" world. It is in the modern world that these extreme cases of sacred authoritarianism or political messianism are to be found.

Totalitarian or monopolistic types of civil religion, with strong nationalistic secular ideologies (as in the case of France, the former Soviet Union, Communist China, Cuba, or Turkey under Atatürk), have been identified as "secular nationalism" (Coleman, 1969: 72; Stevens, 1975). Coleman suggests that secular nationalism is an "alternative" civil religion with a "worldview and symbol system" which either replaces or competes with the traditional religious system of organized churches (1969: 72).

France, for example, after the French Revolution, sought to establish not only a secular but an aggressive anti-Christian civil religion (Bellah, 1967: 13). To replace Christianity with the Cult of the Supreme Being, and to institutionalize the veneration of the goddess of reason, Christian churches were transformed into Temples of Reason, and those churches that did not, or could not, become centres for the new cult were plundered, shut down, or used by revolutionaries and government officials for political activity (De Azevedo, 1979: 11-12; Markoff and Regan, 1982: 335-45; Willaime, 1993: 573). The calendar was also rearranged—the birth of the Republic came to replace the birth of Christ, Sunday was abolished, and priests were urged to resign. In short, the whole nation was forced to secularize. The glorification of the nation, patriotism, and civic virtue were imposed and maintained through a civil religion and a series of rituals and ceremonies devoted to encourage worship of France and the goddess Reason (Giner, 1993: 31). Despite the eventual overthrow of the secular revolutionaries, the French state ever since has occupied a central role in the definition, production, and self-understanding of the French identity.[7]

In a similar vein, the Soviet Union made of Marxism a civil religion where the tenets of faith of historic materialism were not only taught but became compulsory (De Azevedo, 1979:12; Giner, 1993:36; Luke, 1987; Zeldin, 1969). Jennifer McDowell's study (1974) of the political rituals and symbolic power in the Soviet Union is particularly instructive. In her analysis, she shows how public ceremonies or national holidays were intended to strengthen and legitimize Soviet authority. Likewise, Christel Lane, in her interesting study *The Rites of Rulers* (1981), has shown how state-managed rituals and symbols were an important aspect of the general ideology promoting the legitimacy of the Soviet state. These studies suggest a close link between the legitimation mechanisms of the former Soviet Union and the political religion of Marxism-Leninism. Because of the religious quality of Marxism, the former Soviet state has been characterized as "an inverted Roman Catholic theocracy and Russian Marxist communism [as an] inverted Roman Catholicism" (Zeldin, 1969: 110). Zeldin argues that Marxism as a doctrine resembles Catholicism insofar as its principles clearly form a "body of beliefs." As in Catholicism, Marxism has believers, teachers and prophets, and saints and martyrs. There are inquisitorial purges, sinners to be punished, heresies to be eradicated, doctrines to be taught, and rituals and ceremonies to be celebrated. There is only "one truth" (historical materialism), and only "one Church—the Party" (108-9).

The People's Republic of China provides another example of a communist regime where the Marxist ideology, reinterpreted by Mao Zedong in *The Red Book*, became sacralized and enforced through a series of ritual activities. China became a theocratic society, and Mao himself a theocratic ruler. This was particularly evident during the Cultural Revolution, when political and normative demands from the state forced Chinese citizens to act in accordance with party rules and values (Zuo, 1991: 107; see also Demerath, 1994: 113-14; Luke, 1987). Fidel Castro's Cuba may be cited as yet another case. Castro has tended to transform the Cuban political process into a religion.

Franco's Spain, on the other hand, is a classic example of "sacred authoritarianism," as is Shinto Japan. In both cases there is an overt identification of political and religious allegiances. Franco, for example, explicitly assigned a religious function to the state and justified its repressive apparatus by investing it with religious authority. At the same time, the Spanish state demanded a "quasi-religious" commitment to its cause (Coleman and Davis, 1978: 56-57). As Coleman and Davis suggest, a good Spanish citizen was entrusted with a national, religious, and political mission: to defend Christianity and push the "barbarians" (communists, socialists, and anyone opposing Franco's regime) outside the Spanish gates. Political obedience and allegiance to the state thus became a test of loyalty, a way of measuring the degree of commitment to the "Spaniards' view of themselves as the civilizers and Christianizers of a barbaric and godless world" (Stevens, 1975: 362). A political calling to defend Spain was equated with a religious calling to fight atheist Republicans; anyone not accepting this unity became suspect. State and regime took on sacred characteristics that were employed to provide political legitimacy to Franco's rule. Political principles and religious beliefs became indistinguishable. Jose María Beneyto (1983) considers the whole political theory of Franco's regime as a political theology.

Similarly, prior to the Second World War the Japanese government promoted and tried to revive a form of state Shinto that celebrated patriotism, nationalism, and glorification of the emperor. State Shinto has been identified as a civil religion, or a religion of Japanese nationalism, which started at the time of the Meiji restoration in 1868, and lasted until 1945 when Japan unconditionally surrendered to the Allied forces (Takayama, 1988: 329, 330. See also Bellah, 1980d). The emperor was assumed to be linked genealogically to the so-called age of the gods, and the Japanese hierarchical social structure was justified in religious terms. The emperor was "descended from the sun goddess and [took] his preeminence on earth just as she [took] hers among the gods" (Bellah, 1980d: 29). In pre-1945 Japanese society, "divinity, society and the individual" were fused in one organic whole. Bellah has argued that the type of authoritarianism Japanese society has endured for most of its history is the result of a religious ideology that has systematically justified a hierarchical social order, promoted an ethic of "moral heroism" among the peasantry, and consciously manipulated the Japanese civil religion and its Shinto mythology (Bellah, 1980d: 28-37). In sacred forms of nationalism, Bellah notes, "fully and whole heartedly carrying out one's part in society and living up to its values means identification with ultimate reality" (Bellah, 1957: 186, in Coleman, 1969: 70). Japan and the Soviet Union are particularly instructive for they provide sample cases of two different kinds of state-sponsored civil religions. Whereas the Soviet Union used "political religion" to support the authority of the state, Japan used "religion politically" to achieve the same end (Apter, 1963: 61). Japan's type of political solution to the politico-religious problem represents, in Bellah's view, a "theocratic" or "archaic" form of civil religion.

From "Archaic" to "Modern" Civil Religions

For Bellah the crux of civil religion is the conflict between religion and politics, or, what he calls, the "religio-political problem" (1980a: vii). He assumes that different types of solution and different forms of civil religion parallel different stages of religious evolution. Rather than placing the focus of his evolutionary scheme on economics, industrialization or modernization, as others scholars do, Bellah locates the increased development of civil religion with the development of religion itself, in a particular society, at a particular time. In other words, civil religion is seen as varying with the stages of religious evolution (1980a: vii-xiv, see also Bellah, 1970, esp. ch.2).

Primitive and archaic societies do not differentiate between the religious and political realm, hence there is no need for political solutions—the conflict between political and religious power does not really exist. In archaic societies (i.e., the Bronze Age) power becomes more centralized, and the focus of political and religious concern is the divine king. The king acts as a mediator between God and the people. Bellah observes that an ambiguous line of demarcation between the religious and the political, or a low "degree of differentiation between divinity, society and the individual" (1980d: 28) is a typical manifestation of a "full-fledged archaic solution" to the religio-political question. Consequently, such a solution also indicates a "full-fledged archaic civil religion" (1980a: ix). Theocracy is the result of this type of political arrangement. Bellah acknowledges that theocratic or "archaic tendencies" may also appear in modern society, for vestiges of divine kingship have the tendency to re-emerge or develop whenever powerful political leaders appear, as in the cases of Hitler, Stalin, and Mao Zedong (1980a: ix). Under such circumstances, the state, together with its political authorities, becomes sacralized. Leaders assume a monopoly over political morality. They become the exclusive source and sanction of moral principles and justice, making a "rule of law and not of men" virtually impossible (see Apter, 1963: 73). When political authority becomes sacralized, God ceases to be ecumenical and non-sectarian. He is customarily placed on the side of those who command power. Thus, it is not uncommon to find a single leader or a military junta claiming to have become the repositories of truth and the representatives of God on earth. In such cases, a national state or a particular individual assumes a supra-human dimension and becomes the prophet of civil religion.

Bellah argues that the rise of historic religions, while "never fully overcoming" archaic or primitive tendencies, introduces a degree of differentiation between religious and political systems. The relationship between political authority and religious authority, becomes, thus, more problematic and more pronounced. In societies with historic religions, "whether or not there is a clearly differentiated religious structure," tensions and power struggles usually develop between religious leaders and political authority. The most common outcome is a "division of labor," whereby religious authorities legitimize the state, asking in return for political acceptance of their own authority, and for a leading position in religious matters. In such cases, "the state expects the church to help maintain social tranquility and the church expects the state to conform to at least minimal ethical norms." This division of labour is often unstable, giving rise to periods of intense conflict. During these moments of strife two things may happen: temporal authority either "falls back on archaic archetypes," or religious leaders may seize political authority themselves (Bellah, 1980a: ix-x).

Following this evolutionary pattern, another alternative arises: a clearly modern type that exhibits a high degree of differentiation between the sacred, the social, and the individual realms. Here, political legitimacy and moral concerns are not fused with either church or state but are embodied in an independent set of religious symbols (Bellah, 1980a: xi). In terms of Bellah's scheme of evolution, the "unique" political solution that characterizes the American case represents the highest stage of religious evolution.

It is interesting to note that Bellah himself recognizes that the fusion of the political and the religious realms, and the fusion of political and religious power, is "a permanent possibility in human history." Bellah alludes primarily to the case of Japan as "especially instructive," for it represents a modern society in which a civil religion of the archaic type has survived not only "in the recent past [but] to a certain extent even today " (Bellah, 1980d: 28). Discussing political authorities who "fall back" on archaic patterns, he draws examples from Israelite kings, Chinese emperors, the Shah of Iran, or the Ayatollah Khomeini. Only in passing he mentions Hitler, Stalin, and Mao Zedong, as cases of totalitarian societies where "*elements*" of divine kinship have emerged (1980a: ix; my emphasis). Bellah even acknowledges that such regressive archaic tendencies may appear in democratic societies. There is certainly a germ of an interesting idea here but, unfortunately, this critical insight is never fully elaborated in his writings.

Broadly speaking, archaic civil religions, where the sacred and the political are combined, are relegated either to developing nations or to societies in lower stages of religious evolution, while modern types are thought to be representative of advanced societies. It is my contention, however, that what Bellah calls the full-fledged archaic solution to the religio-political problem is characteristic of modern authoritarian regimes wherever they appear, and also of democratic societies at particular political junctures. In such cases, the authority conferred by religion, and the civil religious rhetoric, is appropriated by political leaders and used for specific instrumental political goals.

Likewise, in his discussion of "political religions" in developing nations, Apter (1963: 73) argues that political solutions in the Third World often take the form of theocracies. Through the incorporation of theocratic elements, he notes, the "secular is elevated to the level of the sacred." The sacred is employed as a conscious tool for political rule—"to develop a system of political legitimacy" and as an aid in mobilizing civil society to achieve political ends (77). Apter claims that theocratic political solutions arise in new or underdeveloped nations partly because of these countries' "failure to achieve massive industrialization" (59). This would suggest that theocracies, or theocratic tendencies and praxis, are confined only to new nations in the process of modernization. However, the tendency to sacralize the political order and political authority is not only a characteristic of political religions in developing nations, nor is it a political solution limited to ancient times or to less developed societies. Rather, it is a defining feature of political religions wherever they are found. Hence, although Apter's specific concern is Third World countries, his claim is universally applicable, although he fails to realize this.

This universality becomes clear when one reviews the characteristics Apter attributes to political religions. He notes that these religions strengthen the arm of the state and weaken the flexibility of civil society. In order to retain authority, political leaders make use of force and citizens' indoctrination. The idea is to implant in the citizens "attitudes of respect and devotion to the regime." Apter argues that political authorities are quick to realize that "no ordinary ideology" can overcome the problem of social and political discrepancies. Hence, a "more powerful symbolic force, less rational, although it may include rational ends, seems necessary to them." This force is what he calls political religion, and this political religion, he believes, is to be found within the limits of developing nations alone (Apter, 1963: 59-61).

Zuo (1991) makes a similar distinction between the "political religion" of China and the "civil religion" of modern Western societies. It is my contention that the divide should not be located along the lines of East and West, or new nations and developed ones. Rather, the distinction should be in terms of liberal democracies and totalitarian/authoritarian regimes. As the section in chapter 4, Sacred and Secular Civil Religions, makes clear, such repressive regimes have emerged in the highly advanced countries of the Western world. In addition, civil religions à la Rousseau, in less extreme forms, may also appear in democratic societies. Bear in mind, for example, the civil religion of South Africa, which celebrated and "elevated the dogmas of the Dutch Reformed Church into political virtue" (Apter; 1963: 65, see also Moodie, 1975).

These examples would suggest that there is no necessary linear progression of civil religions. If we take civil religion to be a continuum, ranging from civil religion to political religion, it becomes easier to argue that civil religion, in its two varieties, is found both in democracies (more likely civil religion) and in totalitarian states (more likely political religion). I use the idea of a continuum because the notion of civil religion has both a cultural and a political dimension. The cultural aspect refers to the "world of representations," symbols, and images that emerges from society—that is, society's self-conception or its *ethos*. The political dimension of civil religion refers to both the state and to "the system of mediations" between the political order and civil society—"that is, the political regime" (Garretón, 1989: 3). Political religions à la Rousseau require a more explicit ideology than civil religions à la Durkheim, but it is highly unlikely that civil religion will appear anywhere in pure form. However, even if the line of demarcation is not always clear in practice, we can distinguish between those societies where the blending of the sacred and the secular is imposed, where political ends are elevated to sacred ranks, and where political leaders adopt an autocratic type of civil religion, from those adopting a liberal democratic pattern, where allegiance to the tenets of faith is not compulsory. In the former case, values and goals are often laid down by a single political authority and regarded as sacrosanct. In the latter, values are held together by what Apter (1963: 65) calls a "framework of law" that is itself highly respected and valued. Furthermore, civil religion may vary in the extent to which significant groups come to accept the civil religious discourse. Clearly, one needs to recognize differences in degrees of civil religion.

The idea of a continuum will be discussed in greater detail in the conclusion to this book. What is important for the moment is to make clear that, contrary to Bellah, Apter, and other scholars, I reject the evolutionary view that sees civil religion advancing in a straight, irreversible line. While civil religion may have developed from archaic forms (undifferentiated) to modern forms (in my opinion never fully differentiated), civil religion's tendency to irrupt and oscillate either to the side of society (civil) or to the side of the state (political) is dependent on particular historical and political circumstances. The emergence of one or the other type of civil religion depends on the nature of the state and society at a particular time. Democratic societies with well-institutionalized civil religions may show tendencies towards strong political religions at particular historical junctures, for the tendency to use civil religion as an engine for political rule is found both in democracies and authoritarian regimes. In short, Bellah's model, ranging from archaic and undifferentiated to fully differentiated civil religions, does not really do justice to the complexity of the situation.

This suggests that political religions (civil religions, as Rousseau envisioned them) have not totally disappeared from modern pluralistic societies. They have only adopted new forms and shades. This was the case in the United States, for example, during the McCarthy era or the Nixon presidency, when civil religion was used as a state tool—against the so-called communist conspiracy in the former case and in the defence of the Vietnam War in the latter. As Rouner affirms: "naked power grabbing in the Mexican War and useless slaughter in Vietnam have been justified by appeals to the principles of American civil religion" (1986: 137; see also Bennett, 1979: 123 n. 30).

Civil religion may be more or less repressive to the degree that it uses religious symbolism and religious values to legitimate or advance any kind of domination, including "economic, political, ecclesial, or other forms " (Lamb, 1986: 157). Leo Pfeffer has commented that when civil religion is consciously used for political ends, or when it becomes the handmaiden of national ambitions, programs, and policies, it is far more likely "to be an ignoble than a noble" enterprise (1968: 364). It should be noted that Bellah responded to Pfeffer's commentary by arguing that the proper relation between religious obligations and political ambitions travels in exactly the opposite direction: "national purposes are the handmaiden of the fundamental value commitments of the civil religion." Bellah insists that to use religious commitments for political goals "is a perversion" (Bellah, 1968: 390).

In any case, when civil religion is deliberately used to achieve political objectives, when there is a "flurry of conscious manipulation," to use Bellah's words (1980d: 31), we are undoubtedly moving in the direction of Rousseau. When this happens, the moral or civic claims of the state leave no room for the individual's free or spontaneous endorsement of the political system. I am not necessarily suggesting that a Rousseauan-type civil religion (state-manipulated or controlled) is always and inevitably "ignoble." While some civil religions may be focused on ensuring national grandeur (whether it be modernization, industrialization, or military supremacy), or the survival of the nation, others may be dedicated to the liberty of its citizens, and still others to the suppression of all liberties and rights.

The road from authoritarian rule to democracy does not always follow a straight path, as history so clearly indicates. Even under liberal regimes, which, in the overall history of political systems have been few (Bellah, 1980b: 19), some form of despotism may need only the right opportunity or the wrong charismatic leader to emerge. The question to be asked is, under what conditions might the two forms of civil religion (civil and political) undergo fluctuations in one or the other direction, and what might these changes entail? Another approach is to ask, what role does civil religion play in modern politics either as a political or a cultural resource? Clearly, its democratic or anti-democratic capacity is grounded in political procedures and the uses of civil religion by particular groups at particular times. In other words, the benefits and costs of civil religion would seem to depend, crucially, on the style of politics and the type of government under consideration.

The full political implications of the civil religion concept have not been appraised realistically by most scholars. As mentioned above, one has to leave the sociological field to find a serious effort to acknowledge Rousseau's intention in this area. Indeed, American historians and theologians have been more sensitive than their counterparts in sociology to the dangerous ramifications of civil religion as understood by Rousseau. For example, Richard John Neuhaus, a theologian, recognizes the grave consequences inherent in civil religion of the Rousseauan variety (which he rightly calls political religion). He unambiguously denounces the totalitarian intent of Rousseau's civil religion. Neuhaus writes: "Rousseau spelled it out in theory and, in our time, we have seen its practice in...both Nazism and Marxist-Leninism" (1986: 101). Likewise, Jürgen Moltmann, a professor of theology, has shown the dangers of political religions, or the application of religious ideas and values to political life. In the First World War, he writes, "in the name of the political religion of the German nation 'for God, King, and Fatherland,' our fathers were driven to their deaths in Langemark and Verdun. In the Second World War, in the name of the political messianism of the Third Reich, 'for Fuhrer, People and Fatherland,' my generation was marked by the crimes of the concentration camps and hounded into the mass graves of Stalingrad" (1986: 42). Germany's self-conception and destiny, embodied in the civil religion of the Nazis, "inspired the followers of Hitler to promote...genocide and global warfare" (Bennett, 1979: 123 n. 30).

The ability to organize public rituals on a massive scale, Wuthnow reminds us, is a compelling way used by modern governments (democratic and totalitarian) to reach out and extend their influence into the lives of ordinary citizens—the so-called silent majority. Hitler's genius in this respect is perhaps unsurpassed, as the Nuremberg rally of 1934, in particular, testifies. In fact, the Nazi rallies orchestrated by the German state at the time presented "the first evidence of the importance of such rituals" in the modern world (Wuthnow, 1994: 148). Hitler, through public rituals and political propaganda, sought to make civil religion an instrument of his political agenda. The German civil creed, in short, "celebrated Nazism with a corrupted Christianity" (Rouner, 1986: 1).

The perversion of civil religion often results in political actions that "confuse the sacred investiture of institutions with the notion that institutions (and their official representatives) are the sources of the divine order of politics" (Bennett, 1979: 128-29). The tendency in such cases is to transform the political process into a religious phenomenon, so that political leaders, their actions and programs acquire a sacred character.[8] As a result, all state activity is equated with "virtuous" action, for virtue is embodied in the state (129). In other words, any political objective is invested with quasi-religious characteristics, and ultimacy is conferred on all political and social programs. The dual process of politicizing and religionizing all aspects of life often leads, as Apter indicates, to the disappearance of politics as such. Once the political process is imbued with a compulsory and sacred mystique, political power-holders seem to find it easier to legitimize their mission and justify all kind of ruthless and violent acts "against the enemies of the 'cause'" (1963: 63, 78). Not surprisingly, these types of regimes are of necessity based on distrust and hatred of both internal and external enemies (Moltmann, 1986: 55). What formerly may have been a latent antagonism between different groups in society, is transformed into absolute hostility. Political enemies, seen anywhere and every day, are dangerous for they are cut off from the "divine" political order.

The political tendency to divide the world into friends and foes is apparently a universal phenomenon. The world, in fact, seems to be "divided into a Manichean dualism of good and evil" (Rouner, 1986: 5). The not so distant American obsession to separate the globe between the "free world" and the evil empire, and the recurrent Communist "tendency to reverse the picture," or the Muslim division into "the house of Islam" and "the house of war" are contemporary variants of this phenomenon (Bellah,

1980a: ix). Almost everyone would agree that this tendency is clearly more marked in authoritarian and despotic societies. To be sure, in political religions this enmity is magnified "into an apocalyptic drama" (Moltmann, 1986: 55).

To sum up, political religions in authoritarian regimes represent particular and extreme cases of civil religion à la Rousseau. They function essentially at the state level, and are designed and manipulated by the political elite. Elements of divine kingship appear highly marked—political leaders and their programs acquire quasi divine characteristics. Ideological dominance is achieved by the capacity to impose a program of action and make it viable. This is usually attained by controlling and manipulating the media and mechanisms of repression. The political order, characterized by its authoritarian and exclusionary pattern, requires the use of repressive force to control the political process and to enforce the tenets of faith. The unrestrained power of the state, always omnipresent, fills the role of god that rules over the nation. Thus, the viability of this type of civil religion depends on the capacity of the dominant political group or party to sustain its power.

Religion as a Society-Oriented Institution

Following the Durkheimian tradition, several scholars have argued that, in order to survive, every society needs a religion. Casanova, however, in his book *Public Religions in the Modern World* (1994), contends that whether civil religion is conceptualized "politically" (at the state level) or "sociologically" (at the civil society level) "such a civil religion is unlikely to reappear in modern societies" as a normative force integrating the political or the social community. He further argues that it is both "theoretically untenable and normatively undesirable" to insist on the functionalist existence of civil religion, in the sense that the modern social order "needs" such religion, for the modern nation-state no longer needs a religiously based legitimation (60-61).

Casanova distinguishes three main areas of the modern polity—the state, political society, and civil society—and locates religion in all three areas. He claims that state churches, such as Roman Catholicism in Spain, or "churches in search of a state," as in the case of the Catholic Church in Poland, are the most pristine example of "public religion" at the state level (61). Casanova uses the notion of "the church" in the Weberian sense of being an "obligatory monopolistic community of faith," having "universalist salvation claims" (224). This entails an established church having a "territorially organized compulsory religious community coextensive with the political community or state" (62). The moment a religion surrenders its "compulsory institutional character," Casanova observes, it becomes "disestablished" and it can no longer be considered a church. Rather, it becomes a voluntary association, "either a sect or a 'free church'" (213). Casanova argues that the Roman Catholic Church ceased being a church, in the sociological sense of the term, after the Second Vatican Council, when it accepted the right of "religious freedom" (51).

Public religions at the level of political society, refer to religions that become either "politically mobilized" or "institutionalized as a political party." As examples, Casanova mentions the political mobilization of the Catholic laity and religious groups, such as the Catholic counter-revolutionary movements in France or in Spain, the formation of lay organizations such as Catholic Action, and even the development of Christian Democratic parties in Western Europe or the political activities of the New Christian Right in the United States (61). These movements represent "defensive reactions" of the church to a secularized and hostile modern world. For instance, Casanova notes that to oppose the anti-clerical fury that swept Europe after the French Revolution, or to protect itself from the nineteenth-century European liberal revolutions, or from the rise of socialist power, the Catholic Church swiftly politicized and mobilized the Catholic laity. This represents, in his view, a clear example of the church becoming actively involved at the political level of society (61-62).

Finally, at the civil society level, Casanova places "hegemonic civil religions." These include American evangelical Protestantism in the nineteenth century or contemporary religious groups playing a public role on ethical issues such as abortion (219).

Casanova believes that only public religions whose centre of operation is civil society are compatible with modern differentiated societies where universalistic principles prevail. He believes that public religions, active at the political level of society, are only "transitional types." If they have not yet disappeared, he argues, they are bound to do so. The reason is simple: by deliberately accepting "disestablishment" and religious freedom as a universal right, the church has been forced to switch direction and transfer the defence of ecclesiastical privileges "to the human person." As a result, the raison d'être of political mobilization has tended to dissipate. This has allowed the church to re-emerge in the public arena to defend universal rights or the democratization of political regimes. Casanova concludes that the church, no longer endangered either by an unfriendly state or by adverse social movements, has shifted "from a state-oriented to a society-oriented institution." That is, it has moved its locus of activity from the state to civil society (219-20).

Casanova assumes that once the church becomes society-oriented, it neither needs nor seeks to reenter the state or to mobilize the laity in order to regain control over society. The church becomes both "disestablished" from the state and "disengaged" from political society. Casanova is thus able to claim the Catholic Church, by becoming disestablished and disengaged, no longer needs to "sponsor official Catholic parties" or fight politically for its privileges and interests. This change in "location and orientation" has permitted the Catholic Church a greater role in a variety of processes of democratization around the world, as the cases of Nicaragua, Brazil, or Poland attest. Casanova comes to the conclusion that the "'age' of reactive organicism, of secular-religious and clerical-anticlerical, cultural and political warfare, of Catholic Action, of religious pillarization, and of Christian Democracy has come to an end." Consequently, he proposes that the notion of public religion "ought to be reformulated from the state or societal community level to the level of civil society" (61-63).

What I find problematic in Casanova's argument are the claims that secular-religious warfare is over, that the state "no longer needs" religious legitimation, and that the church "no longer seeks to reenter the state." His assumption that secular-religious warfare is over leads him to conclude that religion at the state level is also dead. Granted, there is much truth in his claim that there has been a reorientation of the church from an institution firmly "anchored in the state" to one more diffusely "centered in civil society" (Casanova, 1994: 62). But whether the church in the Western world has ceased its attempts to penetrate the state is a highly debatable issue.

The mobilization of religious groups, or of interest groups with religious concerns, has increased dramatically in the last few decades in different parts of the world, a fact that Casanova does not deny. On the contrary, he acknowledges that the "deprivatization" of religion in the modern world seems to be a global phenomenon, so religion will likely continue to play a "public role." Religion, as he writes, has gone "'public' in a dual sense": it has become active in the public realm and has attained "publicity" (3, 5). It seems to me that when religion poses a challenge to an authoritarian regime and helps facilitate the transition to democracy, as Casanova claims it does, such religion is involved in the political process of a particular nation. Therefore, it is difficult to agree with Casanova's claim that the church has "abandoned its traditional attempts to enter political society." Catholic resistance in Poland, as he himself recognizes, implied a "struggle first for human and national rights and then,...for the rights of civil society to autonomy and self-determination" (227). The right of individuals to autonomy and self-determination is a political right. In the case of Poland, it required political mobilization and also the mobilization of religion at the political level to achieve this end. Even if the church did not organize under the banner of one political party or religious organization, it was politically involved (at the level of civil society, as Casanova would argue) to achieve political aims.

American religious activism while it may seem to indicate a decline of denominations, also implies a rise of special purpose groups (Billings and Scott, 1994: 176). Some authors have noted the tendency of some religious groups to act together in coalitions concerning particular issues, while, at the same time, agreeing to disagree on others. For example, an "Evangelical-Jewish coalition might form around support for Israel, but...might be divided over the issue of school prayer." Or, a Catholics and Protestant coalition may be "pro-life" on the abortion issue, but have opposing views concerning "scientific creationism" (Jelen, 1995: 279). Religious groups may have a variety of different interests and priorities, but the fact remains that they are often behind the ongoing struggle on issues such as homosexual rights, pornography, abortion, reproductive technology, women's ordination, and so on. The "religious tinge" of these moral crusades is quite obvious and unmistakable (Anthony and Robbins, 1982: 219).

Moreover, as Berger (1967: 137) reminds us, denominations in the United States function in highly competitive religious markets. As with any other competitive market, religious denominations must gain clients (adherents) and beat the religious competition if they want their voices to be heard. They must follow the logic and dynamics of a free market and transform themselves into marketing agencies. This requires active involvement in the public arena. In order to attain goals through the political system, religious groups need the help and cooperation of potential allies. Lobbying, public relations, and fund raising become important ways to gain "a place at the table" of public debate. Another alternative is to engage in civil disobedience or even violence (Jelen, 1995: 279-80). Regardless of the strategy, the final aim is to influence public policy. In other words, religiously based coalitions often use "religio-moral arguments" to legitimize their demands for political activity (Williams, 1996: 375). According to Jelen (1995: 280), in a pluralist political order, such as the United States, interest groups rather than political parties are, perhaps, the most suitable means for practising what he calls "religious politics."

While some scholars have challenged conclusions about how influential religious groups have been (see Billings and Scott, 1994), the news media and some academic observers have suggested that the religious Right in the United States, plays a role in the election of members of the American Congress. Far-right agendas, as some scholars have noted, explicitly seek to "delegitimate democracy," preach a return to "theocratic rule and biblical law," and seek to reinstall religious values in public life. This would suggest that religious activism on the far right has a specific political agenda—to radically challenge and change "the rules of the game in American politics" (Billings and Scott, 1994: 179). Contrary to Casanova's argument, this would also suggest that some religious groups are organized and mobilized at the political level of society.

American religious activism, and the current "culture war" over moral issues, has been the topic of many academic publications (Bennet, 1992; Evans, 1996; Hunter 1991). Even the mass media has adopted the culture war metaphor (Evans, 1996: 17). Culture war theorists explain politico-religious antagonisms in terms of different taken-for-granted assumptions or "ways of apprehending reality" that determine moral values, attitudes, and judgments. It is in this sense, they argue, that people or groups come to have different "cultures" (i.e., different notions of reality). Different world-views represent different ethical "truths," which are "non-negotiable." This means that divisions over moral issues can be solved only "through power politics and perhaps actual shooting wars" (Evans, 1996: 17-23). In other words, debates in American politics over socio-moral issues are being fought within a politico-religious framework. Some religious groups, such as the Unification Church of Reverend Sun Myung Moon, make no distinction between their political and theological messages, so that political struggles and religious struggles become truly inseparable. This would imply that religious-secular warfare is still not over.

Casanova's distinction between political society and civil society seems to obscure the issue rather than illuminate it. When religious groups are actively involved at the level of civil society (regardless of whether or not they belong to any organized political party), and when their goal is to change public policies or even the law, the boundary between civil society and political society becomes very blurred indeed. Under such circumstances, religious groups are actively involved in political struggles, not civil ones.

Leaving the United States and looking elsewhere in the world, we find some quite distinct, yet related phenomena. In Latin America, for example, as Casanova also points out, liberation theology has provided leadership and resistance to all kinds of authoritarian regimes. Eminent Catholic officials around the world have played important roles as arbitrators and conciliators of contending political groups (Billings and Scott, 1994: 182). Catholic-based opposition to authoritarian regimes in Latin America, Poland, and other parts of the globe, tends to confirm the close interconnection of religion and politics, and the continued presence of a religio-political warfare (see, for example, Smith, 1982; Weigel, 1992). It may be argued that the church in such cases is not struggling to defend particular religious values, ideas, or practices. Rather, the church would only be lending its institutional support to a struggle that is essentially secular (e.g., the fight for democracy). Those who opt to think this way, and Casanova does, may be right. But regardless of whether the church is lending its institutional support to achieve secular ends, or whether it is directly involved in order to achieve ecclesiastical privileges (as in former times), the political or secular struggle in which it is embroiled would still be an indication of politico-religious warfare (religion versus the state, or religious authority versus political authority).

Billings and Scott note that more recent and "fluid" understandings of the politico-religious problem seem to be replacing conventional paradigms regarding church-state relations. This relation is being "rethought from a standpoint that focuses attention on the activity of groups rather than systems" (Billings and Scott, 1994:188). Religion as an institution may have little or no direct political influence, but members of a particular religion may play an active role in salient moral issues, such as the death penalty or homosexual rights.

Casanova may be quite correct in arguing that the existence of civil religion on functionalist grounds, in the sense that the state needs a civil religion, is now not only "untenable," but also "undesirable" (1994: 61). But while the modern state may not need a civil religion, there seems to be ample evidence that most organized societies will likely develop one. Of course, how it will be expressed—that is, the world of representations and myths peculiar to a society—may vary from one society to another, and from one era to another within the same society. Moreover, Casanova seems to ignore the fact that the idea of the political utility of religion (as Machiavelli and other social thinkers have so clearly articulated) has not dwindled away. This means that, despite Casanova's contention that the modern state may no longer *need* religious legitimation, there is ample evidence that modern states continue to *seek* it—evidence that applies both to authoritarian and democratic regimes.

Casanova insists, however, that public religions at the state level are incompatible with modern societies, "modern individual freedoms," and "modern differentiated structures" (1994: 219). When he argues that such religions are "unlikely to reappear" in contemporary society (for the modern state no longer needs religious legitimation), he fails to consider state-directed or state-imposed civil religions that may appear in the modern world. He has not considered, perhaps, how frail are the pillars of civility that prevent any society from a total breakdown. No modern nation is immune from political crises that may produce overnight the collapse of its democratic edifice, and the building of a totalitarian political religion. As De Azevedo (1979: 9) reminds us, state-imposed civil religion (in its most extreme form) is always ready to make its appearance, particularly in times of profound political crisis. As he rightly notes, in this category "on trouve surtout les révolutions politiques et sociales et les coups d'État authoritaires, qui transforment leurs doctrines en dogmes obligatoires pour les citoyens." I have provided here some sample cases of states attempting to manipulate or create civil religions to serve their own ends. The chapter that follows presents a concrete case in greater detail.

CHAPTER FIVE

Chile, 1973-1989: A Case Study

I n November 1970, Salvador Allende Gossens became president of Chile. He was the first Marxist candidate in the Western world to win a country's presidency in a free and democratically conducted election. Allende was supported by a coalition that included the Socialist and Communist parties. He promised to adopt "la via Chilena hacia el Socialismo" (the Chilean road to Socialism), and promised to nationalize major foreign and private organizations, particularly in mining, banking, and communications. He also pledged to establish diplomatic and commercial relations with communist nations, including Cuba, North Vietnam, North Korea, the People's Republic of China, and East Germany, but he insisted that he was "not going to imitate either the Soviet Union or Cuba or China" (New York Times, 4 Oct. 1970). Chile would find its own way and take the necessary steps to produce a more just and humane society. His experiment failed, and his regime lasted

Notes to Chapter 5 are on pp. 255-57.

less than three years. The threat of nationalization provoked a series of massive strikes and protests by the opposition. The economy was seriously disrupted by a prolonged truckers' strike, which later spread to other sectors of the economy. The country became ungovernable, and life for many Chileans became unbearable and chaotic, even for those committed to social reforms. Both Allende and the opposition looked to the armed forces for a solution. The military sided with the political opposition and the extreme right. The political and economic crisis of the last months of the Allende's regime gave the military the excuse to seize power. No one could have predicted or even imagined that this would mean the collapse of the Chilean democracy and of Chilean civic pride.[1]

Starting with Bellah's notion that elements of civil religion are moulded especially in times of national crises, this chapter examines the status of civil religion in Chile during the period of the military regime that violently seized power in September 1973 and was swept from power by a national referendum in October 1989. Some of the major assertions and debates surveyed in previous chapters are applied to the Pinochet regime, to indicate how these theoretical disputes are pertinent to an understanding of the Chilean case, and how, in turn, the Chilean case can help to clarify our understanding of civil religion.[2]

Recalling Rousseau, it is proposed that the Chilean state, under the military dictatorship, tried to impose its own interpretation of Chilean historical experience in terms of a civil religious discourse. In the first place, it is argued, the commander-in-chief of the Chilean armed forces, General Augusto Pinochet, cast himself in a "priestly" role with regard to the creation and indoctrination of a militaristic ethic of war and patriotic sacrifice. Second, the ideological "dogma" of Pinochet's political creed drew on well-established religious symbols. However, the "true believers" of Pinochet's civil religion were not the Chilean people (i.e., the nation as a whole), but a select faction of "patriotic," anti-Marxist citizens cast as defenders of the faith. Third, during the first stage of the Pinochet regime, the existing institutionalized religious order—namely, the Catholic Church—offered legitimation to the military authority and provided a resource for the political manipulation of sacred symbols. In Chile, however, it is incorrect to suggest that an undifferentiated, church-sponsored civil religion (of the type described by Coleman, 1969: 70) ever existed, before or during the Pinochet regime. Despite the relative lack of religious pluralism in Chile, the Catholic Church has in no sense monopolized or directed a civil religion. The church did legitimize the military intervention that overthrew the democratic order, but civil religion emerged episodically in Chile, with state sponsorship, to support and legitimate a pattern of political activity at variance with the dominant tradition of constitutional democracy in Chile. Chilean civil religion was an episodic politico-religious discourse fashioned by one civic group over and against another. However, the Durkheimian approach to civil religion remains instructive, for the eventual demise of Pinochet's civil religious discourse is rooted, in part, in its failure to maintain a sufficient sense of moral community. The regime's failure to mobilize Chileans, in a cultural and structural sense, undermined its social plausibility. The delineation of these differences is important, for the ambiguities of Chilean civil religion reflect the diverse and complex ways in which civil religion may be comparatively manifested across history and cultures. It is also important to better understand the theoretical one-sidedness of the civil religion thesis as interpreted by American sociologists. Finally, it is important, once again, to better understand how the concepts of civil and political religion, although related in reality, are analytically distinguishable. What follows is a specific illustration of civil religion in its Rousseauan (politico-ideological) form.

Pinochet's Civil Religious Discourse

On September 11 1973, a violent coup d'état produced a political earthquake that shook the very foundations of Chilean society. The military officers who took power claimed to be acting to restore "freedom" and "moral order" to Chile. Legitimizing the coup, however, posed special difficulties in one of Latin America's oldest and most stable democracies. The breakdown of Chile's democracy "was especially surprising because it occurred in one of the most highly educated and politically sophisticated countries in Latin America" (Puryear, 1994:10). Chile had been committed to a democratic order, with only two small interruptions, for nearly 140 years.[3] Like military governments anywhere, as Sanders notes (1981: 287), the new regime immediately faced a number of problems: it had "to reorganize the political structure to provide for military control, develop an ideology to guide policy, and cultivate the support of various civilian and religious groups." A civil religious discourse was invoked to help achieve these ends. This chapter offers an analysis of this discourse to better understand this turbulent period in the history of Chile and the comparative use of civil religion as a theoretical construct of the sociology of religion.

In Durkheimian form, as I have already argued, the civil religion envisioned for America by Bellah is a common civic faith born, in large measure, of the need to sustain a pluralistic culture by transcending its divergent and particularistic religious perspectives. In Rousseauan form, the civic creed envisioned by the military leaders of Chile arose in response to a religiously nonpluralistic society, polarized by political dissension. Simple positive dogmas (without explanation or comments, as Rousseau advocated) and intolerance were the order of the day for this mode of civil religion.

As mentioned in chapter 2, the symbols of American civil religion and their institutionalization have been delineated largely through the content analysis of national documents and public ceremonies (e.g., Bellah, 1967, 1980b; Cherry, 1969; Donahue, 1975; Pierard and Linder, 1988; Toolin, 1983). By scrutinizing what statesmen, politicians, and religious leaders say on solemn occasions, Bellah and others have pieced together the elements of the civil religious agenda in the United States. Hammond suggests (1980e: 203) that such public documents provide "windows onto [a] sacred code." By analyzing some similar documents and speeches, we attempt to open a window on the sacred code of those who set the agenda during this painful winter of Chilean discontent.

The first declarations of the military junta repeatedly carried the message of a "democratic restoration." The "predominant ideological elements of this stage derived from the Chilean democratic tradition, respect for institutionality, and the rule of law" (Arriagada, 1988: 4). The junta called upon what has been identified as a key element of American civil religion: "democratic faith."

The ideological rhetoric of the new government was expressed through the enactment and publication of edicts, laws, decrees, and so on. As Arriagada notes, these documents provided the rationale used by the armed forces to undertake "the moral duty imposed by the Nation to oust a government that, although initially legitimate, fell into flagrant illegitimacy." The socialist government of Salvador Allende, it was claimed, had "destroyed national unity," endangered "all the rights and liberties of the inhabitants of the country," and the right to a dignified and safe existence (Bando No. 5 de la Junta de Gobierno, 11 Sept. 1973; in Arriagada, 1988: 4-5). Consequently, the junta declared that Chile "is not neutral toward Marxism, and the present government does not fear or hesitate to declare itself anti-Marxist" (*Declaración de Principios*, Mar. 1974; in Sanders, 1981: 291-92). These documents also specified that the armed forces and the national police would hold power "only as long as circumstances so require," based on a "patriotic commitment to restore justice, institutionality, and Chilean identity" (*Decreto Ley* No. 1, 11 Sept. 1973, *Diario Official*, 18 Sept. 1973; in Arriagada, 1988: 5).

To mitigate the incongruity between a repressive regime and deeply ingrained Chilean traditions, an alliance between civil religion and unrestricted power was established. A new sacred canopy was crafted. The fight against Marxism was presented as a holy war; any opposition to the military junta and its policies was a sign of heresy requiring swift and severe punishment. The "war" was symbolically equated with a transcendental view of the destiny of Chilean people, so that it came to be regarded and legitimized as a sacred enterprise. The military junta appropriated for themselves the messianic mission of making Chile "safe" for "democracy." The government's relatively moderate rhetorical style soon gave way to more radical proposals to establish a new social, political, economic, and even moral order (Arriagada, 1988: 12, 22). The armed forces would remain in power for an "indefinite" period to effect the "profound and prolonged action [required] to change the mentality of Chileans" (*Declaración de Principios*, in Sanders, 1981: 292).

Pinochet was presented, and presented himself, as the divinely appointed leader who was to lead his people out of chaos and disorder. The "hand of God is here to save us," Pinochet declared on 13 October 1973, only a month after the military intervention. A year after the coup, he reiterated this theme by declaring, "you know well enough that people prayed for their salvation and that today they feel free and far from evil....Faith and hope are the best roads to get to God, and today Chileans travel these roads with happiness and trust in their destiny" (*Discurso a Líderes Evangélicos en Acto de Apoyo al Gobierno*. 13 Dec. 1974; in Lagos and Chacón, 1987: 15). Four years later, he insisted, once more, that "those who analyze the military intervention of 1973...will inevitably come to the conclusion that the hand of God was present then" (*Discurso para la Delegación Visitante de Evangelicos Bautistas*, in Lagos and Chacón, 1987: 16). Under God's guidance, the military had taken action "at the last minute," because it embodied "the organization that the State has provided to protect itself and defend its physical and moral integrity and its historic-cultural identity" (*Decreto Ley* No. 1, *Diario Official*, 18 Sept. 1973, in Arriagada, 1988: 5). To avoid the "creation of another Cuba," influenced, and perhaps controlled by the Soviet Union, the junta dissolved the Congress, outlawed Marxist political organizations, and placed all other political parties in recess. It also carried out massive detentions of the leaders of Allende's government, of the working class and students, and of anyone else suspected of leftist sympathies. Electoral rolls were abolished, trade unions suspended, and political dissidents were expelled from the country. A state of siege suspended individual liberties (Arriagada, 1988: 11; Smith, 1982: 288). With the notable exception of the Catholic Church, all major social and political organizations in the country were either dismantled or placed under intense surveillance. The Catholic Church became in fact a focal point for the "needs of vast numbers of foreigners and Chileans suffering the brunt of the regime's repression" (Smith, 1982: 289). Any political or ideological difference was perceived as an antipatriotic conspiracy and betrayal of both the army and Chile. A "culture of fear" developed, which was to last for at least a decade (Corradi, Weiss, and Garretón, 1992). Particularly during the earliest day of the coup, the repression unleashed by the military came as a "severe shock. Chileans had little notion of what a military takeover signified; it was not part of their history or vocabulary" (Constable and Valenzuela, 1991: 30).

"Patriotism," equated with anti-Marxism and support for a free market economy, was the first principle of the project of *reconstrucción nacional*. It became the central symbolic pillar of the civil religion of the day, and Pinochet used all his might to propagate and enforce it. Citizens were indoctrinated to love Chile (i.e., fear and hate Marxists), and motivated to civic duty (i.e., fight Marxism). In several speeches Pinochet discussed the nature of the new secular creed and the means by which it should be transmitted to future generations. These speeches and the ideological propaganda of this period are filled with religious imagery and language that has a distinctly "biblical ring" (as Bellah would say it). *La Alborada*, an army newspaper, for example, published on its front page a photograph of a soldier holding a machine gun and guided by a bright star. The caption read: "Just like the star that guided the wise men of the East to Bethlehem, today the Chilean soldier looks to the pure sky of his Homeland and listens to the always renewed biblical message — 'I am the root and the lineage of David, the resplendent star of the morning'" (Lagos and Chacón, 1987: 29).

In addition to the media, Pinochet's regime used the public schools to propagate its creed. A special type of education and cultic celebration of the civil rituals were imposed on the young to socialize them to the official ideology. School children sang a national anthem at the start of each day with a new verse "thanking the valiant soldier" for the liberation of the nation.

Marx was officially exiled from academic discussions, and Pinochet's messianic anti-Marxism was voiced in a religious language of progress towards a redeemed society, a new order divinely foreordained for the happiness of all Chileans. Thus began the military re interpretation of Chilean history.

Pinochet's national calling was associated with a global call to regenerate humankind by extirpating the Marxist cancer. Marxism, he insisted over and over again, is "an intrinsically perverse doctrine, and everything that springs from it, as healthy as it might appear, is consumed by the poison that corrodes its roots." Its danger is "intrinsic" and "global" and "no dialogue or transaction is compatible with it." In the face of the global threat posed by Soviet imperialism, power must be placed in the hands of the armed forces, for only "they have the organization and the means to confront Marxism transformed into permanent aggression" (*Mensaje Presidencial*, 11 Sept. 1974; cited in Arriagada, 1988: 22). Admiral Jose Toribio Merino, one of the four military men who composed the junta, emphatically declared during an interview: "Let us put it realistically: the world today has one enemy—communism. A monolithic, impenetrable enemy that has acquired technology as good as that of the democratic system but used exclusively for destruction. And it is attempting to dominate the entire world. So, what system should be chosen to combat this monolithic bandit that does not show its face, whose religion is the lie?" "Can there only be military governments," asked the journalist, if the only means to eliminate the enemy is war? His reply was immediate: "What other way is there? Which way? How?" (*Ercilla* 2, 165, Feb. 1977: 20-24).

In a national newspaper in 1977, Pinochet stated that God gave him "faith in the destiny of Chile." Communists, he said, are dangerous, they are working in clandestine ways. "We ought to recognize this. They have a mystique which is given by Satan, but they do have a mystique nonetheless" (*Diario Las Ultimas Noticias*, 22 Aug. 1984, in Lagos and Chacón, 1987: 19). He, as an individual, and Chile, as a nation, had been elected by God to fight and eliminate these Satanic forces. He had been blessed with a special, God-given faith and counter-mystique.

Accordingly, any opposition to his policies was perceived as a moral problem, and the torture and repression of Marxists was the price for saving Western Christian culture and Chilean morality. Pinochet, the saviour, was to be in charge of finding and punishing the infidels.[4]

Illustrating this state of affairs, on the thirteenth anniversary of Pinochet's appointment as commander-in-chief of the army, General Santiago Sinclair, the president's chief of staff, addressed an audience of several thousand soldiers. His speech, as Arriagada notes, took the form of an instruction to the Chilean troops on the idea that military leadership may never be opposed, for it represented a "noble" and "sublime" task involving the defense of the moral order and of the homeland. Pinochet, soldier and priest, "wise leader" and noble statesman, was the sacred figure entrusted with this military and moral duty.

> In you, First Soldier of the Republic, we see the wise leader, the Commander who has been able to illuminate the difficult path of these years. You have had but one ambition: the greatness of Chile; a single motto: "Duty is above question."…And so my General, we wish to publicly renew our obedience and loyalty to the inspiration of the hierarchical authority of Command and the moral authority that flows from your position as military leader.…Providence willed that you carry the torch of the pledge that we make to the Fatherland; thus, our loyalty to you is loyalty to Chile.…Beneath the gaze of the Mother of God…and with the sacred inspiration of God,…the Army of Chile acts with a profound and undeniable sense of justice to demonstrate before the citizenry the recognition and honour owed the first soldier of the Republic, Captain General Augusto Pinochet Ugarte. (*El Mercurio*, 24 Aug. 1986; in Arriagada, 1988: 119)

This view of the commander-in-chief endowed with sacred characteristics was reaffirmed by Sinclair fifteen days later, when Pinochet escaped an assassination attempt: "my general, the sacred figure of our Commander in Chief has been the victim of an assassination attempt. The Army repudiates, condemns, and will not forgive this act" (*El Mercurio,* 9 Sept. 1986).

The dogma of a sacred war against communism was a recurring litany throughout the regime. It was mitigated during times of less fierce repression, but was always ready to make an appearance when Pinochet's government felt the need to resort to a harder line (Arriagada, 1988: 25). By early 1984, after a little over ten years of largely unchallenged rule, economic difficulties besieged the regime, and Pinochet's opponents began to organize, planning strikes and rallies. Demonstrators went into the streets, banging pots and pans to protest his tyrannic rule. When asked, in an interview with *Newsweek,* how he had survived the strife—for many had predicted that he would be "squeezed out"—Pinochet without hesitation replied: "As for the secret of my survival, it is not a secret. I am a man fighting for a just cause. The fight between Christianity and spirituality on the one hand, and Marxism and materialism on the other. I get my strength from God....Destiny gave me the job....I never wanted to be President" (*Newsweek,* 19 Mar. 1984: 67).

Pinochet's Civil Religion and the Catholic Church

Despite the Catholic Church's apparently congenial relations with the Allende government, most church leaders privately believed the military coup was not only inevitable but necessary to prevent civil war. The deep-seated respect for constitutionality traditionally exhibited by the armed forces would, they assumed, make the military takeover relatively peaceful and short-lived (Smith, 1982: 287). Two days after the coup, Cardinal Silva Henríquez deplored the flood of "blood which has reddened our streets," asking for "respect" for those "fallen in battle" and, specially, for "him" [Salvador Allende] who was until Tuesday, September 11th, the President of the Republic" (Smith, 1982: 288). But a common thread running through early church declarations was the public justification of the coup. "We recognize the service rendered to the country by the Armed Forces in liberating it from a Marxist dictatorship that seemed inevitable and that would have been irreversible." It is "just to recognize" that, in staging the coup, the military had listened to the voices of the majority and, in so doing, had "put aside an immense obstacle to peace" ("Evangelio y Paz," *Working Document of the Permanent Committee of the Episcopacy,* in Villela, 1979: 266). Less than a month after the coup, Cardinal Silva declared: "The Church has always maintained cordial relations with governments of this country. We desire to be of service. The Church is not called upon to install governments or to take power away from them, nor to give or withhold recognition of government. We accept the governments which the people want and we serve them." He further added that Church and state had a task to accomplish "the task...of removing the great difficulties in which the country now finds itself" (*Diario La Tercera,* 10 Oct. 1973, in Smith, 1982: 290). But it was believed that repression would be only a short-term emergency measure needed to restore social order and economic stability. Accordingly, Cardinal Silva Henríquez refrained from direct criticism of the regime. The church, after all, expected to play a prominent role during the period of *reconstrucción* (Smith, 1982: 291).

A number of other prominent church leaders were more direct than the cardinal in their initial reaction to the regime, and publicly voiced their satisfaction with the military takeover. On 11 September, the same day of the coup, Bishop Francisco Valdés of Osorno made public a prayer whereby he thanked God for having liberated the nation from the "worst clutches of lies and evil that have ever plagued poor humanity," a view echoed by at least six other bishops, one of whom even presented his episcopal ring as a "modest contribution" to the long task of reconstruction. Archbishop Emilio Tagle of Valparaiso appeared on television and thanked the military for having saved the homeland from the claws of Marxism. He admitted the loss of blood but implied that it was an inevitable price to pay to restore Chile to "its former status of a free and sovereign nation" (Smith, 1982: 292). Bishop Augusto Salinas of Linares went so far as to place 11 September "on the same level of importance as national independence from Spain in 1810" (Smith, 1982: 293). This view was reiterated, twelve years later, by Monsenor Jose Joaquín Matte, Bishop "castrense," (army chaplain) in a mass celebrating the anniversary of the coup. He declared, "twelve years ago, the rosary began to be prayed without a break, and the Virgin Mary brought about the miracle: it was the second independence of Chile" (in Lagos and Chacón, 1987: 24).

In general, during the first months of the regime the pronouncements of the church complemented the new civil religious message of the military regime: mild criticism went hand in hand with moral endorsement of the coup, while the people were exhorted to seek reconciliation and peace. Needless to say, such pronouncements were given extensive coverage in the government controlled media. In short, an alliance between civil religion (in its Rousseauan meaning) and institutional religion was established early on, although it would soon deteriorate as parts of the church began to protest the actions of the government. Even those who criticized the government were quick to admit the beneficial effects of the military intervention. As Smith ruefully observes, "some of the same bishops who had condemned [the group called] Christians for Socialism for going against episcopal guidelines regarding clerical involvement in politics and identifying their priestly office with partisan political movements, now were guilty of even worse actions themselves, condoning bloodshed and lies"(1982: 293). It is possible, Smith argues, that the promises of the military junta "to restore order and constitutional rule" reinforced the mistaken expectations of church leaders (290-91). It is more likely, however, that fear of Marxism was more deeply ingrained than fear of fascism.

During the period of consolidation of the junta's power and its methods of repression (1974-76) this attitude evolved towards a more open, yet still cautious criticism. The international press carried a message abroad presenting the Chilean bishops as forthright opponents of the regime. As an institution, however, there is little doubt that the Church in the early months of the coup provided important moral legitimacy to the regime. To be sure, ecclesiastical authorities and prelates were ambivalent and even divided. But contrary to the comments of some analysts (e.g., Alexander, 1978: 367-70), it was only when the repression of the regime "touched the bishops personally and lay elites close to them" (after mid-1976) that church leaders unambiguously began to condemn human rights violations and demand a return to a democratic regime (Smith, 1982: 287).[5]

The Church had to restructure and redefine its position in Chilean society, and it began to play a more central and "prophetic" role in the civil life of the nation. It started bringing into the open questions of repression and the arbitrary arrest and disappearance of prisoners, and it began providing meals, work-shops, and other forms of aid to the "victimized masses" of the economic distress brought on by the regime. The new activism and protection of the Church created a socio-political niche of considerable importance within which different sectors of the population found some space for free expression (Villela, 1979: 269-71). In the last analysis, the Church, while it became extremely critical of the regime, never broke with the military junta. Both elected to hold each other at a diplomatic distance, while seeking to avoid any direct confrontations. It is fair to say, therefore, that civil religion during the Pinochet regime was state-sponsored and, for a short while, church-supported. Pinochet, however, never quite succeeded in making the church an instru-ment of his own civil religion. On the contrary, the Church came to be perceived as a serious threat to his political agenda. Hence, Coleman's (1969: 70-71) either/or distinction concerning undif-ferentiated civil religion (i.e., either state or church-sponsored), is not really applicable to the Chilean case. Neither is Coleman's claim that examples of "the church performing the role of civil religion can be found throughout Latin America."

Analysis of Pinochet's Civil Religion

As Pinochet's exploitation of religious symbolism testifies, civil religion "has not always been invoked in favor of worthy causes" (Bellah, 1967: 14). Indeed, both "self-less and oppressive actions can be masked in the cloak of civil religion" (Toolin, 1983:47). As things were, the junta's moral agenda gave Chileans little choice: one could either be with the junta or against it; one could either serve God (Pinochet) or Satan (Marxism). In short, the rhetoric presented the choice as one between good and evil— one could chose to belong to the kingdom of light or to the kingdom of darkness. It is not difficult to see both millenarian and messianic elements in this situation: the promise of a "reconstructed" Chile, of a better world to come, and the belief in a holy mission connecting Chile with a global struggle to defend the universal ideals of "freedom and liberty."

Yet the messianic rhetoric was not reflective of a prophetic civil religious development. Rather, the Chilean case more clearly calls to mind Marty's (1974) notion of the priestly mode of civil religion. When the discourse of civil religion shifts from a focus on a transcendent deity to the promise of national self-transcendence, "the signal of priestly civil religion is raised" (Marty, 1974: 151). As the Pinochet regime confirms, such a civil religion "will have as its main priest the president, since he alone stands at the head of all the people… and he has greatest potential for invoking symbols of power" (146). In general, Marty argues, modern fascisms combine a "cosmic vision" with national purposes in ways that almost by definition produce a priestly "'this-worldly transcendent' civil religion" (151). Hence, while American civil religion is an attempt to bring America's own life under a higher ideal and its role is to make "any form of political absolutism illegitimate" (Bellah, 1970: 172), Chilean civil religion under Pinochet sought to make a mode of political absolutism sacred and legitimate.

The general tendency to characterize civil religion as a national, non-sectarian faith loses validity in the face of dictatorial regimes, as does the portrayal of civil religion as a canopy of common values fostering social integration. In line with Weber, we must remember the dual functions of legitimating ideologies and theodicies. They serve to reconcile subservient groups to their fate. But they also serve to assure ruling groups of the righteousness of their rule and privileges. The latter was probably the primary function of a civil religious discourse in the case of the supporters of Pinochet.

In the end Pinochet's quest to unify and strengthen the nation through a civil religious discourse was not entirely successful. He succeeded in maintaining the rulers united, and in discouraging a "deviant" consensus from emerging among those who opposed the regime. This, however, was accomplished as much by military might as by the influence of a civil religious discourse. No one is, after all, attempting to argue that a civil religion played a prominent role in the coup or its aftermath. More simply, we are drawing attention to a political use of religious ideology that has been neglected, not only in the analysis of the Chilean situation, but in the analysis of American civil religion as well.[6]

In Chile a religious lexicon was systematically used to ensconce Pinochet's personal dream of what Chile should be. Yet, the state-sponsored civil religion led not to cohesion but to social disruption, to a constant state of internal war. It offered only a very fragile integration based primarily on the elimination of all alternative political ideologies from public discourse. In the end, the religious dimension with which military repression was masked proved to be insufficient to silence protests against the misuse and abuse of power.

When large sectors of the population were deprived of freedom and justice it became increasingly difficult to agree with the military's conception of moral imperatives and civic duty. The treatment of "non-believers" was too brutal. As the gap between the political ideals of the anti-communist creed and the political reality widened, Pinochet's civil-religious language became increasingly a rhetoric devoid of content, a macabre ploy. His trumpet call to patriotic battle was heeded by ever decreasing elements of the population, including the Church and the bourgeoisie. So in the end, the Chilean experiment with a Rousseauan civil religion supports Marty's (1974) and Richardson's (1974) suspicion that civil religion is used to fulfill different purposes at different times. Such being the case, civil religion tends to be "episodic."

Thus, contrary to Bellah's notion, every civil religion is not necessarily a national civil religion. The Chilean state, personi-

fied by the military junta, and specifically by Pinochet, appropriated the destiny of Chile as its own, but it never represented
the whole nation. The rhetoric of patriotism fell into the hands
of fascist forces that tried to impose the idea that "loving Chile"
and "being patriotic" was synonymous with hating Marxists,
leftists, and even moderate democrats who opposed the regime.
For several years, the religious-military ideology, combined with
total repression, effectively rendered invisible any opposition to
the junta. Repression and pious pretense joined hands in Chile,
and, in the name of non-violence, institutionalized violence ran
rampant for seventeen years.

Chilean Civil Religion in Comparative Perspective

Sociologists have made only tentative inroads into the investigation of the factors affecting the relative "success" of civil religions. A survey of the comparative literature leads us to postulate
five interrelated factors responsible for the demise or survival of
civil religions, factors relevant to the failure of Pinochet's civil
religious discourse.

First, the Pinochet government did not develop sufficient
organizational vehicles to carry the religious message of the new
civil religion. In his excellent comparative analysis of civil religion in the United States and Mexico, Hammond (1980a) has
argued that a true civil religion never developed in Mexico
because there is no set of institutions imbued simultaneously
with political and religious significance. Despite the seeming
similarity in conditions between the United States and Mexico
(e.g., the events of the Mexican revolution and the dominance of
religion in the life of the people), historical circumstances made
Mexicans much more ambivalent to the introduction of religious
themes into their public ceremonies, political speeches, educational system, and judiciary. In Mexico, a much sharper distinction was drawn between the realms of the sacred and the profane. The former was clearly assigned to the Church, and the
Church, which backed the losing side in the revolution, was pur-
posefully excluded from the affairs of the state.[7] In contrast, in

the United States, "the Puritan method of harmonizing politics and religion led to institutional changes, which in turn facilitated development of civil religion" (Hammond, 1980a: 79). Churches became voluntary associations and, like other such associations, engaged in much political activity. Americans "found it easy to be simultaneously 'religious' and 'political.'" As a result, by extension, political, educational, and legal institutions could more readily become imbued with certain general sacred meanings and duties.

Similar patterns of institutionalization of civil religion have been noted in the cases of Iran and Japan (and one can readily speculate about other cases such as Poland, Myanmar, and so on). As Braswell (1979) delineates, the Shah of Iran, in a Rousseauan fashion, strove explicitly to create a complete religious organization, loyal to the government and its objectives, which paralleled and was intended to supplant the traditional Shiite hierarchy of Iran. In the case of Japan, Bellah argues that the roots of the almost Machiavellian exploitation of the institutions of state Shintoism during the 1930s and 1940s run deep into the nation's past, and that the practice remains a live option for the future (Bellah, 1980d; see also Takayama, 1988).

In Chile, however, the Pinochet regime was content to anchor its civil religious discourse in a more traditional alliance of government bureaucracy, the army, and the Church. Attempts to fashion independent religio-political organizations were resisted because of Pinochet's autocratic suspicion of mass political movements, his confidence in the army, and his firm identification with the Catholic Church. In May 1975 the Movimiento de Unidad Nacional (MUN) was founded to support and extend the efforts of the regime. Among its leaders was the most influential civilian advisor to the junta, the right-wing, authoritarian, and staunchly Catholic Jaime Guzmán.[8] In principle, however, the movement was established to be independent of the government, and by March 1977 the youth group of MUN actually began to issue public criticisms of the policies of the government, and the movement rapidly disappeared. The proposed Movimiento Pinochetista of 1979 never moved ahead for it never received official support. Likewise, the Movimiento Cívico Militar, which was supposed to coordinate political activity at the municipal level, also failed to receive official endorsement and just withered away. Following announcement of the movement in 1980, less than 700 citizens joined in the entire city of Santiago. The fact that the Pinochet government failed to develop an organized mass support, even at the height of its popularity, provides a clear indication of its fear of an independent center of political power (Remmer, 1989: 140).

Second, in like manner and for similar reasons, the Pinochet regime did not give sufficient attention to the development of relatively independent civil religious symbols and ceremonials. Markoff and Regan (1982) place much emphasis on the empirical manifestations of civil religion, noting the consequent need to mark the differences of "tone" in civil religions. On the one hand, revolutionary France presents us with a "dazzling and changing hodgepodge" of civil religious ceremonies and texts. On the other hand, Malaysia presents us with a minimalistic civil religion that is a "model of consistency and coherence" (Markoff and Regan, 1982: 339). Yet in each instance specific events and activities can be pinpointed that reveal the presence and character of the civil religion in question (cf. Liebman and Don-Yehiya's discussion of Israeli civil religion [1983], or McDowell's analysis of Soviet civil ceremonies [1974]). Alternatively, the Pinochet regime was content to infuse the existing occasions of state and church activity with elements of a civil religious rhetoric. There were no new equivalents to the Nuremberg rallies, Israeli commemorations of the Holocaust or Masada, no new "Fourths of July." Likewise, no new symbols were consistently fashioned, like the French tricolour, Nazi swastika, or the Soviet hammer and sickle. Yet such symbols are required to galvanize independent commitment to the cause and to socialize the population to the values of the regime. Rather, it seems likely that Pinochet's role model in these matters was Franco in Spain, and not the more revolutionary figures of fascism like Hitler or Mussolini.[9] His objective was the preservation of tradition in matters symbolic and cultural, more than the cultivation of change and new configurations. This factor, combined with the first one, left Chilean civil religion too dependent on its alliance with the Church and the Catholic and conservative heritage of the country, and hence too susceptible to delegitimation in the face of the mounting disaffection of the Church and the populace.

Third, the civil religion of the Pinochet regime was founded on insufficiently broad core values. The litany of war against communism wore thin with time, while the traditional values of patriotism, religious piety, and the defence of freedom were insufficiently unique to justify the perpetuation of dictatorship. More "successful" civil religions call upon rich heritages of distinct values, like the "promise" of America, the first and greatest modern democracy, or the "salvific suffering" of the Jewish or the Polish people (Morawska, 1987), the glory of Persia or Islam, or the ancient lineage of Buddhist culture (Seneviratne, 1984).

Fourth, the civil religion of the Pinochet regime was also too dependent on the notion of an external ideological threat to the nation. Such a preoccupation is a prominent feature of many civil religions, for example, Afrikanerdom (Moodie, 1975), Israel (Liebman and Don-Yehiya, 1983), Poland (Morawska, 1987), and contemporary Iran and Iraq. Yet such threats change or dissipate, requiring a change in interpretive frameworks. The very success of the severely oppressive measures instituted by the regime soon undermined the credibility of this threat in the eyes of the populace. Moreover, towards the end of Pinochet's rule, the Cold War began to come to an end and the Soviet "evil empire" began to crumble. Hence the negatively framed civil religious discourse of the Chilean junta lost much of its raison d'être.

The Pinochet regime, nevertheless, maintained its hold on power for a remarkably long period of time, and the strong impression persists that its eventual delegitimation and defeat in the referendum of 1988 were primarily the result of its autocratic actions. The continued abuse of civil and human rights and the repression of political dissent, were flagrantly at odds with the civil religious rhetoric of defending "endangered rights and liberties," "restoring justice," and providing all Chileans with a "dignified and secure existence" (i.e., the language of Edict No. 5

and Decree-Law No. 1). It was also at odds with Chile's long tradition of institutional life and rule of law. As Liebman and Don-Yehiya (1983) argue, it was the ability to perpetuate the sense of moral community that uniquely sustained a civil religious discourse in Israel, as the nation and its civil religion passed through three successive phases of development, precipitated by internal demographic changes and a shifting external political environment. But the Chilean military junta, factional in its support from the beginning, lost the capacity to maintain even the pretence to being founded on a moral community. In line with the Durkheimian approach to civil religion, then, we suggest that the inability to create a sense of moral community was instrumental to the demise of Chilean civil religion. Pinochet's endeavour, like many others, may have been Rousseauan in nature, but its failure is perhaps best explained with reference to Durkheim.

In general, the comparative literature suggests that most civil religions are self-limiting and hence episodic. There are several reasons for this state of affairs. First, when the political agenda is masked by religious symbolism, "the symbols become tarnished and lose their transcendent and unifying potential" (Gehrig, 1981a: 56-57). Second, when those in power approach politics "as if ultimate moral and religious issues are at stake," the political process is bound to be misused or destroyed. For the more justified political leaders feel in zealously carrying out their mission, the less likely they will be to accept criticism or seek compromise (Richardson, 1974: 165). Third, as Richard Fenn has argued, civil religion "weakens" and loses power when the state itself deviates from its standards while still invoking its symbols (in Gehrig, 1981a: 57). Yet, political officials "of a particular state will no doubt from time to time, if not all the time, violate the canons of their own moral yardsticks," creating the "openings for the deligitimation of regimes, institutions, and policies" (Markoff and Regan, 1982: 350). Fourth, by and large, civil religions "fail to evoke deep and lasting commitments because [their] symbols are too closely associated with values and beliefs; they lack independent validity; they are not perceived to be rooted in the very nature of reality, the way religious symbols are" (Liebman and Don-Yehiya, 1983: 225).

Consequently, when the political environments change, or when values do, civil religions are simply rejected.

All civil religions are probably self-limiting in some combination of these ways. Certainly each of these points is pertinent to the assessment of civil religion in Chile. Less pertinent, but worth noting, is Markoff and Regan's contention that "it is the experience of a gap between parochial identities and the claims of the state that generates the felt need for civil religion" (1982: 342). Accordingly, they conclude that even a successful civil religion contains the seeds of its own destruction. Why? Because, they suggest, "when citizens embrace it, they come to see a larger, civic meaning in their everyday activities and grant the executors of the state further power to extend their hold over the periphery. The political center's authority is enhanced—which, in turn, renders the civil religion gratuitous" (1982: 349). Chile poses a counter-instance to this hypothesis because Pinochet's religious ideology was not a response to the problems of pluralism (at least not in any traditional sense).

The creation and maintenance of a civil religion clearly depend on a confluence of contingent historical, cultural, and structural conditions. But, as the case of Chile reveals, there is a crucial strategic or purposeful component to the development of a civil religion. This component comes to the fore in consideration of both the structural factors affecting the "success" of civil religions (e.g., the creation of organizational carriers and symbol systems) and the consistency of the words and deeds of the moral entrepreneurs who chose to bring civil religious discourses into play. In Bellah's own words (1967: 12), civil religion, like any other religion, may suffer "deformation and demonic distortions." The civil religion Pinochet and his military junta tried to impose in Chile bears witness to such deformation and distortion.

CHAPTER SIX

Civil Religion and the Spirit of Nationalism

I noted in previous chapters that American civil religion is assumed to provide legitimation to the political order and, at the same time, to challenge institutional authority. On this issue, Bellah tells us, the Declaration of Independence speaks for itself. It makes reference to the "'Laws of Nature and of Nature's God' that are clearly transcendent to and stand in judgment on the laws of the state" (1976b: 167). This is the reason why Bellah insists that civil religion is "oriented to a level of reality that transcends the state and institutions" (167). Given that the American nation (or any nation for that matter) is, to some extent, sanctified, or endowed with sacred attributes, it should come as no surprise that the religious authority, conferred by civil religion, may be used and "marshaled" not only for a great variety of political programs and agendas, but also for "an extraordinary range and variety of American nationalisms" (Wilson, 1974: 137 n. 4). When a nation acts in the name of God,

---

Notes to Chapter 6 are on pp. 257-61.

there is always the danger that the nation itself or its particular nationalist agenda may become sacralized. This chapter considers this danger.

Patriotism as a Civic Duty

Critics have rightly observed that the theories of both Rousseau and Durkheim provided an intellectual milieu favourable to the development of nationalist ideologies. Indeed, both thinkers conceive patriotism as a civic duty to be orchestrated and encouraged by the state. On the issues of nationalism and patriotism, Durkheim moves closer in the direction of Rousseau. One may say, in fact, that it is at this juncture that their theories really converge.

Rousseau's writings belong to an age when modern nation-states and national consciousness were only beginning to emerge.[1] While he is well known as a political philosopher, he is less well identified as a champion of nationalism. Asked in 1772 to advise the Poles on constitutional reforms, Rousseau, in line with his idea that the love of the country and the love of its law are inseparable, admonished the Poles to deepen their patriotism. Macfarlane has argued that Rousseau made the development of patriotic and nationalistic sentiments the centerpiece of his proposals for constitutional reforms in Poland. Indeed, Rousseau assigned to national institutions a fundamental role in forming its citizens' character, tastes, and customs needed to inspire the ardent love of a country. He therefore counselled the Poles that they did not need to bring about drastic constitutional amendments: just a few legal changes would suffice to establish a government capable of carrying patriotic virtues "to the highest point of intensity." Individuals should be taught to love their country and protect their homeland. If this were done, they would naturally respect and obey the law, not out of fear, but because the law represents nothing other than the "inward assent of their will" (Macfarlane, 1970: 108-9).

Rousseau's brand of nationalism is characteristic of the democratic, republican tradition of the eighteenth century. It is a humanitarian nationalism. Most commentators agree that it is devoid of any narrowness or sense of exclusiveness. His concern is not the pursuit of national supremacy or even national uniqueness often associated with modern nationalism. Rather, his focus is on the common good, and on instilling in people a love for, and a deep sense of being a part of, the national community. Nationalism thus understood requires a sense of belonging, a concern for the common good, and a moral attachment to the nation (Sandel, 1996: 5). But a sense of moral obligation does not just happen. In order to have a conscious attachment to the community, individuals must be educated (one may say even forced) to become good citizens and patriots. This role Rousseau assigns to civil religion and to education. Both are necessary to promote social unity; both are indispensable for engendering a sense of "public-spiritedness" (MacFarlane, 1970: 196). Sandel is quite right in asserting that the republican spirit (to which Rousseau's writings certainly belong) was never "neutral toward the values and ends its citizens espoused" (1996: 6).

Rousseau's ideas (and modern European thought, in general) crystallized around some basic concepts such as "liberty, humanity, and patriotism."[2] Rousseau was convinced that a truly free state and the welfare of a free community depended for its character upon the individuals who composed it. Corrupt rulers would be unable or unwilling to create a free state. To overcome moral corruption, civic training was required—all members of the community should be taught civic responsibilities and should be encouraged to co-operate (Kohn, [1944] 1967: 263). Patriotism was to be the "most efficacious" means to develop civic virtues. Only then would the general will prevail (Rousseau, [1755] 1973: 130). Republican virtue, civic duty, good citizenship, and a healthy patriotic spirit came to be considered central elements for the integrity, preservation, and welfare of the society.

Education was to be essential to cultivate the civic virtue and moral perfection of individuals, necessary to maintain the common good. Education should not only provide instruction but should form good citizens and "direct their opinions and tastes in such a way that they will be patriotic by inclination, by passion, by necessity" (cited in MacFarlane, 1970: 109). Rousseau insists that it is not sufficient to tell citizens *"be good;* they must be taught to be so" ([1755] 1973: 130). A good government, Rousseau writes, "vigilant incessantly to maintain or restore patriotism and morality among the people, provides beforehand against the evils which sooner or later result from the indifference of the citizens for the fate of the Republic....Wherever men love their country, respects the laws, and lives simply, little remains to be done in order to make them happy" ([1755] 1973: 137-38).

To rekindle national patriotism, Rousseau also proposes awarding special honours to deserving and exemplary citizens, reawakening national customs, holding national games, producing national plays, and celebrating and commemorating holidays that should "breathe patriotism" (Hayes, 1960: 48).[3] Rousseau, in short, is convinced that "a passionate patriotism [is] needed as the expression of a community's self-consciousness" (Sherover, 1984: xxxix). He expresses disdain for what he calls "vain and futile declaimers," who travel the land trying "to sap the foundations of our faith," by showing contempt for "patriotism and religion." These pseudo prophets waste their time and talents trying to defame "all that men hold sacred" (Rousseau, [1750] 1973: 15-16). Rousseau has been called the "prophet of nationalism" primarily because his concept of citizenship cannot be divorced from that of patriotism (Sherover, 1984: 212).[4] It is here that a major difficulty arises. While Rousseau's intentions were good—he is undoubtedly committed to a benign kind of nationalism—the role he assigns to the state in orchestrating national sentiments and love of country is potentially coercive and may lead to national chauvinism. Rousseau did not foresee (as many students of civil religion do not today) that his brand of nationalism could (and would) develop into those tyrannous excesses of the twentieth century. The problem confronting us, therefore, goes beyond his intention and must be detached from it.

Let us now turn to Durkheim's sociology, where it is also not difficult to find an explicit philosophy of nationalism. Several critics have emphasized this aspect of his work (Bellah, 1973b; Giddens, 1986; Lukes, 1973; Mitchell, 1990; Wallace, 1990, 1973).

Wallace indicates that Durkheim's nationalism is evident not only in his teaching and writings, but also in his own patriotic efforts during the First World War (1990: 221). One critic has claimed, however, that although scholars have recognized Durkheim's interest in encouraging and preserving French national self-consciousness, no scholar has specifically considered his work "from the standpoint of his nationalism" (Mitchell, 1990: 113).

Just as Rousseau before him, Durkheim assigns a fundamental role to education in the inculcation of patriotism, which he defines as "the ideas and feelings as a whole which bind the individual to a certain State" ([1950] 1986: 202). Morality and citizenship go hand in hand: a good patriot is a moral citizen. Morals, however, do not exist *a priori* in the individual conscience. They are the "product" of society and have "force" only insofar as society itself is stable and organized (203). Thus, he argues, the state cannot be just "a spectator of social life (as liberals would have it)." The state is "supremely the organ of moral discipline" (201). As such, the state must "be present in all spheres of social life and make itself felt" (194). One field open to its moral mission is education.

The specific agencies of civic education, the public schools, should be in charge of inculcating public responsibility and of moulding the character of its citizens. Conceived by Durkheim as a mini "political society," the school is to be the primary social institution in charge of preparing every new generation for a life of civic responsibility. Its most fundamental goal is the formation of patriotic citizens (Mitchell, 1990: 121; Wallace, 1973: 4). French education, in short, should be unquestionably secular, moral, and, above all, national—the French spirit of nationalism and patriotism should be spread across the land (Durkheim, [1925] 1961: 4).

In 1916 Durkheim gave a lecture entitled "The Moral Greatness of France and the School of the Future," in which he praised the public school system for accomplishing its task. The war had proven Frenchmen to be heroic, courageous, noble, and ready to sacrifice their life for the nation. The war had shown the *"moral greatness of France."* But this idea needed to be implanted in every heart and fixed in the *conscience collective* of every French individual, not only in times of crisis, but also in times of peace (Durkheim, [1916] 1979: 159). To accomplish this task, education should be infused with moral ideas and ideals. Young people should be taught to act morally—that is, to cultivate civic virtue—and to act in the public interest by doing their duty. "For to be free is not to do what one pleases; it is to be master of oneself, it is to know how to act with reason and to do one's duty" (Durkheim, [1922] 1956: 89). In short, Durkheim saw in patriotism the civil religion of modern times (Wallace, 1990: 220). Not surprisingly, Bellah (1973b: x) has referred to Durkheim not only as a great philosopher of moral order, but also as "a high priest and theologian of the civil religion of the Third Republic."

We have already seen the fundamental importance Durkheim places on public gatherings for strengthening collective identity. Through collective ceremonies, individuals can overcome the moral isolation that characterizes modernity. In his view, sacred symbols and rituals are as important for modern individuals as they were for Australian aborigines. For example, he assigns to the flag a crucial symbolic importance—it is to be the new symbol or "'rallying point' for *la patrie*, just as the totem [had been] for the clan" (Mitchell, 1990: 120).

Wallace (1990: 222) has argued that patriotism is, for Durkheim, a sort of intermediary association between the nation and the world. Indeed, as an ardent patriot, Durkheim was convinced that every Frenchman had duties to France that they did "not have the right to cast off." But he seemed equally convinced that "beyond this country, there is another in the process of formation, enveloping our national country: that of Europe, or humanity" (in Lukes, 1973: 350). For it is not national but "human aims that are destined to be supreme" (Durkheim, [1950] 1986: 202). Durkheim is emphatic about this. It would be "a cause for despair," he writes, "if one were condemned to think of patriotism only in terms of putting France above all" (in Lukes, 1973: 546). Durkheim's proposal implies that the nation, as an intermediate group, should serve as the bridge for the "realization of humanity." It would do this by linking members of a particular society with humanity in general. Each particular state or nation would become the agency through which the "human ideal" would be carried into effect. In other words, Durkheim sees the need to move beyond narrow nationalism so as to harmonize "national patriotism with world patriotism." Nationalism, in this sense, was meant to be "a stepping-stone to internationalism"(Wallace, 1990: 222).

Durkheim was against the type of nationalism characteristic of the German state. German nationalism was, in his view, unethical, immoral, and regressive, an unfortunate relapse into "tribal or pagan" mentality whereby national interests were placed above the idea of humanity (Wallace, 1990: 221). The idea of an internationalist future had no place in such type of nationalism. This did not mean, however, that nationalism *per se* was either evil or that it should be rejected. There is nothing wrong with having national pride, Durkheim reflects. In fact, as "long as there are States, so there will be national pride, and nothing can be more warranted. But societies can have their pride, not in being the greatest or the wealthiest, but in being the most just, the best organized and in possessing the best moral constitution" (Durkheim, [1950] 1986: 204). Patriotism would prepare the individual to work for the celebration of humanity. If all the nations of the world would develop a sort of humanity consciousness, international relations would not only be more effective, but international troubles would tend to disappear. "Each national state would become 'a special point of view on humanity'" (Mitchell, 1990: 122).

Durkheim thus envisions a decline of national difference and the eventual formation of a supra-national community.[5] He puts forth this idea frequently. In his course "The Teaching of Morality in the Primary School," which he taught in Paris, he argues for the "possibility of a non-exclusive patriotism committed to internationalist ideals." Then, again, in "Patriotism and Cosmopolitanism," he insists that national ideals should be broadened and universalized (Lukes, 1973: 118, 350) And in his lecture "On Patriotism and Militarism," his cosmopolitan vision is emphasized once more. He insists that no matter how much individuals may be attached to their native land, "they all today are aware that beyond the forces of national life there are others,...unrelated to conditions peculiar to any given political group"(Durkheim, [1950] 1986: 201). He was hopeful, particularly before the war, that internationalism would eventually emerge, that men would break free of "local" or "ethnic" chains and rise above particular interests so as to "approach the universal" (202). Although in later writings Durkheim's optimism seemed to have waned, for he was not sure if internationalism would ever come, he never completely renounced the idea that "it is the tendency of patriotism to become, as it were, a fragment of world patriotism" (Durkheim, 1950/1957: 75).

In a typical Durkheimian fashion he envisioned the "religion of humanity" as a powerful integrative force, capable of becoming a universal religion embracing, or even substituting for, all other religions (Wallace, 1990: 222). The "cult of the individual" or the "cult of man" would be capable of achieving world peace and world integration. The creation of this world religion was, in his view, of the utmost importance, for sooner rather than later "members of a single social group will have nothing in common among themselves except their humanity." This modern form of individualism, he believed, originated not from egoistic sentiments but from a desire for greater justice and from "sympathy for all that is human" (Durkheim, [1898] 1973: 51, 48-49).

Thus, the essence of moral individualism, at its "most abstract level," refers to humanity in general rather than to individuals of any particular nation (Giddens, 1986: 21). A national *conscience collective* would eventually be supplanted by an international or universal *conscience collective*. As Giddens notes, the notions of patriotism and love for humanity were not in opposition. Rather, they complemented each other. From Durkheim's point of view, there was a "basic compatibility, in the modern world, between national ideals, patriotism, and the growth of a pan-national community" (Giddens, 1986: 29; see also Mitchell, 1990). Durkheim, however, never directly explained how clan religion could become "intertribal" and civil religion "international" (Schoffeleers, 1978: 48).

Lukes notes that interpretations of Durkheim's work, based on "selective misreading" of his writings, have led to exaggerated charges that he paved the way for fascism or totalitarian nationalism. There seems to be substantial evidence, he argues, that Durkheim did not espouse a narrow or chauvinistic form of nationalism. Durkheim's writings offer "a conclusive refutation" against those who have portrayed him as an anti-liberal "right-wing nationalist, a spiritual ally of Charles Maurras and a forerunner of twentieth-century nationalism, even fascism" (Lukes, 1973: 338).

Durkheim's theory becomes problematic, and even contradictory, when we consider the role he assigns to education and the state for moulding patriotic citizens. Social integration is not so spontaneous after all, nor is it the sense of belonging or the moral bond attaching citizens to the collectivity and the state. Certain sentiments necessary for the social order require reinforcement, not only through rituals, but through education. The idea of a national (moral) community has to be inculcated, taught, and transmitted from generation to generation. Individuals are induced to acquire civic responsibilities by a moral authority exercised by society and the state. Durkheim insists that the moment education turns into an "essentially social function, the State cannot but be interested in it." In fact, "all that is educational must to some degree be subordinate to its action" (Durkheim, [1938] 1986: 177).

There are obvious similarities here between Rousseau's and Durkheim's ideas. By insisting that the state be highly involved in education, both are paving the way for possible manipulation and control. Moreover, by stressing the sacred character of state and society, their theories may awaken in individuals a fanatical devotion to a particular collectivity and, by the same token, hostility to other collectivities, nations, or states. To be sure, Durkheim's theory goes much further than Rousseau's in this respect, insofar as he argues that the object of religious concern—the divine—is nothing other than society.[6] The idea of society as sacred may foster, in turn, a need for "any society to set itself up as god and to create gods." Simply put, the "idea of a nation-god," or the idolizing of the nation, is an "obvious conclusion" that can be drawn from Durkheim's writings (Mitchell, 1990: 123).

Rather than solving a problem, Durkheim actually creates one by affirming simultaneously, and perhaps inconsistently, the love for humanity (the human ideal) and the love for one's country (the national ideal). Although his nationalism is pacifist, humanitarian, and anti-militaristic, his theory may lead, unintentionally but perhaps inevitably, to an aggressive type of patriotism. Individuals may be inspired not only to honour their country, but to deify or worship a particular collectivity, nation, or state. The possibility always exists that they may shift "from a conception of the nation as the supreme reality, and humanity as the highest ideal, to one in which the nation fulfills the requirements of both" (Mitchell, 1990: 124). Any particular nation may, thus, become "heteronomous vis-à-vis other peoples and nations" (Mead, 1974: 69). Even though Durkheim's arguments are presented in a more universal form, his doctrine may give rise to international hostility, national self-glorification, and rejection of national minority groups. This problem is also present in most theories of civil religion.

It seems to me that it is not enough to make clear that Durkheim's sociology points in the direction of universalism. It is also not enough to explicitly acknowledge that he condemned narrow nationalism as either immoral or as a regression to tribalism. What needs to be acknowledged is that Durkheim proposed "a conception of the nation and the state, which came dangerously close to the very thing he condemned" (Schoffeleers, 1978: 14).

In sum, Rousseau, recognizing a socio-political need, *designed* civil religion to encourage patriotism—a love of the nation and its law. Durkheim, by contrast, *found* patriotism to be the civil religion of modern times. But in the final analysis, both presented a proposal that required instruction, indoctrination, and a measure of state control to keep the spirit of patriotism alive.

If we turn to Bellah's theory, which, as already noted, is very much in the Durkheimian tradition, it is not difficult to see that it manifests the same weakness and tends to produce the same result. Implicit in his notion of civil religion is the same kind of ambiguity and tension found in Durkheim's theory of religion and society—the tension between "particularism and universalism" (Schoffeleers, 1978: 14).[7] Bellah also envisions the emergence of some type of world civil religion. The global community, according to him, needs "a global concord"for its survival—a global order of civility and justice. Accordingly, Bellah alludes to a "trans-national sovereignty." Yet this would require the "incorporation of vital international symbolism into our civil religion, or, perhaps...it would result in American civil religion becoming simply one part of a new civil religion of the world" (1967: 18). He believes that American civil religion with its "tradition of openness, tolerance and ethical commitment" might play an important role in the development of "a world civil religion that would transcend and include it" (Bellah, 1980a: xiv). Bellah, true to his American heritage, assigns a "noble mission" to American civil religion and a special place for it in the world order. This universal civil religion would be a "fulfilment," not a "denial," of American civil religion (Bellah, 1967: 18). It is clear that, under Bellah's proposal, American civil religion also points towards a "global, cultural resource," or towards a "global civil religion" (Wilson, 1979: 147, 170).

As in Durkheim's case, there is no doubt that Bellah is far from having chauvinistic national aspirations. However, while it is true that he envisions a world civil religion, it is no less true that the American civil religion he describes is highly nationalistic. By explicitly sacralizing the nation (as Durkheim did before him), he can also be interpreted as encouraging nationalism or, perhaps, a nationalist mentality. This is a charge that Bellah has repeatedly denied.

To sum up, neither Bellah nor Durkheim, nor even Rousseau, constructed their theories with premeditated condemnable intentions. However, the fact that their theories can be interpreted in a nationalist sense, together with the fear that civil religion runs the risk of becoming aggressive nationalism, remains problematic (Schoffeleers, 1978: 49).

All nationalisms involve a state ideology, and a sacralization, so to speak, of the national culture. Likewise, all civil religions, whether in their Rousseauan, Durkheimian, or Bellahian varieties also involve an ideology that sacralizes national life. In this sense, civil religion is no different than nationalisms, which always involve a "spiritual core" and an ideology (Mead, 1974: 58). The nation, as one of the most powerful "repositories of symbols," comes to have religious significance and even "replace religious institutions in the minds of the people" (Marty, 1974: 140). One hardly needs to be reminded that Hayes (1960) has called nationalism "a religion." It is at this intersection that civil religion and nationalism seem to meet (see also Hudson, 1970).

Apter (1963: 89) has argued that most nationalisms take a form similar to theocracies. Both attempt to establish a system of transcendental values, which provides state legitimation and the "moral underpinnings" necessary to achieve political ends. Apter's description of the instrumental political objective of nationalisms and theocracies fits very well the role often assigned to civil religion—that is, to provide legitimacy and common moral values. Like civil religion, nationalism exalts national existence and national values. Nationalism, in short, seems to operate in the same way and play the same role as civil religion. It follows that the concept of civil religion touches the "tangential but no less important issue of *nationalism*" (Demerath, 1994: 114). As belief systems, both provide identity, meaning, and purpose for the collectivity (see Apter, 1963: 91). It seems odd to me that, while other systems of beliefs such as communism and fascism have been included in the literature as categories of civil religion, nationalism per se has not.[8]

In dealing with the issue of civil religion or nationalism, we are confronted with a serious dilemma—a dilemma that haunted both Rousseau and Durkheim. That is, how to instill in citizens, a healthy love of their country (as advocated by Rousseau) or a national pride (as Durkheim wished) and avoid the dark side of nationalism and its excesses? History tells us that, while the French Revolution may have given birth to the idea of nationalism in its more civilized form, Nazism and Fascism unveiled its most perverted face. Fascism "pushed nationalism to its very limit, to a totalitarian nationalism, in which humanity and the individual disappear and nothing remains but the nationality, which has become the one and the whole" (Kohn, [1944] 1967: 20). The danger that civil religion might be transformed into a sort of totalitarian nationalism (or national religious absolutism) looms large and deserves serious attention. It may be the reason why some people "despise the notion of a civil religion, out of fear that symbols of transcendence will be perverted to the uses of the state" (Novak, 1992: 302).

On the level of ideological discourse, for example, the civil religion Pinochet tried to impose in Chile was highly nationalistic. National security, national unity, and national power were justifications often given by Pinochet in support of military action. Enemies of the nation (i.e., dissidents) were seen as compromising the nation's survival. An identification of nation, state, and armed forces (or military government) was established—citizens were viewed only as "subordinate subjects." Because the essence of the nation and its tradition were said to be in danger, it fell to the armed forces, the guardians of that tradition, "to restore order, to take into its hands the destiny of the nation, and to reestablish national unity" (Garretón, 1989: 70). Structural problems, conflict of interests, and disagreements among groups were ignored, rejected, or "discredited as prejudicial to unity." Conflicts were the machinations of the "enemies" of the nation or of their "infiltrators." Because national security was defined in terms of protection from subversion by internal enemies, conflicts had to be avoided, and enemies punished. The war required that all the resources of the nation be mobilized in order to achieve national objectives— the most important one being the confrontation of Marxism. The national program devised by Pinochet, and announced through various official documents, was a project to which the entire nation ought to be devoted. The military regime left no room for dialogue, disagreement, or even compromise. Any conflict over what the Junta considered national interests and purposes was considered illegal—it desecrated the principle of national unity, and disrupted the project of *reconstrucción nacional* (Garretón, 1989: 68-72).

In recent years we have seen nationalistic passions spread with epidemic intensity. As evidenced by the war and ethnic cleansing in the former Yugoslavia, and the emergence of new countries from the former Soviet Union, nationalism can be a fierce and destructive force. In Canada, the resurgence of Québécois nationalism after the Quiet Revolution, and particularly during the last two decades, has pushed the unity issue to national centre stage. Although the federal government is apparently willing to show Québécois and other Canadians the possibility of reforms and compromise, Quebec's increasingly militant attitude and self-asserted right to declare independence unilaterally are raising serious concern about the country's future. The sovereignist movement, and its message of independence and separation, may be interpreted as a civil religion with strong political and nationalist overtones, i.e., a civil religion shifted radically towards the Rousseauan side of the continuum.[9]

As Geertz (1973: 253) declares, "Rather like religion, nationalism has a bad name in the modern world, and, rather like religion, it more or less deserves it. Between them (and sometimes in combination) religious bigotry and nationalist hatred have probably brought more havoc upon humanity than any two forces in history, and doubtless will bring a great deal more." Geertz is probably correct. This is why the link between civil religion and nationalism seems to me not a "tangential" issue (as Demerath argues), but rather a question of utmost importance—one that seems not to have attracted the attention it deserves. The possible connection between civil religion and nationalism clearly demands that this matter be re-examined.

Nationalism in the United States

In chapter 2, I discussed some of the issues relating to the origins of American national self-understanding. However, for the sake of clarity, in the context of the present discussion, I briefly return to this topic.

Unlike European nations, which over a period of centuries slowly evolved into self-conscious nationhood, the American nation, Hudson notes, seemed to "spring into existence almost overnight." Before the American Revolution, the possibility that the thirteen Colonies could ever become one people was generally considered too impractical and remote. After the revolution, even George Washington expressed surprise that "the divisions had been bridged" (Hudson, 1970: xix). The War of Independence seemed to "confirm the belief that independence was a design of Heaven, effected by God himself to further his own purposes for the world" (Hudson, 1970: xxi).[10] The colonists came to believe that,

> by God's intention, America was destined to be a purer and freer England, strong, healthy, undefiled, and more firmly devoted to freedom. The American continent and the American people became blended in a universally accepted myth of great symbolic significance. The continent was the Promised Land. The people were Israel, escaping from Egyptian bondage, crossing a forbidding sea, living a wilderness life, until, by God's grace and their own faithfulness, the wilderness became a new Canaan. Their pilgrimage was part and parcel of God's scheme of redemption for the whole human race. Viewed from this perspective...the American Revolution was a religious revival. (Hudson, 1970: xxxii)

Alexis de Tocqueville was intrigued by the American experiment—a society that, according to him, comprised "all the nations of the world." Writing to a friend, he asked him to imagine, if he could, a people "differing from one another in language, in beliefs, in opinions; in a word, a society possessing no roots, no memories, no prejudices, no routine, no common ideas, no national character, yet with a happiness a hundred times greater than our own" (in Hudson, 1970: xxi).

The diversity, as Hudson notes, was more apparent than real, and certainly not so profound as de Tocqueville believed. At the time of the American Revolution, more than 80 per cent of the colonists had a common historical heritage—they were from British stock. English was the established language. Historical records and legal documents show that English was the official language even in documents of the Dutch Reformed churches. While the new settlers identified themselves as "Virginians, Pennsylvanians, and New Yorkers rather than as Americans," most of them considered themselves "Englishmen." And while there certainly was religious diversity, it was diversity within a common tradition—Puritan Protestantism. Clearly, the new country possessed a "predominant national origin" and, most importantly, a "predominant religious faith" (Hudson, 1970: xxii-xxv).

Historians and students of American society broadly agree that, since their early beginnings as a nation, Americans have been possessed "by an acute sense of divine election" (Cherry, 1971: vii). In this sense, to understand American national self-consciousness is to understand the religious heritage of the American people. God was fundamental to the colonists' self-understanding. Hence, Chesterton's famous remark that America was founded "on a creed" that preceded the creation of a national community, or the foundation of the state. Until the First World War, "theological language, religious metaphors, and biblical allusions were as characteristic of political discourse and historical writing as they were of sermonic literature" (Hudson, 1970: xi). In fact, the Protestant clergyman enjoyed for a great number of years a special place as a "central spokesman" for American culture and identity. American political leaders merely mirrored him. This tradition has continued even up to modern times. One has only to think of men such as Reinhold Niebuhr and Martin Luther King, for example (Bellah, 1975: 56).

Several basic themes gave early Americans a sense of identity: a tradition of a chosen people "in covenant with a God," who was to judge, discipline, and guide the American people; a free people endowed with a quasi-religious devotion to liberty, the "cause of liberty" being "the cause of God"; a special mission in the world, that is, America's role as the guardian of liberty and as a haven for the oppressed; a vision of a special destiny and of "future greatness" that "God held in store for America" (Hudson, 1970: 19-56). Settlers convinced themselves they were the very embodiment of the general trend human evolution would follow. They would establish in the New World a "better rational order," with "greater individual freedom," and perfect social equality. For this reason, America came to view itself as the "trustee of these blessings for Europe and mankind" (Kohn, [1944] 1967: 291, 293).

In 1850 Herman Melville described Americans as the "peculiar, chosen people," "the Israel of our time."[11] He wrote, "we bear the ark of liberties of the world...God has given to us, for a future inheritance, the broad domains of the political pagans...God has predestined, mankind expects, great things from our race; and great things we feel in our souls. The rest of the nations must soon be in our rear. We are the pioneers of the world....And let us always remember that with ourselves, almost for the first time in the history of earth, national selfishness is unbounded philanthropy; for we cannot do a good to America, but we give alms to the world" (in Bellah, 1975: 39). Likewise, J.L. O'Sullivan, founder (in 1837) and editor of the *United States Magazine and Democratic Review,* was convinced that America had been blessed with a manifest destiny and a holy mission, the "mission of going before the nations of the world as the representative of the democratic principle and as the constant living exemplar of its results" (in Henry, 1979: 88). As Henry rightly notes, the idea of a "'noble mission' and ideal foundation" required a strong degree of nationalist spirit (1979: 88).

Hence, the sentiment of being "chosen," and the idea of a "special mission" have been important components of the American national self-consciousness. Following Weber, Wilson has distinguished two patterns of missionary zeal: the exemplary and the emissary traditions. In the former version, rooted in Puritanism, America is portrayed as showing to the world the achievement of a "perfected society." The aim is to set up America as an example—as the land of liberty and democracy. America stands as a model, sanctioned by God, which others may emulate. Wilson argues that the exemplary construct is the source of American isolationism that lasted well into the Second

World War. The idea was for the United States to stay removed from international conflicts and entanglements so that it could preserve its own "continuing purity." The emissary version, on the other hand, entails a mythical program of national mission. Under this construct, the idea is to preach a way of life to others, to reveal "the truth" to the rest of the world. Such a vision includes wars in defence of democracy and crusades against communism (Wilson, 1979: 29-31).[12] This model has contributed to the image of the United States as a "Messiah, the 'last best hope' of human kind" (Novak, 1992: 288).

Denis Brogan has argued rather cynically that the key function of American civil religion is "not the doing on earth the will of the Christian or Jewish God, but of securing for the United States the blessing of the God whose Chosen People is the American People" (1968: 357). Myths die hard: they repeat themselves like endless litanies from generation to generation. What is important for this discussion is to recognize, as Wilson does, that this "complex of mythic materials" was central (and perhaps still is) to the cultural nationalism of the American republic (Wilson, 1979: 32).

In the context of American society, the connection between civil religion and nationalism presents an interesting and perhaps unique case. America was not only founded on a creed, but this creed has defined American identity. Huntington, in his excellent book *American Politics: The Promise of Disharmony* (1981), claims that nationalism in the United States has been defined more in "political rather than in organic terms." He argues that for most other people national identity is "organic" in character. By this he means, it is "a product of a long process of historical evolution involving common ancestors, common experiences, common ethnic background, common language, common culture, and usually common religion." This is not so in America. Here, the political convictions of the American creed have provided the rationale of American national identity (Huntington, 1981: 23). This was particularly true in its early years as a nation, when the community was "a community decided not by blood but by faith" and united by a "fierce spirit of liberty" (Hudson, 1970: xxix, xxv). Several scholars have echoed the view that America was not formed by "natural" foundations of blood or common history. Rather, it was shaped by "a universal idea. Loyalty to America meant therefore loyalty to that idea" (Kohn, [1944] 1967: 324). This basic idea can be summarized as the right to life, liberty, and the pursuit of happiness.

The main political values of the American creed—"liberty, equality, individualism, democracy and the rule of law under a constitution"—set forth in the Declaration of Independence, are a critical element of American national identity. The other source of ideas of the political and social ethos of Americans, seventeenth-century Protestantism, added elements of "moralism, millenialism, and individualism" to the American social and political landscape. Protestant values, stressing the importance of the individual, joined hands with republican and democratic ideals to provide "the underlying ethical and moral basis for American ideas on politics and society" (Huntington, 1981: 15-16). Protestantism, in a sense, married the spirit of liberty with the spirit of religion. America's religious self-understanding and America's republican and democratic self-understandings are, in fact, inseparable.

Huntington thus claims that the United States, as a nation, originated in "a conscious political act" whereby national identity was equated with "allegiance to political principles." What distinguished Americans from their British brethren, he argues, was not religion, ethnicity, culture, or language, but the fact that America, from the moment it came into existence, held these democratic and republican truths to be self-evident. This body of political ideas constitutes, for Huntington, the true essence of Americanism. In this sense, he claims, Americanism is "virtually unique." Huntington writes, "it is possible to speak of a body of political ideas that constitutes 'Americanism' in a sense in which one can never speak of 'Britishism,' 'Frenchism,' 'Germanism,' or 'Japanesism.'" He further notes, "There is no British Creed or French Creed; the Académie Française worries about the purity of the French language, not about the purity of French political ideas" (Huntington, 1981: 24-25). Political ideology and nationality are so intimately interwoven in America that "the disappearance of the former would mean the end of the latter." In Europe, by contrast, political ideology and nationalism never married each other. On the contrary, they "crossed each other." Ideologies represented social class interests while nationalism represented ethnic and linguistic groups (1981: 27-28).

American nationalism, Huntington concludes, is, in some ways more "intellectualized," less emotional and less irrational than in most other nations since political ideas and principles are at the basis of its definition. At the same time, compared to European ideologies such as liberalism, conservatism, and Marxism, which were linked to particular social groups and class interests, the American creed is "less systematic and intellectualized." It "reflects a national consensus and is identified with American *nationalism*" (1981: 29, emphasis added). Huntington sees American national identity as "very fragile." While the political system has been remarkably stable (there has been only one constitution and one system of government since 1776), wave after wave of immigrants have changed the nation's ethnic, religious, and cultural makeup.[13] For Huntington, the danger of national disintegration in America is not to be found in ethnic warfare or the threat of separation (as, for example, in the former Soviet Bloc or among the Basques in Spain or the Québécois in Canada), but in "disillusionment" with its political values or political institutions. "Destroy the political system," Huntington warns, "and you will destroy the basis of community, eliminating the nation." In other countries constitutions are abrogated, but the nation remains the same. Americans do "not have that choice." Americanism implies adherence to concrete political values. This is the reason why "to be an American is an ideal; while to be a Frenchman is a fact." In the former case, national identity is defined "normatively," while in the latter it is defined "existentially" (Huntington, 1981: 30). Novak (1992: 45) has also reflected that "being an American is a state of soul."

I am afraid it is difficult to briefly summarize and give full credit to Huntington's eloquent and well-elaborated discussion. What is important to note is that Huntington directly links the American creed (i.e., civil religion) with nationalism. Hughey has also pointed in this direction. He notes that America nationalism "has been committed far less to a territorial definition than to America as the embodiment of a national faith" (1992: 539).

I have already argued that what might have been true in nineteenth-century America appears much less true today. For example, in its early stages American nationalism contrasted itself with Europe and celebrated enlightened, democratic ideals. Now, one may argue, it differentiates itself from the world and tends to celebrate economic success. Indeed, in more recent times, being a great nation is often translated as "having a standard of living that is the envy of other nations, or a defense system that cannot be challenged, or a governing system that other nations try to emulate" (Wuthnow, 1988a: 243). It follows that at the dawn of the new millennium American national self-understanding seems to involve less religious, more mundane, more materialistic, and more pragmatic interests. American national self-understanding appears to have much to do with justifications about its "power, privilege, and wealth (243). A blatantly materialist and pragmatic ideology proclaims that "America is right because it is rich," or that Americans are "virtuous" because they are "successful" (264).[14] America's position of leadership and privilege in relation to the rest of the world has given rise, in turn, to the myth (and mission) that what is good for America is good on a global scale.

I do not want to imply that the political ideals of the American creed have lost all relevance. On the contrary, republican ideals are still very much a part of the American heritage. Yet, divorced from their Puritan ethical foundations, these ideals have lost their original religious meaning. Individual freedom, for example, no longer means restraint and voluntary submission to authority, nor does it mean a religiously grounded obligation to do good for the community, as it meant for early Puritan settlers. Rather, liberty is understood today as a free ticket for the pursuit of personal gain, and the freedom to do what one wishes (Bellah, 1975: xii). In any case, modern American civil religion weaves together "patriotism, competitive individualism, and a boundless faith in the potentialities of economic growth and prosperity." The new ethos or "moral dimension" calls for a "sanctification of American society, its laissez-faire economic processes, its democratic political processes, and its military and international might" (Anthony and Robbins, 1982: 216-217). The nation is exalted and deified through its political and economic policies, rather than through its moral and religious principles.

Summing up, the way American civil religion has been portrayed as operating (as a covenant between God and nation) tends to blur the boundary between civil religion and a religiously informed nationalist ideology. Moreover, the claim that civil religion "is clearly an element in nation building" (McGuire, 1987: 161), coupled with Bellah's espousal of the use of civil religion as an instrument to achieve national goals, has helped to confound the problem even more.[15]

This should come as no surprise since, from its beginnings in western Europe, modern nationalism has been conceived as having some of the qualities of religion (Hayes, 1960: 164). In this sense, linking religion proper with nationalism is not a novel idea. As Kohn notes, social scientists have long been aware of the close connection that appears to exist between nationalist and religious movements. "Both have an inspirational and sometimes revivalist character" (Kohn, [1944] 1967: 23). Both are essentially cultural forces with profound political resonance. What is indeed surprising is that the linkage between civil religion and nationalism has not received a similar attention.

Drawing a distinction between civil religion and nationalism is not a simple task. Hayes's interesting book *Nationalism: A Religion* (1960) is a case in point. What Hayes examines under the rubric "nationalism: a religion" bears a strong resemblance to any discussion of civil religion. Hayes indicates that nationalism, like all traditional religions, has a god—a "god of a chosen people." Like other religions, it involves "not simply the will, but the intellect, the imagination, and the emotions" of the people. Like other religions, again, nationalism is eminently social, and its central rituals and public ceremonies are performed for the "salvation of a whole community." Its "driving force is a collective *faith*, a faith in its mission and destiny" (Hayes, 1960: 164-65).[16]

Hayes further shows what he considers "striking parallels" between modern nationalism and medieval Christianity. He argues that the chief mission of the "national State" and the "universal Church" is a "mission of salvation." Just as Christianity adapted some elements from paganism, modern nation-states have borrowed heavily from the Christian church. Modern secular rites tend to emulate religious rites. Public ceremonies take on a quasi-liturgical form. The reverence for saluting, lowering or hoisting the flag is a case in point.[17] Modern nationalism has its ceremonies and places of pilgrimage, its holy days and its temples. In the United States, Hayes notes, the "Fourth of July is a nationalist Christmas, Flag Day an adaptation of Corpus Christi, and…Veteran's Day a patriotic version of All Souls Day, while in imitation of the saints' days of the Christian calendar are observed the birthdays of national saints and heroes, such as Washington and Lincoln" (1960: 165-67).

Clearly, civil religion embraces much of the same range of phenomena identified by Hayes as the religion of nationalism. Consider, for example, the striking parallels between Hayes's description of modern nationalism and Bellah's portrayal of civil religion. Wilson summarizes some of the elements of Bellah's model: the most salient theme is America's mission of salvation and the idea of Americans "carrying out God's will on earth." Bellah has also identified a series of "religious figures," heroes and martyrs, sacred events, sacred places, and sacred rituals such as "deferential behavior toward the flag and civic officials, solemn proceedings on Memorial Day or the Fourth of July" (Wilson, 1974: 127, 129; see also Wilson, 1979).

Critics have sporadically charged that Bellah's notion of civil religion represents a glorification or the worship of the American nation, but no serious attempt has been made to approach Bellah's work from the standpoint of nationalism. It should be evident, however, that the symbiotic relationship between nationalism and civil religion is very noticeable in the United States. If the religion of nationalism has borrowed from Christianity, American civil religion has borrowed from both Christianity and nationalism. Like most nationalisms, American civil religion also "appeals to man's 'religious sense'" (Hayes, 1960: 176). Derived mostly from events in American history, civil religion, as I have already noted, includes the belief in the theme of America as the new Israel and the ascription of sacred meanings to secular symbols (Kim, 1993; Richey and Jones, 1974; Wilson, 1971). It tends to sacralize and exalt national sentiments and national myths. It makes quasi-religious claims (both implicit and explicit) about American national character, about the validity of America's actions, and of its place in history and in the world. In short, it is a celebration of the nation's culture and way of life. These claims certainly are important components of cultural nationalism. They provide the most fundamental assumptions on which the nation, and its political order, is legitimated. One has to remember that legitimation not only means "tacit acceptance of the nation and its policies" but also a certain degree of trust, allegiance to, "or conviction about," the nation's destiny, mission, procedures, and political goals (Wuthnow, 1988a: 242). Finally, the outcome of civil religion mirrors the outcome of the religion of nationalism. That is, a "nationalist theology of intellectuals becomes a nationalist mythology for the masses" (Hayes, 1960: 168). In the case of nationalism, this usually takes place when national and religious feelings are "fused" and nationalism itself turns into a surrogate religion (Hayes, 1960: 10). It seems to me that, in the final analysis, civil religion, at least in its cultural form (the Durkhemian variety), is indistinguishable from cultural nationalism. Both stress collective identity, both refer to the ethos of a people, both are a "state of mind" (Kohn, [1944] 1967: 10). Needless to say, the political ideological form (the Rousseauan variety) might also emphasize nationalism as the locus for civic-religious practices.

What constitutes national identity is an old and unresolved debate. Scholars have been trying to explain national identity or the character of national groups since the eighteenth century, when the idea of national consciousness first unfolded in Europe (Huntington, 1981: 13; Kohn, [1944] 1967). It is not my intention to enter into a debate about the exact meaning of national identity. What is at issue here is the relationship between civil religion and nationalism. My concern is the degree to which values, beliefs, and ideas of the American creed or civil religion in general, can be identified with or are manifestations of nationalism.

The Structural Ambivalence of Civil Religion

In chapter 3, I examined the problem of legitimacy and argued that legitimacy of a government could be strengthened by appealing to national sentiments (Kokosalakis, 1985: 374; Wuthnow, 1988a: Richardson, 1974).[18] Richardson explicitly notes the crucial role of nationalism as a legitimizing factor. He claims that political power in the United States often tends to be legitimated through appeals to the principles and values of a nationalist ideology, framed in religious terms, whereby the nation assumes self-transcendence. The "religionizing of the nation and politics" and the idea of national self-idolization are central to Richardson's discussion of civil religion in America. Some scholars have referred to this type of civil religion as "the religion of patriotism" (Jones and Richey, 1974: 16).

Richardson has linked the power of modern states to the workings of nationalism. Modern states are often composed of different cultural groups. In order to retain a degree of autonomy in pursuing their own objectives, each group competes for social power either against the state or against each other. He argues that when nation-states began to emerge in Europe, the state's interests became linked with the interests of "its more powerful constituent nations: the German state with Prussia, the Soviet state with Russia, and the United States with the 'north.'" This association was usually sanctioned by the creation of a strong national civil religion or national political ideology. In such cases, the history, culture, and destiny of a nation are appropriated by the state and its dominant culture or group. Inevitably, other cultural groups are either ignored or "vigorously suppressed" so that the dominant culture be "diffused throughout the land" (Richardson, 1974: 168).[19] Richardson notes that the birth of American nationalism, and its accompanying civil religion, went through two stages: an inward and an outward stage. The former was concerned with domestic policy and a strong attempt to force a melting pot culture. The main task of the latter, on the other hand, was foreign policy and the incorporation of other countries "within the web of its culture and commerce." Not by "mere coincidence," Richardson notes, "the American Civil War was followed by an American imperial age" (1974: 169).

Despite evidence indicating that civil religion provides an ideological framework for nationalism, a number of scholars have repeatedly denied this claim. Mead (1974: 61) insists that the "religion of the Republic does not mean worship of the state or nation." Bellah has also frequently maintained that civil religion is not a form of national self-worship and political chauvinism. He writes, "the American civil religion is not the worship of the American nation but an understanding of the American experience in the light of ultimate and universal reality" (Bellah, 1967: 18). Elsewhere (1970: 168) he reiterates that civil religion "is not a form of national self-worship but...the subordination of the nation to ethical principles that transcend it and in terms of which it should be judged." In a similar vein, Novak (1992: 144) notes that civil religion "is not the same as the glorification of the status quo; it is not the absolutizing of 'the American way of Life.'" For Hughes (1980: 76), it is not "intrinsically idolatrous." In short, most students of American civil religion have taken the position, advanced by Mead, that civil religion in America "is not to be equated with crass American nationalism" (Wilson, 1974: 119).

Despite Bellah's repeated claims, he has recognized that American civil religion is not always "a good thing" (1974a: 257), and that it can be "idolatrous" at times. However, he seems to suggest that this happens "when the gap between the nation and its ideals is closed, so that the dimension of transcendence is lost and America falls into laudatory self-congratulation" (Richardson, 1974: 164). The problem, as Richardson notes, is that Bellah assumes that when the gap is closed, it is a misuse of civil religion (in Durkheimian terms, a "pathology"). The logic of Bellah's argument allows him to conclude that "Richard

Nixon...misuse[d] civil religion; but Abraham Lincoln and John Kennedy used it properly" (Richardson, 1974: 164).[20] Bellah insists that to compare civil religion with a "vulgar" form of nationalism is to ignore, or fail to perceive, its crucial role in maintaining a "cohesive and viable"social order. He believes that while civil religion may be, occasionally "abused for chauvinistic ends, [it] always confronts the nation with a potential judgement over nationalistic idolatry" (Stauffer, 1975: 390). This means that insofar as there is a pathology or deviance it is not to be found in civil religion per se, but rather in the errors or unscrupulous behaviour of those responsible for its proper functioning.

But, as Richardson rightly notes, the misuse of civil religion is not merely the result of some individuals using it improperly. Rather, such misuse is very likely to be engendered by or be part of "the very structure of civil religion itself" (1974: 164). From his standpoint, "the pretensions of American nationalism, the national self-idolization," are not civil religion's pathology, error, or malfunctioning: they are the unavoidable manifestations of civil religion itself (Jones and Richey, 1974: 11). I agree with Richardson's suggestion that the so-called misuse may have little to do with error or usage and more to do with the way civil religion works. This would mean that the idolatry of the nation is a natural expression or an inevitable aspect of any civil religion.

Bellah has asserted that one of the most important aspects of American civil religion has been, and still is, to affirm that a higher principle underlies civil laws. This means that "civil power stands under the sovereignty of God and that the nation must judge its own acts in the light of divine righteousness" (Richardson, 1974: 164). Bellah's claim is not without its problems. Richardson notes the "built-in doubleness" of Bellah's transcendental construct, or of any such model. If what is "finite" is characterized as "infinite" we may also "claim infinite characteristics for what is finite." Thus, by seeking to relate "American politics to God's sovereignty, we are also relating God's sovereignty to American politics." In so doing, he reflects, piousness may be confused with pride (Richardson, 1974: 164). If we accept Richardson's argument, and I do, then the sacralization of the nation is not only inevitable, it is a defining characteristic of civil religion itself (if it is understood at a national level). Richardson is quite unambiguous about this. He writes: "the 'best' politics in America...always becomes idolatrous," so it seems ironic "that American civil religion always tends to generate the very situation it seeks to prevent" (Richardson, 1974: 165).

In *The Broken Covenant* (1975), which is a reformulation of his earliest work, Bellah takes a prophetic stance and seems to assign a nationalist role to civil religion. Due to the social and political problems caused by the Vietnam War (a war that Bellah opposed), he admits that the American civil religion has become disjointed. Americans, he laments, have lost their sense of direction, the covenant has been betrayed by high political officials, and American society "is to the edge of the abyss" (1975: 142-58). Bellah writes, "no one has changed a nation without appealing to its soul, without stimulating a national idealism, as even those who call themselves materialists have discovered. Culture is the key to revolution; religion is the key to culture. If we win the political struggle, we will not even know what we want unless we have a new vision of man, a new sense of human possibility, and a new conception of the ordering of liberty, the constitution of freedom" (162). If my reading of Bellah is correct, it follows that he is assuming that civil religion, if well used, may be utilized to inspire nationalist sentiments of the right kind. America needs to reaffirm the covenant, and recover the republican civil religion and its spirit of civic virtue "in its most classical form" (151). But who is to decide if civil religion is well used or misused? How can we prevent the use of civil religion by high officials to exalt and glorify certain agendas or groups to the exclusion of others? How can we prevent a totalitarian form of nationalism from developing?

Most scholars either leave unanswered the question of whether civil religion is or is not the worship of the nation, or simply deny that it can be equated with national self-glorification. Others, few in number and often not sociologists, recognize the threat of civil religion becoming a self-glorifying and politically useful nationalism, "as it does when a particular regime or policy is defended in civil religious terms as an absolute, unquestionable good" (Wuthnow, 1994: 131). Still others, such as Coleman (1969) and Richey and Jones (1974), do not conceive civil religion per se as encouraging nationalist tendencies. Such a danger is limited to certain types of civil religion, often of the less "advanced" sort.

In Coleman's view (1969: 72), nationalist tendencies and praxis are found in totally desacralized civil religions, in what he calls secular nationalism, which he associates with authoritarian, undemocratic regimes. He conceives secular nationalism as a functional alternative to civil religion. It provides a legitimating symbol system that comes to replace religious symbol systems. Coleman argues that secular nationalisms emerge in situations where traditional religion is too closely linked to a "pre-revolutionary" regime.

I alluded to Coleman's typologies of civil religion in chapter 2; let me briefly consider it here again. According to Coleman (1969) civil religions in Western society have followed an evolutionary pattern. This pattern exhibits three phases: undifferentiated (either state-sponsored or church-sponsored), secular nationalism, and civil religion differentiated both from church and state. Undifferentiated stands for the most "primitive" type of civil religion, as was the case in State Shintoism in Japan in the 1800s, or in cases where the church performs the role of civil religion. Coleman claims that examples of the church performing the role of civil religion can be found throughout Latin America, but I have already argued that this claim is highly debatable (Cristi and Dawson, 1996, see also chap. 5 above). As for secular nationalism, he mentions three cases: the Soviet Union, Turkey under Atatürk, during which time political nationalism came to serve as civil religion replacing Islam; and France during the French Revolution. Coleman implies that the sacralization of a nation in cases such as these leads inevitably to outcomes not compatible with a democratic system.

It seems obvious from Coleman's discussion that he sees American civil religion as in no danger of ever becoming self-glorifying nationalism. After all, Coleman approaches the issue in evolutionary terms. Social evolution and differentiation are concomitant concepts, so he expects religious evolution to parallel general cultural evolution. In his eyes, the civil religion found in America represents the most advanced stage of evolution; it uniquely illustrates the case of a differentiated civil religion. The "peculiar genius" of American civil religion, he claims, is to be "general enough" to embrace all religions and peoples and yet "specific" enough to provide a "clear statement of the role and destiny" of every American as a citizen and of the nation in relation to questions "of ultimate meaning and existence" (Coleman, 1969: 70-75). One may add that, in his eyes, American civil religion is advanced enough not to be equated with crude nationalism.

Coleman detects some major difficulties in cases of undifferentiated civil religions sponsored by the church, and in cases of secular nationalism: the danger that civil and religious liberties of minorities will be jeopardized, the failure to provide national symbols that would integrate religious or ethnic minorities, and the undue pressures exerted on the national loyalties of the religious and other minorities. Coleman fails to realize that what he attributes to undifferentiated types of civil religion (exclusion of minorities, clash of loyalties, and so on) are problems endemic to any civil religion, American civil religion included. For example, it is doubtful that Americans of African and Native descent ever subscribed to the "history of salvation" designed by the Americans of European descent: "what is seen by the latter as a journey to the promised land was to the former the way to a profoundly degrading life of slavery" (Schoffeleers, 1978: 20). This failure on Coleman's part should come as no surprise, for he is one of those scholars who insist that "by definition" American civil religion is a religious system "given to the social integration of society" (Coleman, 1969: 76).

In other words, the problem of exclusion of religious or ethnic minorities is not to be found, as Coleman suggests, in the evolutionary phases of civil religion. Rather, as Richardson claims, it is more a result of the structural characteristics of civil religion itself, and of the pluralist nature of modern nation-states. Most modern societies embrace a variety of ethnic groups that do not share a common historical past or common values. The history that civil religion interprets and represents is often the history of the dominant culture. Moreover, by linking only a specific type of civil religion to nationalism, Coleman also fails to realize that any civil religion, at any stage of its evolution, (American civil religion included) may encourage and foster nationalist tendencies. Simply put, the nationalist impetus may come to dominate the language, rhetoric, ideals, values, and beliefs of the discourse of any civil religion.

Under such conditions, religious nationalism and/or civil religion may be used to justify and legitimize either the status quo or to advance a particular political agenda. Some scholars have noted, for instance, that the current revival of religion in the United States goes hand in hand with the pretensions of American nationalism (Kokosalakis, 1985: 371). Conservative Protestantism in America has also borrowed the civil religious discourse, showing a strong tendency to articulate its political demands in religious-nationalistic terms. Conservative Protestantism not only shrouds its political claims in nationalist terms, but connects "the a priori approval of the Almighty with the actions of the American body politic" (Demerath and Williams, 1985: 164-65; see also Wuthnow, 1988a). Demerath and Williams do not relate this to a structural problem of civil religion. Instead, they seem to agree with Bellah's idea on the misuse of civil religion. Thus, they claim that the "rhetorical display of patriotism and national pride are a form of bravado from a confused body politic rather a true reaffirmation of civil religion itself" (1985: 164).

Jones and Richey (1974) have identified five meanings or interpretations of civil religion found in the literature, only three of which are relevant to this discussion: folk religion, the transcendent universal religion of the nation, and religious nationalism. The main representative of the folk-type civil religion is Will Herberg. He sees the common religion of Americans as emerging from "folk" life itself (Jones and Richey, 1974: 15). Folk religion is the American way of life or Americanism—a system of "ideas, values and beliefs that constitute a faith common to

Americans as Americans." Sociologically, Herberg notes, it is the American religion "undergirding American national life and overarching American society." He further claims that the American way of life is a "civil religion in the strictest sense of the term, for, in it, national life is apotheized, national values are religionized, national heroes are divinized, national history is experienced as a *Heilsgeschichte,* as a redemptive history" (Herberg, 1974: 77-78). This type of civil religion has a political, social, economic, and spiritual dimension, all of which celebrate national ideals. It is embodied in the Constitution, and it glorifies free enterprise, egalitarianism, and individualism. In its spiritual dimension it refers to the central place given to religion. The most fundamental element of this civil religion is the "religionization" of the American nation and its culture (79-80). Taking a theological stance, Herberg charges that civil religion is an inherently idolatrous faith. He claims that to conceive America's civil religion as a religion "somehow standing above or beyond the biblical religions of Judaism and Christianity, and Islam too, as somehow including them and finding a place for them in its overarching unity, is idolatry" (87).

Mead is the best-known proponent of the transcendent universal religion of the nation. Mead writes that the religion of American society in the late nineteenth century, "was articulated in terms of the destiny of America, under God, to be fulfilled by perfecting the democratic way of life for the example and betterment of mankind" (1963: 135). As a result of religious freedom, no religion "could plausibly claim to be or to function as 'the church'" in America, so "*the nation came more and more so to function,*" giving rise to what he calls the religion of the Republic (1974: 66). But, as mentioned earlier, Mead emphatically rejects the claim that the religion of the Republic means the deification or sacralization of the American nation. Despite this denial, his model of a transcendent religion both implicitly and explicitly foments nationalist sentiments and sacralizes the nation.

The third meaning of civil religion is expressed by the phrase religious nationalism. Jones and Richey associate it with the work of Charles Henderson (1972; 1975), who examined Richard

Nixon's exploitation of "public theology" or civil religion. Hayes's work, which they do not mention, certainly also belongs in this category. As we have already seen, Hayes considers American nationalism a religion. The nation itself becomes the object of adoration, taking on a self-transcendent character.

What needs to be stressed here is that only certain forms of civil religion are associated, directly or indirectly, with a nationalist ideology. However, the spirit of civil religion and the spirit of nationalism cannot always be easily dissociated. Civil religion, particularly in its Durkheimian form, and cultural nationalism are comparable in their methods, functions, and goals. Both define a nation's key goals and aspirations, and both provide the essential definition of who are the chosen ones—"who belongs to the nation and who does not" (Wuthnow, 1994: 131). For a very long time, this definition was restricted only to "white, male, property holders who [were] members in good standing of their churches." As for purposes, they are also fluid and subject to change. At one point, they may be defined in economic terms; at others, in terms of national security or participation in international wars (Wuthnow, 1994: 131).

To be sure, civil religion's nationalist tendencies may be attenuated or aggravated in response to particular national or international crises. These tendencies may also be dependent on, or vary according to, a particular political regime (democratic and undemocratic) and the use (or appropriation) of the civil religious discourse by politically powerful individual. In the late 1960s, for example, American patriotic piety was subjected to severe criticism, as there was a generalized sense of disenchantment or loss of faith in the nation. The United States underwent a series of upheavals, including student protests against the Vietnam War, racial conflicts, and the Watergate scandal. Theodore White, a distinguished American historian, observes: "In 1968 this faith [in the nation] was to be shattered—the myth of American power broken, the confidence of the American people in their government, their institutions, their leadership, shaken as never before since 1860" (in Sandel, 1996: 295). Yet, at this very same time the nationalist discourse increased. Both

George McGovern and Richard Nixon used civil religious language while campaigning for president. McGovern, even more directly than Nixon, articulated a version of civil religion "replete with Bible quotations" and references to events and symbols of the American tradition. Bellah argues, however, that McGovern's version was quite different from the one expressed by Nixon. McGovern's was more in tune with the classic tradition of civil religion in America. Nixon's vision of America and his version of civil piety, by contrast, were "hopelessly inadequate" and even unethical (Bellah, 1974b: 261-64).[21]

In line with my argument that the symbols of civil religion are vulnerable to manipulation, it is not really surprising that politicians, in the United States or elsewhere, may try to arouse and exploit popular patriotic sentiments for political ends (see Henderson, 1972 and 1975). Civil religion, thus, may vary in its political, religious, or nationalistic intensity, depending on a society's particular history and social and political circumstances. Perhaps this is another reason why civil religious endeavours appear to be short-lived "with periods of weakness and ultimate failure, although not necessarily total disappearance" (Markoff and Regan, 1982: 348).

The myths of American civil religion constitute a strong blend of biblical imagery and nationalist sentiments. Rites, rituals, and symbols are associated with national heroes, national accomplishments, and national historical events. Undoubtedly, civil religion's myths are a powerful ingredient in American nationalism (Henderson, 1975: 474). Or, as Wilson writes, "there have been mythic elements within the culture amounting to a religious sanction for the national polity" (Wilson, 1979: 20). In short, if what has been described and analyzed in this chapter as civil religion is not the method of nationalism (to borrow Richardson's phrase), it is without any doubt its spirit.

Berger's (1961: 52) reflection that the process of secularization in America has produced a "political religion that resembles more a national ideology than a transcendent religion" seems to me quite correct.[22] Leo Pfeffer has stated, perhaps sarcastically, that "idealistically, not realistically," it is true as Bellah has repeatedly insisted that "American civil religion is not the worship of the American nation but an understanding of the American experience in the light of ultimate universal reality." However, he reflects, "the more civil religion is used to pursue national purposes, the less true [Bellah's claim] will...be" (Pfeffer, 1968: 364). It should be stressed once more that emphasis on the instrumental aspect of civil religion (i.e., a national ideology to pursue national or political goals) by no means prevents understanding civil religion as culture-bound (i.e., loyalties and ideas expressed in everyday life concerning a people's national identity, values, and traditions).

The analysis presented here demonstrates a certain affinity between civil religion and nationalism. This affinity may bring about alarming consequences (ethnic cleansing, anti-semitism) depending on whether or not civil religion and its nationalist tendencies ceases to be a cultural phenomenon and adopts the character of a political ideology serving the vested interests of a particular social or ethnic group. It should be obvious, therefore, that whether or not one finds this relationship distressing depends on the type of nationalism the civil religious rhetoric advocates. The key point here is whether the civil religious discourse promotes social and cultural integration or whether it demands political, cultural, or ethnic segregation. It seems to me that the Durkheimian-Rousseauan axis that characterizes the civil religion phenomenon may also be valuable for explaining the shift from cultural to political nationalism.

Durkheim versus Rousseau Revisited

T he discussion in the preceding chapters makes it readily apparent that the notion of civil religion has been too narrowly conceived. Too much emphasis has been placed on the religious and cultural aspect of the concept and its political ramifications have been neglected. There has been little attempt to understand the political and ideological forces that shape civil religion. The problem, as I have argued, stems from a lack of conceptual understanding of the civil religion phenomenon in its wide variety of forms and manifestations. At the risk of belabouring the point, I will go back, once more, to the problem of the origins of the concept—an issue that emerged at the beginning of this work and has re-appeared in several chapters. Indeed, I have insisted throughout that a comparison along the Durkheimian-Rousseauan continuum is essential for a proper understanding of the civil religion phenomenon, particularly if it is to be applied cross-culturally or from one period to

Notes to Conclusion are on pp. 261-63.

another within the same society. This is also required in order to assess politically motivated uses of civil religion wherever they occur, including in American society.

I

Williams (1996: 368) reviews two perspectives often used to explain the socio-political significance of religion: religion as culture and religion as ideology. He notes that, while in some studies culture and ideology are conflated, in others the two notions are treated as mutually exclusive realities. Williams underscores the importance of drawing an analytical distinction between culture and ideology, but recognizes, at the same time, the need to see their "interactive and often complementary natures." His central thesis is that religion is both culture and ideology. This distinction, he notes, has theoretical and empirical significance for the study of politics and group action. Conceptualizing religion either as culture or as ideology helps to understand "the varied ways religion affects politics and political action" (1996: 368, 377).

The culturalist approach focuses on individuals' values and beliefs, and presupposes an "implicit" definition of culture. Religion as culture "influences political relationships because religion is central in the creation of symbolic worlds." As a cultural system, religion provides clear guidelines of "'what is' as well as 'what ought to be.'" Religion in this sense is "less about beliefs" and more "about the meaning in the world." Williams notes that to embrace a religious world-view "is to absorb a set of taken-for-granted assumptions about one's duty to God and to society." Religion as culture works "'behind the backs' of participants." Its political presence, and influence, is "often effective without the active awareness of those experiencing it" (Williams, 1996: 370).

Williams reminds us that there is another way of looking at religion—as an "explicit" ideology rather than as an "implicit" culture. He conceives ideology as "belief *systems*—articulated sets of ideas that are primarily cognitive...primarily articulated by a specific social class/group, which function primarily in the interests of that class or group, and yet are presented as being in the 'common good' or as generally accepted" (in Williams and Demerath, 1991: 426-27). As Williams notes (1996: 374), this definition separates ideology and culture, associates ideology with power and privilege, but acknowledges at the same time that ideologies are not the patrimony of only powerful groups, for any group may produce ideologies.

Clifford Geertz (1973) understands ideology as a "system of meaning" that emerges during periods of political or social crisis, when other "cultural systems" weaken and are unable to handle social turmoil and change. Ideology is not given a negative valuation: it is not understood as a "distortion of reality," as something powerful groups inflict on powerless ones, or in terms of false consciousness. Ideology, in this sense, "is the articulated idea systems that emerge when culture 'fails.'" In a Geertzian sense, ideology is an "organizing principle" intended to regulate political understandings, to reorder social and cultural life, and to mobilize collective activity (Williams, 1996: 371, 374). In other words, ideologies are "highly articulated, *self-conscious* symbol systems that promote a *general* ordering of human relations" (Evans, 1996: 19; emphasis added).

Williams's excellent discussion is relevant to my analysis of civil religion.[1] Parallels can be drawn between Williams's model for studying religion and politics and the study of civil religion. When we think of civil religion as culture we are at the centre of the Durkheimian camp. Civil religion thus conceptualized refers to a set of taken-for-granted assumptions about one's society or group. As a cultural system, it provides a world view or the ethos of a nation or a collectivity. It refers to the cultural dimension of a people's identity. Like religion proper, it helps to establish a clear sense of what is as well as what ought to be, and provides "frameworks of intelligibility," or "frameworks of self-understanding" for individuals and collectivities (Wilson, 1979: 94). Durkheimians would argue that civil religion emerges from the culture itself as a result of deeply held and shared values that are the basis for social cohesion. Culture-wide religious values are, so to speak, naturally or spontaneously translated into aspects of the socio-political system (Williams, 1996: 370).

Moreover, the ordering of human social relationships, which Williams considers "part of the essence" of both politics and religion, is also part of the essence of civil religion.

When Williams argues that religion "affects political life 'behind the back' of participants," so that those experiencing its influence are not actively aware of it, one is reminded of the way civil religion is conceptualized by Durkheim—as a cultural given rather than as something calculated and imposed upon citizens. The cultural approach appeals to common sense beliefs about one's society or group. Ann Swidler (1986: 279) has defined common sense as "a set of assumptions so unselfconscious as to seem a natural, transparent, undeniable part of the structure of the world." In his original essay, Bellah himself explicitly acknowledges "reifying and giving a name to something that, though pervasive enough when you look at it, has gone on only *semiconsciously*" (1967: 12; emphasis added). Civil religion as culture (or civic piety) exists "at the threshold of consciousness, if not below it, and is only vaguely perceived from time to time by members of the society as self-conscious behavior." Yet, the fact that it is primarily implicit indicates how important it is for society (Wilson, 1979: 83).

This is no doubt the classic position adopted by Durkheim, in the sense that every society has a religious dimension or naturally represents itself as sacred. Since the collective body is the sacred object, "a religious dimension or aspect of social life exists without reference to the self-consciousness or intentionality of the members of the social group" (Wilson, 1979: 150). It expresses itself in terms of ceremonials and rituals, and it points to the social behavioural patterns of the group—that is, to distinct "patterns of behavior which confirm membership in the culture" (Wilson, 1979: 88). Finally, it is the result of a "gradual and spontaneous" development rather than of a "conscious political determination" (De Azevedo, 1979: 9). This would imply that civil religion of the Durkheimian variety, is more "diffuse" than political religion, and often integrates cultural elements in an unofficial or semi-official way (Giner, 1993: 42). Symbols, rituals, feelings, beliefs, and values are more important than ideas.

By contrast, civil religion as ideology is concerned primarily with "rights, duties, and obligations," where symbols and functions play only a minor role. As Wilson writes, "this is the classical language of political thought" (1979: 160). Conceptualized this way, civil religion refers to imposed organizing principles required to regulate political understandings and good citizenship. It addresses the problem of the civic ordering of society. When we think of civil religion as an explicit ideology, we are at the heart of the Rousseauan camp. Here, the organizing principles and the ordering of political existence are imposed on people from above (Demerath and Williams, 1985: 156). Civil religion as ideology, fits quite well Swidler's definition of ideology in general: a "highly articulated, *self-conscious* belief and ritual system, aspiring to offer a unified answer to problems of social action" (1986: 279, emphasis added).

In civil religions of the Rousseauan variety the ideological component is more explicit and it is directly linked to the political order. As a religion designed for the support of the state, it requires state control and demands citizens' obedience. It may even take the form of unconditional commitment to a program or doctrine (Selznick, 1992: 409). In other words, beliefs and behaviours signify "loyalty to a sharply defined political structure—indeed, in the extreme case, to a particular regime at a particular time" (Wilson, 1979: 163). This means that it may even emerge in support of a particular political party or political authority. Loyalties and identity are to be found in the political realm, specifically in citizenship. In this way, individuals are located in relation to their civic and political obligations (Apter, 1963: 90). Civil religion as ideology requires a specific, sustained, and serious effort to impose its tenets of faith. In its more extreme version, its aim is total mobilization and/or total control of the national community. In the Rousseauan model ideas are more important than feelings and values.

Ideologies tend to emerge during cultural turning points, or times of crisis, when "patterns of meaning (with regard to politics) fail to keep the world in some sort of interpretive order."[2] In a Geertzian sense, ideologies are "cultural responses" to social strain. They are also representations of what is as well as what ought to be, and are potentially accessible, at least in principle, to any social group (Williams, 1996: 371). Ideologies, to a certain extent, need to be "inscribed into the collective memories" and need to be taught to group members (Evans, 1996: 20). They are functional insofar as they articulate collective needs and aspirations and provide the basis for collective action.

Now the "dynamics of ideology," as Selznick notes, "are not *inherently* pathological." The mere fact that a system of beliefs or a coherent doctrine tries to endorse group interest, to provide a basis for collective action and goals, is "neither harmful nor repugnant in itself." Only when "ideologies harden," when they explicitly demand unconditional commitment, a "destructive virus takes hold." All ideologies, however, carry "some risk of creating a closed world...impenetrable in conviction, mindless in obedience, fierce in hatred of heresy and opposition" (Selznick, 1992: 410-11).

Swidler has proposed a model for analyzing cultural influence on individuals or collectivities. She notes that culture affects action in different ways in "settled" as opposed to "unsettled" social conditions. Ways of behaving during settled times have a taken-for-granted quality. Under these circumstances, culture acts as a model *"of"* and as a model *"for"* social experience (Swidler, 1986: 278). During settled periods, "culture 'holds' people, binding them to legitimate ways of acting, thinking, and feeling" (Williams, 1996: 371). This means that during settled times, culture indirectly influences action "by providing resources from which people can construct diverse lines of action" (Swidler, 1986: 273).

During "unsettled" cultural periods, a radical rethinking of existence takes place, and innovative methods of constructing, defining, or understanding reality emerge (Williams, 1996: 371). Ideologies come to play an essential role in organizing social experience. As a result, different ideologies and new "styles or strategies of action" are addressed by competing groups trying to gain influence. What group or ideology eventually survives depends "on structural opportunities for action." Hence, during unsettled cultural periods "explicit ideologies directly govern action" (Swidler, 1986: 273, 278). During settled times people are "held by" their cultural beliefs, whereas during unsettled periods people "come to hold" "explicit, articulated, [and] highly organized meaning systems." In short, they come to hold *ideologies* (Swidler, 1986: 279; Williams, 1996: 371).

The Durkheimian variety of civil religion, with its taken-for-granted character, lives during settled periods. In Geertzian terms, it refers to the "assumed 'givens' of social existence," what he calls "primordial attachments" (Geertz, 1973: 259). Its power to shape or direct human action is rather weak. As an ideology, however, civil religion abandons its taken-for-granted character. Under such circumstances, it has, or at least it is intended to have strong and direct control over action (Swidler, 1986: 282).

Though polarly opposed, culture and ideology are continuous rather than dichotomous variables. Correspondingly, civil religion and political religion are interrelated poles rather than absolute antinomies. The relationship between them is inherently dialectical, and so is their relation to the political order. Civil religion can never be totally separated from political religion. One may speak of degrees or shades of civil religion—the distinction being one of emphasis. At certain historical crossroads, civil religion may be more confined to certain groups within society (more civil); at others, it may be limited to the state (more political). In other words, civil religion may have an overt political component, even if a relatively minor one, while political religion may have many cultural components, even if largely confined to the background.[3] This distinction rests on the capacity of civil religion to provide a meaning system or "a picture of the universe in terms of which the moral understandings make sense" (Bellah, 1975: ix), in either a coercive or a non-coercive manner. It also depends on the degree of control the state has to produce and reproduce the sacred symbols and belief systems. What is at issue here is whether the state demands an unusual amount of control and "centrally regulated 'force'" to secure conformity, or whether the civic faith is, or seems to be, "sufficiently *internalized*" by a majority of the citizens so that conformity to societal values and norms is accomplished in an "enthusiastic and primarily voluntary" basis (Anthony and Robbins, 1975: 411).[4] The central focus is the political referent. We want to know how patterns of belief and behaviour common to the culture are transmitted to citizens and future generations. In other words, we want to know what are the requirements placed upon citizens in order to assure loyalty and the preservation of civic piety and/or civility.

II

The form civil religion takes in a particular society largely depends upon specific historical circumstances. Civil religion may shift its meaning and become more or less political, more or less nationalistic, more or less oriented towards civil society or the state. Broadly speaking, therefore, any civil religion (even in the United States, where it is said to be totally independent from both church and state) has the potential of being used as a political religion.[5]

On a societal level, civil religion à la Rousseau implies a conscious, rational manipulation of the myths of the nation for political aims. In contrast, civil religion à la Durkheim does not require direct enforcement by external agencies of social control. The integration of self and society appears to be more voluntaristic. The Durkheimian culturalist approach, where undoubtedly Bellah and followers should be placed, emphasizes shared values and cultural elements: "society itself is the object of religious behavior and the reference for religious symbols in given social orders" (Wilson, 1979: 159). Civil religion thus conceptualized is more of a "given" rather than the result of a specific political agenda or policy (Demerath, 1994: 113). It may indeed have a political orientation, but this would appear in a less coercive, or even non-coercive, form. As a cultural phenomenon, civil religion is assumed to exist "somewhere between...religion and government" (Wimberley and Christenson, 1980: 36). In democracies, the process of socialization, not mere force or threat, facilitates its production in society. However, particular institutional structures or carriers are instrumental for the support, maintenance, and reproduction of cultural beliefs and values.

In the Durkheimian/American model, the processes of civil religion are assumed to generate collective understandings that represent the moral sentiments of a people and the spontaneous affirmation of the social order (in the sense of proceeding from the will of the people, or from one's own choice). One may say that individuals are "born" into the national faith; no particular commitment or act of joining is necessary. No one is legally compelled to follow or support the ideals of the civic creed against their will. Those who choose not to accept the tenets of faith are in no special danger. Civil religion is institutionalized through education or the legal system, so people experience "faith" largely in an unconscious or taken-for-granted fashion. The values characteristic of a people become embodied in institutions that help perpetuate them. This would imply that civil religion (if considered at a societal level) is *instilled* in citizens and, to a certain extent, required of them, but it is not forced on them. Civil religion in its cultural form is part of what Durkheim calls the "collective representations" of the society.

Political religions, by contrast, are anchored in specific ideologies. In political religions the role of the state is fundamental. It is essential to transform the individual through the tutelary agency of an "Etat éducateur" (Willaime, 1994: 574). The state and its political officials become guardians of the most fundamental values and "needs" of the society. Values and needs, in turn, are raised to the "status of transcendental beliefs" (Apter, 1963: 93).[6] These fundamental needs, may include things as varied as the desire to achieve modernity and industrialization, the desire for cultural survival of a particular group, or the dreadful desire for ethnic cleansing, or may even include the desire to become a superpower by attaining scientific, technological, military, and nuclear superiority. But as an ideology of the state or political organizations, civil religion is always the prerogative of the government. Civil religion as ideology is thus *imposed*, with varying degrees of success, from the top down, without "explanation or comment" as Rousseau advocated. In this case, we will have a highly articulated self-conscious symbol system, the result of conscious political determination (Swidler, 1986: 279). As such, civil religion (like any religion involved in political struggles) becomes an organizing principle for the specific purpose of mobilizing the masses, "clothed in the universalist language of God's will and transcendent justice" (Williams, 1996: 374).[7]

In short, civil religions of the type Rousseau advocates are truly political religions representing the extreme end of the civil religion spectrum. In the Rousseauan variety, a belief is imposed upon the people (often in an arbitrary manner), while in the Durkheimian form people experience faith, civic piety, or simply a common religion. While Durkheim's doctrine yields a civil religion of integration and co-operation, which does not contemplate submissive acceptance to the creed, Rousseau, by contrast, creates a civil religion of constraint that demands unquestionable loyalty and unconditional commitment.[8]

Selznick (1992: 387) draws a distinction between civility and piety as two different sources of morality and moral integration in society. He argues that they parallel Durkheim's distinction between organic and mechanical solidarity. The former engenders "rules of civility," while the latter focuses on shared history and group identity. Although Selznick's claim may be true, and civility and piety may be compared within Durkheim's theory in terms of advanced and "primitive" societies, it may be more illuminating to contrast civility and piety in terms of the contrast between the Rousseauan and Durkheimian models of civil religion. One may argue that Rousseau's intention was to foster and enforce civility, while the central focus of Durkheim was piety. For piety, as Selznick acknowledges, "expresses devotion" and implies integration, whereas civility "governs diversity, protects autonomy, and upholds toleration." Rousseau protects autonomy, individual rights, and toleration, provided that individuals are good citizens.

The continuum ranges from what Willaime has called *religion civile communitaire*, which functions at a local, regional, national, or even international level, and *religion civile politique* which functions at the state level (Willaime, 1993: 573). One needs hardly to be reminded this is an ideal-type construction. I am not suggesting that any given civil religion is in fact cultural or ideological in any absolute sense. In fact, it is highly unlikely that we will ever find civil religion in pure form. Either type can turn into the other. In the most literal sense, all civil religions are partially mixed. I have made a sharp distinction between two ideal-types only for analytical purposes.

The dialectical relation between civil religion and political religion can be approached as a tension between spontaneous and enforced values, beliefs, and ideas. This same dialectical tension exists *within* each type of civil religion as well as *between* them. The degree of freedom granted to those who do not subscribe to the tenets of faith is an important element that should be taken into account. In other words, the ratio of externally imposed force to voluntary compliance may be taken as an index for identifying the type of civil religion under consideration (Anthony and Robbins, 1975: 412).

The degree of freedom dissident groups are allowed legally to enjoy in different societies has been measured according to the following criteria: the level of repressive action against such groups, politically motivated arrests of "significant persons," arrests of "insignificant persons," government-sanctioned and politically motivated killings, and the "frequency with which the constitution is suspended and martial law is declared" (Cole and Hammond, 1974: 182). We may ask, then, what methods are used to subject people's behaviour to a national belief system? Is consensus inauthentic and manipulative rather than genuine? How is consensus maintained and the solidarity of citizens encouraged, and among whom? What influence does the government have in controlling ways in which basic values and beliefs are mobilized or articulated? Finally, does civil religion exert a cultural or political influence?

It follows that the political or civil character of civil religion is primarily determined by its particular structural location, either to the side of the state or the side of society. This depends, in turn, on the nature and structure of the state (or the particular process of state formation in less developed societies), the national religious environment or culture, and the relations between political and religious authorities. It would also appear to be conditioned by the "availability of more or less coherent, alternative ideologies to interpret the national experience" (Markoff and Regan, 1982: 342-45).

Total state-appropriation of civil religion, and the transformation of a totalitarian ideology and its political rituals in an official religion, is more likely to appear in societies with a weak civil society. As Markoff and Regan have argued, the "propagation of an elaborate belief system rejecting older religious beliefs and institutions is clearly enhanced if the political arrangements include a monistic state uncontrolled by civil society" (1982: 347). In such cases, the political process itself becomes a religion that everyone is forced to embrace. The most notable twentieth-century examples, although not the only ones, are "either totalitarian regimes or regimes with a recent totalitarian past" (347). A strong civil society, or to use Durkheim's phraseology, societies with a strong sense of moral community, are less likely to develop a totalitarian type of political religion. Needless to say, a strong civil society has always presented dictators with a more difficult barrier to trespass (Giner, 1993: 43).

The differences between civil and political religions may be discernible not only between societies, but from one historical moment to another within the same society. Markoff and Regan, in comparing and contrasting the French and Malaysian civil religions, have already pointed in this direction. To Bellah's assertion (1974: 257) that "all politically organized societies have some sort of civil religion," Markoff and Regan respond, "Perhaps, but what sort?" (1982: 341). Their study suggests a profound diversity in civil religions. They see "not only differences between national cases, but striking distinct versions of civil religiosity within either instance" (341). As they mention, the possibility exists of the not always easy "co-existence...of multiple civil religions within a nation-state and rival images of the future—each, perhaps, associated with a particular group" (340). Thus, one may speak of different social, historical, religious, and political determinants or bases of civil religion.

Both civil and political religions tend to "consecrate essentially profane components of social life," especially through civic rituals and public ceremonies (Giner, 1993: 55). Both concepts seek to examine the "intrusions of religious codes" into the public political realm (Luke, 1987: 109 n. 1). Both embody the terms of reference in which the political system is explained, legitimized, and justified. This may incorporate "politics of opposition," for civil religion is not only "a claim for legitimacy; it is a moral yardstick that permits such a claim, or counterclaim" (Markoff and Regan, 1982: 342). In other words, civil religion's rhetoric may be used to legitimize both a just and an unjust social order. It may also be used as a justification to eliminate opposition or as a means to facilitate collective action (Cole and Hammond, 1974: 182).

While civil and political religions are linked with politics and may be used to give legitimacy to political ideologies, the nature of the religious-political element varies. In civil religion, the religious factor is provided by linking the political system with a transcendental power, meaning, or symbolism, often derived from an established religion (the Judeo-Christian tradition, for example, in the case of American civil religion). By contrast, in political religion the religious factor is more markedly embedded in the "sacralization" of a particular political order, program, or leader (Zuo, 1991: 104). This may happen with or without the sponsorship of the church or of a national religion, as in the case of Marxism-Leninism (in the Soviet Union and China), or in revolutionary France. By the same token, the political element is less salient in civil religions and more evident in political religions. As Lane (1981: 45) effectively argues, the link between the religious and the political aspects of life, the connection between religious and political authority, and the demands placed on citizens in terms of their civic and political duties is not the same in civil and political religions.

It follows that civil religion is neither simply civil nor purely religious, but is also centrally political.[9] Wilson (1979: 172) has even suggested that it may be reasonable to explain the civil religion phenomenon more "as a latent political revitalization movement than as a manifestly religious one."[10] As a political solution, a "minimalist version" of civil religion may be established. A minimalist civil religion would be one that is neither too religious nor too political (Markoff and Regan, 1982: 346).[11]

It should be clear that civil religion, insofar as it entails the application of religious ideas to political life, always carries some risk of becoming an ideologically closed system. As long as civil religion is consciously manipulated by the state and state officials to sanction the political order, we are in the presence of a political religion. Simply put, at particular historical moments democracies may show tendencies towards the development of a political religion, even if in a mild form. Thus, I find myself in disagreement with scholars who claim that political religions belong to communist regimes and dictatorships found in the Third World, while civil religions are primarily found in modern industrialized societies (Zuo, 1991).This distinction is misleading. One may also find civil religions in the West, which in their content, form, and substance are truly political religions of a mild variety.[12] I also find myself in disagreement with those who make exactly the opposite claim, that the political religions of totalitarian regimes are not civil religions (Giner, 1993). Giner's central thesis is that under a totalitarian regime both civil religion and civil society cease to exist. In his view, civil religions are located in civil society not in political society (the state). It is worth pointing out that it was Rousseau, after all, who coined the term *civil religion,* and undoubtedly he placed it in the realm of the state not in civil society.

Rousseau clearly spelled out his ideas on civil religion and "was prepared to follow through on the totalitarian implications of that claim" (Neuhaus, 1986: 99). What is astonishing is the lack of rigorous attention to the conceptual meaning of Rousseau's theory. As we have seen, Bellah and his followers have been unable, or perhaps unwilling, to clarify the distinction between the Durkheimian and Rousseauan approaches. Sociologists have not only failed to understand the extraordinary political resonance of Rousseau's doctrine, but they have also failed to address the issue of whether civil religion is distinguishable from political religion. Granted, this is a distinction that is difficult to make, and for some scholars it is even difficult to accept. Some authors, like Carl Schmitt (1970) and Jürgen Moltmann (1986), use the term *political theology*. Wilson (1986: 111) considers it a mistake to misinterpret civil religion and "confuse" it with political theology or political religion.

III

The purpose of drawing a distinction between Durkheimian civil religion and Rousseauan political religion is not to dismiss or dispense with one notion or the other. It seems reasonable to assume that both the Durkheimian and Rousseauan approaches to civil religion remain instructive. Following Durkheim, one may say that any collectivity develops its own sense of identity, destiny, and mission. This means that every group, community, or nation is likely to develop a system of beliefs by which it celebrates and sanctifies its self-understanding. This sacralization engenders a sort of collective piety that is experienced by most (in Durkheim's view, probably by all) members of the group (Willaime, 1993: 572). This means that every stable, functioning society/group has to an important degree a "common religion" (Williams, 1951: 312).

If one accepts Durkheim's thesis, no functioning society or group can exist without a common faith. Likewise, most collectivities will tend to produce some sort of moral community. It follows that a "religious expression of [the] collectivity as a social reality must exist" (Wilson, 1979: 154). This would imply that if a society (or collectivity) wants to survive as a viable social system it must possess a set of shared values and common aspirations (Demerath and Hammond, 1969: 204). Durkheim tells us that without collective representations, without a commonality of values and goals, the collectivity would dissolve and society would die (Mitchell, 1990: 115). Perhaps this is what Sidney Verba had in mind when he referred to the "primordial emotional attachment that is necessary for the long-term maintenance of a political system" (in Wilson, 1979: 69).

This Durkheimian notion is considered to be an unquestionable assumption among "functional social theorists (if not all social theorists)" (Demerath and Hammond, 1969: 203). Coleman writes: "Durkheim's contention that every group...has a religious dimension" seems to hold a "permanent validity" for some authors (1969: 69). Indeed, Bellah recognizes that his argument was "premised on the sociological idea that all politically organized societies have some sort of civil religion" (Bellah, 1974b: 257). On the basis of this Durkheimian assumption, a civil religion is not only an unavoidable phenomenon, but it is essential to the life of any society or collectivity (Wilson, 1979: 154). Needless to say, Durkheim's thesis has been phrased and rephrased in countless different ways.

There can be little doubt that any collectivity or society needs integrating symbols and shared meanings and purposes. Collective life requires some sort of common faith; otherwise we would live in a Hobbesian world of anarchy, moral confusion, or brute force. If Durkheim's assertion is correct, then, there must be some point of convergence between different groups. To be sure, short of coercion people need to trust each other to conduct their affairs. And trust presupposes a commonality of basic principles, and a "*common* acceptance of the higher aims toward which activity is directed" (Demerath and Hammond, 1969: 204). In other words, for processes of cultural solidarity and identity to take shape and form, it is essential to maintain a sense of moral community or some kind of common moral beliefs (Bellah, 1975: ix). Obviously shared understandings or meanings do not have to be based upon religious understanding (Anthony and Robbins, 1975: 407). Neither do they have to be perceived as necessarily embracing the nation as a whole. Some groups may be excluded because they have not been invited, or may exclude themselves by refusing to attend the civic banquet.

At the same time, in order to reinforce Durkheim's moral community, or collective identity, a coherent and intellectually elaborated idea-system is needed—which is exactly what Rousseau proposed.[13] As some have rightly noted, "any collective political action requires both cultural processes of solidarity as well as ideological justifications" (Williams, 1996: 372). Perhaps Gramsci was right when he reflected that "political control requires both consent and coercion" (Williams, 1996: 373). The preceding analysis suggests that whereas the Durkheimian variety tends to move in the direction of consent, Rousseau's starting line is, undoubtedly, coercion.

But Durkheim's idea of a moral community is not without its problems. It is certainly controversial and equivocal in its American usage. By definition, a moral community is not, or need not be equated with, the whole national experience or with the society as a whole, as Bellah and most American sociologists would often seem to imply. It seems highly unlikely that, in America or anywhere else in the world, we will ever find evidence for a total commonality of values and beliefs, or "for a monovalent and highly coherent national meaning system." What we might find is a series of "frameworks of intelligibility," espoused by a diversity of groups for a diversity of purposes (Wilson, 1979: 95). This implies that different groups may belong to different moral communities, not to a single overarching one. Different groups, in turn, may produce different civil religions.

The concept of nation-state as moral community, has come under increasing attack. How can we share a common worldview when modern society is afflicted by all kinds of class, ethnic, racial, religious, and ideological conflicts? From this perspective, the formation of a national, moral community is virtually impossible, not only because of conflicting group interests but also because of the concern the modern individual has with the self. Few are willing to sacrifice personal interest for the common good. And this applies both to individuals and groups alike. In stark contrast, there are those who argue "normatively" that national moral communities spell danger, that "allegiance or loyalty to a nation-state is evil because moral communities are dangerous" (Liebman and Don-Yehiya, 1983: 215). Implicit in this idea is a fear that the conception of a moral community may give rise to abusive or repressive practices, or to authoritarian and totalitarian regimes. Indeed, as Liebman and Don-Yehiya indicate, most, or perhaps "all totalitarian states view themselves as moral communities entitled to suppress individual freedoms in the name of collective purposes" (1983: 215). The idea of moral community may also lead to narrowness, chauvinism, and exclusiveness, building a wall between friends and foes (whether this is expressed in national, religious, social, ethnic, or political terms). A national moral community that identifies individuals primarily as citizens of a particular nation (or state) may give rise to a dangerous nationalist mentality, as suggested in chapter 6. It may provide a fertile soil for nationalist ideologies, which may be expressed in either a benign or destructive form.

To sum up, one of the major weakness of the civil religion thesis is its exclusive reliance on the Durkheimian tradition. From this rather simple fact stem most of the problems one finds in the literature. We have seen that a conceptual clarification of Rousseau's and Durkheim's theories lead to two quite different conceptions of civil religion—each perspective resting upon a distinctive set of premises. Throughout this book, I have identified a number of problems, and raised several major objections against the civil religion thesis, particularly in the context of American society. Perhaps the most important one is that civil religion is not *by definition* an integrative force in society. In modern, pluralist society, where the idea of the individual reigns supreme, it is difficult to find an overall binding belief system. Even if we accept the assumption that post-industrial societies still require a general set of values and/or a public symbol system that would provide individuals with "ultimate meaning," it does not follow that a single civil religion will automatically accomplish this task. Religious pluralism, different world views, and social and ethnic heterogeneity make this possibility very unlikely. True, civil religion may be a binding glue for a large number of people, or sectors of the population. In this sense, it may serve to "sanctify different subgroups within the larger society" (Liebman and Don-Yehiya, 1983: 11-12). As Wilson notes, it is an "incontrovertible proposition" that certain symbolic elements, ceremonies, or national rituals may assume a religious character for some groups or individuals (1971: 20). In the specific context of American society, the values Bellah describes have, no doubt, "been prominent throughout American history, and remain so" (Hughey, 1983: 68). This is also an incontrovertible proposition. Obviously, those values have not always repre-sented *all* Americans. Values and symbols "do not lead a rela-tively autonomous existence"; they are immersed in the arena of everyday conflicts and political struggles. They are important vehicles for the expression of group interests and aspirations (Hughey, 1983: 172). They are also of crucial importance for the mobilization and sustenance of collective action. The values of the American creed have clearly expressed white, Anglo-Saxon values—the values of the dominant group in America. This means that either as a dominant culture or as a dominant ideol-ogy, civil religion does not successfully incorporate all social groups and segments of society.[14] By arguing that civil religion exists "out there," expressing the experiences and aspirations of all Americans, proponents of the Durkheimian tradition have effectively disengaged civil religion from specific groups or carri-ers (Hughey, 1983: 68). Moreover, as indicated especially in chap-ters 4 and 5, civil religion may, at times, be quite disintegrative, leading to moral confusion and conflict rather than integration.

The analysis presented here contradicts Bellah's notion of a well-established American civil religion that expresses the reli-gious self-definition of the American people as a whole. It also calls into question the total moral unity that civil religion allegedly produces. Civil religion cannot and does not mobilize the entire nation on behalf of socially approved tasks and responsibilities. I have also argued that in the civil religion phe-nomenon one can find the coalescence of both spontaneous cul-tural elements and ideological coercive ones. Finally, contrary to arguments found in the literature, the alleged structural differ-entiation of American civil religion has been called into question. As Bellah himself has recognized, there is a necessity, built into the American republican tradition, "not only for the assertion of high ethical and spiritual commitments, but also for molding, socializing, educating the citizens in those ethical and spiritual beliefs so that they are internalized as republican virtue" (Bellah, 1978: 21). This suggests (and I believe I have given enough evi-dence to prove) that civil religion has an institutional basis or a set of carriers that provide organized and ritualized reinforcement of ethical standards (the courts, educational system, media, political system, and so on). If this proposition is accepted, then civil religion can never be totally differentiated—it can never constitute a symbol system separated from political institutions.

In short, the civil religion notion, in its Durkheim/Bellah formulation, has proven to be deficient on several grounds: it does not provide an adequate solution to the problem of conflicting interests that divide society, whether this conflict is expressed in terms of race, class, or political ideology; it is often not useful to evaluate significant differences or shades of civil religions, both between societies and within them; it is inadequate to investigate civil religious beliefs as expressions of ideologies produced by some groups; it is inadequate, again, to analyze politically motivated uses of civil religion.

The critique presented in this study does not necessarily mean that the civil religion concept is sociologically useless. On the contrary, I remain convinced that it addresses an important sociological topic of investigation—the "religio-political problem" (Bellah, 1980a: vii). As Bellah has rightly observed, this problem "will not go away, whether we use the term 'civil religion' in thinking about it or not" (1989: 147). Civil religion either as a cultural phenomenon (i.e., a group understanding of itself) or as a political phenomenon (i.e., a matter relating to the government or the state) seems inevitable in any collectivity. By suggesting that the American civil religion model is inadequate, I have by no means implied that it is also false. While I have raised numerous criticisms, my intention has been to identify the limitations and, particularly, the one-sidedness of the Durkheim/Bellah tradition, not its falsity. I have provided an alternative model for the study of civil religion, which, I hope, will make it easier to understand and identify different varieties of civil religion. For, each society, and perhaps each civil group, will give different responses to the problem of collective identity, to the problem of meaning and purpose, and to the politico-religious problem, and thus they will likely produce different civil religions.

NOTES

Introduction

1 Outside the sociological field there is, perhaps, no concept of Rousseau's political theory that has been more severely criticized than his philosophy on civil religion. His ideas on this topic have been judged the intellectual cradle of "totalitarian democratism" (Merquior, 1980: 36). Some critics have even gone as far as to consider Rousseau's chapter on civil religion in *The Social Contract* (1762) "unfortunate" and "an embarrassment" (Noone, 1980: 133, 152). It is essentially this chapter that is responsible for the charges levelled at Rousseau, blaming him "for heralding modern despotism" (Merquior, 1980: 36), or accusing him of being the "spiritual father of totalitarianism" (Macfarlane, 1970: 12) and "the first apologist of unfreedom" (Merquior, 1980: 36). Certainly, Rousseau's warning that anyone who "behaves" as if he does not believe the tenets of the civic faith is to be punished by death, does have a frightening ring in the light of the tyrannies of the twentieth century.

2 This criticism has been levelled against Durkheim's legacy in the sociology of religion. Giddens notes that this tradition "nowhere confronts the possibility that religious beliefs are ideologies, which help legitimate the domination of some groups over others" (1978: 103).

3 I am indebted to Wilson (1979: 149) in his use of a model based on "a continuum of religious representations." In Wilson's construct the

243

locus of analysis is the "religious referent." He seeks to identify where the sacred is located (whether sacrality is attributed to the group or to ritual elements and symbol systems, or to cultural values, etc.). Wilson's suggestion that other continua could be constructed provided the inspiration for the model I present in this book.

Chapter 1. Theoretical Foundations

1 It has been the tendency in sociology to refer to "civil religion," while political scientists or historians tend to use the terms "political religion," "public religion," "public theology," and so on. Perhaps the reason is to be found in the fact that, generally speaking, sociologists have taken the consensus approach, which sees civil religion as stemming from culture in a rather spontaneous way. As such, they tend to see the locus of civil religion in civil society. Historians and political scientists, on the other hand, tend to emphasize the role of the state in the production of civil religion. For a discussion of Fascism and Nazism as political religions, see Gentile (1990) and Moltmann (1986). See also Apter (1963) for an examination of political religions in the developing world, and Wilson (1979), for a discussion of public religion in American culture.

2 Durkheim certainly gives the state a role in the organization of the cult. However, as the "organ of consciousness of society" the state is the repository of higher, universal, and sacred principles such as the "cult of the individual" or "moral individualism." As Hughey has rightly noted (1983: 67), in Durkheim's terms, "it is the universal, humanistic values which transcend the state,...and not the state itself which is important."

3 Neither Durkheim nor Rousseau had any intention of incorporating women into their general theories. Unless they specifically made reference to women, they spoke from a male world and to a male audience. Rousseau, in particular, is referring to political society, an area from which he explicitly excluded women. In discussing their ideas, I have opted to use "man," "he," "him," for I do not want to give them more credit than they deserve.

4 The influence of Machiavelli's views on Rousseau's political philosophy is quite marked. For example, Machiavelli thought it essential that rulers encourage a religion that "teaches that he who best serves the State best serves the gods" (Allen, 1960: 459).

5 Rousseau's concern is how to avoid the bitter struggles that may develop between spiritual and temporal power, or between the representatives of religious and political authority. The confrontation "between pope and emperor in medieval Europe, the tension between Confucianism, Buddhism, and Taoism at the T'ang court, and the struggle between the mullahs and the politicians in Iran today," are some historical examples of the problem Rousseau was trying to identify (Bellah, 1980a: x).

6 Machiavelli's argument is not very dissimilar. Religion, he notes, "has glorified humble and contemplative men, rather than men of action. It has assigned as man's highest good humility, abnegation, and contempt for mundane things....This pattern of life...appears to have made the world weak, and to have handed it over as a prey to the wicked, who run it successfully...since they are well aware that the generality of men, with paradise as their goal, consider how best to bear, rather than how best to avenge, their injuries" (cited in Larrain, 1979: 18).

7 The indispensability of religion as a prerequisite for political stability is an idea that can be found throughout the history of socio-political thought. Social thinkers and politicians throughout the ages have been concerned with the connection between religion and the political order. A belief in a divinity has been considered by many as absolutely necessary. Rousseau, for example, writes in *Emile*: "if there is no God, the wicked is right and the good man is nothing but a fool" ([1762] 1911: 255). From a similar orientation are Voltaire's maxim "If there were no God, it would be necessary to invent him" (cited in Noone, 1980: 135) and, in more modern times, President Dwight D. Eisenhower's famous observation that "our government makes no sense unless it is founded in a deeply felt religious faith—and I don't care what it is" (cited in Bellah, 1976a: 156). Undoubtedly, Eisenhower's remark was inspired by Anthony Trollope's comment after a visit to the United States in 1860. In America, he stated, "everybody is bound to have a religion...[but] it does not matter what it is" (cited in Hammond, 1980a: 69).

8 Rousseau equates the common good with the aims of the general will. In his terms, the intent of the state is the common good. He notes that the "clashing" of private interests has made society "necessary," but it is the harmony of "these very interests" that has made it "possible." There must be some point of convergence between all interests, otherwise no society could exist and survive. Hence, that which is common to these "different interests is what forms the social tie" (Rousseau, [1762] 1973: 182).

9 Phillip E. Hammond (1980a) takes the position that civil religion, in Rousseau's meaning of the term, is independent of both church and state. I strongly disagree with Hammond's interpretation. I will return to this point in chapter 4.

10 This is in opposition to Soviet Marxism or China's Maoism, for example, where the state ideology, while certainly imbued with a certain sense of "sacredness," is devoid of a transcendental meaning. For an interesting study of Soviet Marxism-Leninism as a political religion, see Lane (1981); for an examination of the religious quality of Russian Marxism and its civil ceremonies, see Zeldin (1969), McDowell (1974), and Lane (1979). For an argument that communism or Maoism cannot and should not be considered a religion, see West (1980). West

argues that insofar as these political doctrines deny "the reality of the Holy as an objective and transcendent reality," they are just "substitutes" for religion, not real religions (1980: 35).

11 I take the term "wall of separation" from the metaphor that, since its introduction by Thomas Jefferson, has traditionally been used to refer to church and state relations in the United States (see for example, Bellah, 1978: 17; Hammond, 1981: 227).

Chapter 2. American Civil Religion and the American Debate

1 I am referring here to civil religion in the United States. I am fully aware that civil religion in "America" should include civil religions ranging from Canada to Chile (i.e., the Americas). However, even a superficial review of the literature makes clear that when scholars argue or debate about civil religion in America, they are referring solely to the United States. For the sake of clarity, I have decided to follow the conventional usage in this chapter.

2 One might see Mormonism as a good example of this—as a people possessed with a covenant, and America as a land literally visited by Jesus Christ. Joseph Smith, a farmboy turned prophet and the founder of the Mormon church in 1830, taught that "the New Jerusalem was here, smack dab in the middle of America" (*Time*, 4 Aug. 1997: 38).

3 In Bellah's view, a modern expression of this corruption is to be found in the "purely private pietism" that emerged during the nineteenth century, and whose emphasis was individual gain. Bellah even interprets fundamentalism in America, not necessarily as an "expression of backward yokels," but rather as a strong reaction against the utilitarian ethos of modern America, by the heirs of the biblical tradition that remained "uncorrupted or only minimally" so (1980c: 171).

4 For a bibliographic review of the American civil religion literature see Hammond (1976); Kathan and Fuchs-Kreimer (1975); and also Mathisen (1989). For more articles and books dealing with the subject, see Caplow (1994); Casanova (1994); Gamoran (1990); Giner (1993); Hughey (1983); Kim (1993); Mitchell (1995); O'Toole (1984); Shanks (1995).

5 This is worth noting, for the Social Sciences Index did not have a descriptor term for civil religion until 1980. Now it regularly includes the notion in its subject headings. The term has also become prevalent in non-American case studies and in cross-cultural analyses. See, for example, Breslauer, (1993); Larson, (1995); Liebman and Don-Yehiha, (1983); Morawska, (1987); Neeman and Rublin, (1996); Schieder, (1987); Woocher, (1986).

6 Coleman's construct is similar to a model advanced earlier by David Apter in his article "Political religions in the New Nations" (Reynolds, 1977: 267). Apter distinguishes three types of political reli-

gions: 1) theocratic systems characteristic of virtually all premodern societies; 2) reconciliation systems, typical of modern Western society where religion and state are separated, where "secular ends can never become sacred," and where there is individual liberty, religious tolerance, and political freedom; 3) mobilization systems or "political religions," which represent an alternative to the two other models (Apter, 1963: 57-104). These types would roughly correspond to evolutionary trends associated with the process of modernization. Both Apter and Coleman fail to realize that even in modern Western society "secular ends" may become sacralized. They also fail to realize that political religions may emerge in the East and in the West, in highly industrialized countries as well as in those in the process of development. This issue will re-emerge in chapter 4.

7 This parallels Durkheim's idea that religion is not only a system of practices (such as feasts, rites, cultic celebrations), but also a system of ideas whose primary object is to offer an explanation of the world. The first is "turned towards action...the other towards the thought" necessary to organize the group (Durkheim, [1912] 1961: 476).

8 Accounts of civil religion portrayed as religious nationalism, democratic faith, or Protestant civic piety are often found outside the field of sociology, specially in the work of church historians, theologians, and philosophers (Gehrig, 1981a: 52).

9 The fact that Wilson uses a religious referent does not make civil religion less political, or less in tune with behavioural issues. Certainly, behavioural issues are implicit in the first two models. If they were not, it would be difficult to accept Wilson's own claim that the central analytical focus of the cultural model is the "symbolic unity" of the collectivity as expressed "in and through the action-guiding provisions which define the culture." If the cultural model centers on "patterns of behavior common to the culture," how can it not have a manifest behavioural content? Moreover, insofar as the political and theological models are concerned with the political order, both are either explicitly or implicitly political (Wilson, 1979: 151).

10 Although to a large extent Hammond is correct, his suggestion needs to be qualified. One should remember the attacks on the Supreme Court as being unelected and so failing one of the primary requirements of legitimacy. One should also consider the various impeachment efforts that have resulted from this situation. Moreover, as Wilson rightly notes, the case law tradition, characteristic of the American system, does not derive political rights from natural rights, so that "the law is far less sacrosanct than in a natural rights formulation, and the jurists far less remote and god-like." However, legal institutions, as Wilson notes, do provide structural support for civil religion by defining and setting boundaries beyond which particular patterns of conduct will not be permitted in America. That is, the law

determines a "range of life styles appropriate to and acceptable in the American culture" (Wilson, 1979: 130-32).

11 On this issue Novak (1992: 127-28) writes, civil religion is not "some lowest common denominator, of all the beliefs of all our citizens. It is not discovered by taking an opinion poll. It is discovered by analyzing experiences, interpretations, and institutions of our national life."

12 But a few empirical studies (using questionnaires and sample surveys) have suggested its existence. Wimberley et al. (1976: 890) conducted a series of surveys specifically designed to test Bellah's thesis at the individual level. They concluded that civil religion "is found to exist empirically" in America. Their study indicates that civil religion is, or emerges as, a "distinct factor" separate from other types of religious commitments. In 1982, Wimberley and Christenson explored the issue of civil religion as an indicator of policy preference. They concluded that civil religion appeared to be a "significant but fairly ineffective" indicator of differences in matters of public policy. In an earlier study, Wimberley (1980) found civil religion to be more effective as an indicator of support for presidential candidates—allegiances to civil religious commitments seemed to correspond with a "conservative profile." A separate study (Christenson and Wimberley 1978) found that, while civil religious commitments and allegiances had "no relationship to whether people voted, the 'civil religious' were slightly inclined toward Democratic [*sic*] party membership and conservative political identities" (cited in Wimberley and Christenson, 1982: 212). See also Cole and Hammond (1974); Jolicoeur and Knowles (1978); Thomas and Flippen (1972); Wimberley (1976).

13 In *Habits of the Heart* (1985) Bellah does not make any reference to civil religion. By this time, he had stopped writing about it and did not even bother to answer some of the critiques still sparked by his ideas on American civil religion (Mathisen, 1989: 137). Bellah himself acknowledges that, although *Habits* deals with the "same substantive issues" as his other writings on civil religion, he is pleased to have dropped the term. He observes that his decision has liberated him from the often "irrelevant" disputes and arguments about civil religion commonly engendered by his earlier publications (Bellah, 1989: 147). For further discussions on the definitional debate see Cherry (1971); Cutler (1968); Gehrig (1981b); Hammond (1976); Marty (1974); and Richey and Jones (1974).

14 A civil group is understood here as any group active at the level of civil society. For example, one could mention groups ranging from environmentalists to Boy Scouts and other voluntary associations. At an international level, one could include organizations such as Doctors without Borders, Greenpeace, Amnesty International, and so on.

15 I must add that this problem is not unique to Bellah. Most American authors use the concept of civil religion or civil creed in a Durkheimian fashion. Not surprisingly, there is the tendency to com-

bine into a composite whole the beliefs of the elite with those of the masses. However, the problem was not created by Bellah; rather, it antedates him. Lipset (1963), for example, in discussing American values, "Americanism," or the "American Creed" falls prey to the same error. In a recently published article, Grabb, Baer, and Curtis call for a reconsideration of Lipset's argument. In their view, one of the most fundamental weakness of Lipset's thesis is the "tendency to conflate values at the elite level with values at the mass level when describing the American Creed" (1999: 513-14).

16 See the argument advanced by Abercrombie, Hill, and Turner in *The Dominant Ideology Thesis* (1980). The authors argue that a dominant ideology is more likely to bind together the dominant class itself, rather than integrate or incorporate the subordinate classes into the existing social system.

17 Such was the case in Malaysia in the aftermath of the riots of May 1969. Regan shows that the government, searching for a means to restore political stability and national integration, turned to civil religion. Civil religion seems to have emerged as a interim solution to "consociational politics of accommodation" (Regan, 1976: 95).

18 Islam, for example, represents a special case of civil religion. In Islamic countries the religious and political spheres are hardly separable. There is little or no distinction between religious affiliation and national identity. Muslim and citizen are synonymous terms. However, in the last few years, some countries such as Egypt and Syria, as opposed to to Iran and Pakistan, are clearly trying to separate the two spheres. The case of Israel requires some qualification as well. Clearly, the most salient belief of Israeli civil religion is Israel as a Jewish state. Ninetythree per cent of Israelis believe that "Israel ought to be a Jewish state." This applies even to atheists or agnostics. What unites all Jews under a moral community and a common moral cause, is fundamentally their Jewishness. Thus here too, religious affiliation and national identity are intimately linked. It goes without saying that Arabs, who represent approximately 17 per cent of the population of Israel proper (excluding the West Bank and the Gaza Strip), are not part of Israel's moral community. This does not mean, however, that Israel has had a single civil religion. Throughout Israel's history there have been a variety of interpretations of what a Jewish state ought to be (e.g., Zionism-socialism, revisionism, statism, etc.). When a particular interpretation has been dominant, other significant segments of the Jewish citizenry have been excluded. Political, ideological, and religious confrontation and disagreements on how to express the Jewish identity, and how to transmit it to future generations, have not been uncommon. Even in this unique case, then, the outcome has been a civil religion that has not led to consensus and integration (Liebman and Don-Yehiya, 1983: 13-14).

19 It is interesting to note that the term civil religion proved to be "far more tendentious and provocative" than even Bellah at first realized. Paradoxically, Mead's "religion of the Republic" or terms such as "political religion," "public piety," or "public philosophy," as Bellah himself has noted, appeared to be more "neutral." For some reason, they never provoked the "the profound empirical ambiguities that the terms *civil religion* with its two thousand years of historical resonance inevitably did" (Bellah, 1978: 16).

20 Some scholars have argued that the term *secularization* has become almost useless ("unserviceable") for social research due to the confusion and great variety of processes to which it applies (Casanova, 1994: 19-39). While theories of secularization have tended to predict the decline and eventual disappearance of religion, some authors question whether secularization is taking place at all, and others deny that it is. For a good review of different theories and of the various meanings given to the term, see Hamilton (1995), especially chapter 15.

21 Despite the alliance of religion and politics in the United States, studies have shown that the use of religious rhetoric in political campaigns is not a reliable strategy for winning votes. It might even be counterproductive. This means that the use of politico-religious discourse in campaign speeches "does not of itself win or lose elections for candidates," at least not in North America (Donahue, 1975: 52). See also Demerath and Williams (1985: 160-66).

22 This has been the message conveyed by the moral ethos of civil religion, and by political propaganda. However, the crude reality has not been the preservation of freedom and democracy but the support and preservation of a global free-market system, to maintain and enhance America's economic interests. Reminders of this situation include American support for right-wing military dictatorships around the world, the granting of "special status" to China in spite of the bloody suppression of the Tiananmen Square democracy movement in 1989, and of China's continuing violation of human rights. Hans Morgenthau has put it very forcefully. "The United States," he writes, "is repression's friend...with unfailing consistency, we have since the end of the Second World War intervened on behalf of conservative and fascist repression against revolution and radical reform...we have become the foremost counter revolutionary status quo power on earth" (cited in Huntington, 1981: 247). The American civil religion ethos has called for a "sanctification of American society, its laissez-faire economic processes, its democratic political processes, and its military and international might" (Anthony and Robbins, 1982: 217).

Chapter 3. The "Problem" of Legitimacy, Power, and Politics

1 One notable exception is, of course, Karl Marx. Unlike Hobbes, Locke, and Rousseau, Marx does not consider religion essential for the stability

of the political order. On the contrary, he argues that religion should no longer be the "spirit" of the state, but should be expelled from the political sphere. Religion is the "catalogue of the theoretical struggles" of humankind—his own concern is practical struggles ([1843] 1978: 14). He laments that the philosophers have only "interpreted" the world—his intention is to "change it" ([1888] 1978: 145). Marx's aim is human emancipation, but this requires first political emancipation. The question of the relation between political emancipation and religion becomes for him "a question of the relation between political emancipation and human emancipation." Marx is not really interested in criticizing the "religious failing" of the state. Rather, his intention is to criticize the bourgeois state "in its secular form, disregarding its religious failings" ([1843] 1978: 31).

2 In fifteenth-century Florence, Savonarola had such a vision; so did the Anabaptists in Germany and Calvin in Geneva during the sixteenth century (Bellah, 1978: 16). In America it was the dream of the Mormons, and in England it was the aspiration of the sectarians during the Civil War. Bellah (1978: 17) claims that even the civil theology of Hegel "shows that the yearning for the union of Christian and citizen was still vigorous at the end of the eighteenth century."

3 There is a whole school of thought in sociology that denies that religion has anything to do with legitimation in the modern world. Legitimation is thus linked to non-religious factors such as economic, technical, and/or functional rationality (see chap. 2).

4 I use the term man to refer specifically to modern men, for although Weber has been characterized as "an outspoken feminist," he was not really interested in explaining modern woman at all. For claims regarding his alleged feminism, see, for example, Collins (1986: 270); Mitzman (1969: 279).

5 As any Weberian scholar knows, Weber's unsystematic usage of the words "rational," "rationality," and "rationalization" presents some serious difficulties. The precise meaning of these concepts often remain obscure in his writings. In the words of Lukes (1971: 207), Weber's notion of rational or rationality is, "irredeemably opaque and shifting." This problem has been acknowledged by several scholars (see Casanova, 1984; Kalberg, 1994).

6 Weber distinguishes between an "ethic of responsibility" and an "ethic of absolute ends." Those who follow the former, take responsibility for consequences. Those who follow the latter, use "dubious means or at least dangerous ones" to achieve their ends. In this case, the means and the outcomes are irrelevant—responsibility is taken for achieving ends not for the consequences that follow (Weber, [1919] 1958: 120-22).

7 This criticism would have hardly surprised Weber. He was the first one to admit that he used the concept of charisma "in a completely 'value-neutral' sense" ([1921] 1958: 245).

8 It is interesting to note that *The Marx-Engels Reader*, edited by Robert Tucker (1978), has no rubric bearing the name legitimacy or legitimation.

9. New Right leaders, for example, define morality as essentially a public issue and tend to frame their discussion in public contexts. On the issue of abortion ("a national sin") a 1979 Moral Majority leaflet stated that those "moral Americans who still believe in decency, the home, the family, Bible morality, the free enterprise system, and all the great ideals that are the cornerstone of this great nation must rally together and make their voice heard across this land and in the halls of Congress and the White House" (in Wuthnow, 1988a: 213).

10. Nineteenth-century social thinkers anticipated and laid the ground for this approach (i.e., ideas, values, and beliefs do not have an independent existence—ideas originate from society). These thinkers were conscious that ideas and beliefs were shaped by or came about because of human activity. They were also eager to demonstrate their dependence on social forces (Wuthnow, 1994: 21). A classical example is Marx, for whom the ruling ideas were in every epoch the ideas of the ruling class, and religious leaders were in the business of manufacturing religious beliefs. Religious beliefs, ruling ideas, and intellectual forces were nothing more than products of the material, economic circumstances in which rulers and leaders lived (Marx, [1932] 1978: 172). Weber was not so much interested in the sources or causes of religious beliefs. Rather, his concern was the relationship between different religious ideas and the particular social groups that carried those ideas. He examined, for example, the social role of the prophet and the priest, and how the two produced very different styles of religious orientations. Weber's sociology of religion was fundamentally an attempt to understand the ways that different social strata or groups (such as bureaucrats, artisans, warriors, or traders) "became the carriers of new ethical orientations," and the impact their religious ideas had on society (Wuthnow, 1994: 22).

11. For an interesting study on the restitution of power to the sociology of religion, see Beckford (1987).

12. I am referring here to power in politics or political power in a Weberian sense. That is, politics is to be understood as "only the leadership, or the influencing of the leadership, of a political association," in particular the state. Hence politics means "striving to share power or striving to influence the distribution of power either among states or among groups within a state" (Weber, [1919] 1958: 78).

13. See for example, Regan (1976) for the Malaysian case; Braswell (1979) for the Iranian case; McDowell (1974) and Zeldin (1969) for the Soviet Union; Zuo (1991) for the case of the Cultural Revolution in China as a "political religion"; Takayama (1988) in the case of Japanese civil religion.

14. Although Bellah takes a strong Durkheimian position, in this he is very close to Rousseau's ideas. Rousseau notes that the general will obligates "all members of the State without exception." Magistrates have the power as "ministers of the laws" to enforce the laws, and the

right to use the power assigned to them (Masters, 1968:190). Rousseau assumes that this power is always used and directed towards the common good and public utility. The general will is "always upright and always tends to the public advantage." While it may be "often deceived," it is "never corrupted" (Rousseau, [1762] 1973: 184-85). Rousseau recognizes that if the law ceases to be legitimate, people are no longer bound to obedience. Individuals in this case have the right to return to their natural freedom. In Bellah's terms, if the nation does not live up to its ideals, citizens have the right to civil disobedience. But as with Rousseau he tends to assume that civil religion is always directed towards the common good.

15 Several commentators have noted that, historically, Western conceptions of natural law and justice have grown out of biblical and theological roots. This is clearly visible in the writings of John Locke and Thomas Hobbes, for example. Carl Schmitt, the *éminence grise* of the National Socialist dictatorship in Germany in the thirties, notes that all crucial political concepts are nothing more than "secularized versions of theological notions: constitutional monarchy corresponds to the deistic conception of God, democracy is a version of pantheism, and so forth" (Rouner, 1986: 4). Richardson, echoing this view, notes that notions such as "God as a 'sovereign,'" or "the world as ordered by a 'law'" imply not only the use of "political categories to describe God," but also the use of "theological symbols to describe politics" (Richardson, 1974: 162).

16 Huntington believes that there has been no equivalent change in the way in which Americans think about the authority and autonomy of government. In his view, the notion of the state "as a legitimizing authoritative entity [has remained] foreign to American thinking" (Huntington, 1981: 36).

17 One may argue, perhaps, that civil religion itself is part of the changing process. Scholars may have disguised, consciously or unconsciously, the exercise of power and presented it as something else.

18 Throughout history, religious wars and religious persecution have been more often tied to issues of power rather than faith. For example, behind the surge of persecutions of Christians by the Roman authorities lay the threat that Christianity posed to the legitimacy of the Roman Empire. Christians were persecuted not so much for being "godless," but rather for being "irreverent and defiant of the sacrality and authority of the Emperor." In fact, the growth of Christendom from a "small millenarian movement to a universal church by the 4th century is incomprehensible outside the dialectic of religion and power" (Kokosalakis, 1985: 369). On the other hand, once the Roman Empire was Christianized, "the Christian mission was changed into a state mission involving the expansion of the Imperium Romanum." The Reformation has also been related to the challenges presented by local princes and lords to the authority and power of the pope.

Likewise, the great missionary zeal of the eighteenth and nineteenth centuries has been linked to European colonialism and its expansion of world markets (Moltmann, 1986: 51).

19 I owe the idea of these contrasts to Clifford Geertz, who uses them in the context of the role ideologies play either in "defining or obscuring," "maintaining or undermining," "strengthening or weakening," social norms, tensions, etc. (1973: 203).

20 Needless to say, the power of the American presidency can be enhanced as a result of wars (Gulf War, Cold War, any war) and the needs of "national security." Civil religion's most important ritual ceremonies and state holidays are "remembrances of glorious battles and its courageous dead soldiers." It is "not mere coincidence," Richardson argues, that the "great American leaders have been generals and 'war presidents'" (Richardson, 1974: 174).

Chapter 4. State-Directed Civil Religions in Comparative Perspective

1 Bellah has made a brief reference to Judaism and Islam (1968: 391), to France (1976a: 155), and to England, where he claims that civil religion goes "back at least to Shakespeare and Milton" (1968: 389). He has compared the Japanese and American cases (1980d), and has discussed civil religion in Italy in a more detailed fashion, describing it "as a land not of one religion" but of five different cases of civil religion (1980c). Hammond has compared the civil religion of the United States and Mexico (1980a), and Markoff and Regan have analyzed post-Revolutionary France and contemporary Malaysia (1982).

2 This, in opposition to a Durkheimian type of civil religion that can manifest itself at different levels (group, local, regional, national, state, etc.)

3 For an excellent analysis of the breakdown of democratic regimes in the context of Europe and Latin America, see Linz and Stepan (1978). The rise of fascism in Italy, the National Socialist takeover in Germany, the tragic consequences of the breakdown of democracy in Spain, Argentina, Brazil, and Chile, and some other less well-known cases are carefully examined.

4 For revolutionary France, see Demerath and Williams (1985:155) and Markoff and Regan (1982: 344); For Italy under Mussolini, see DeGrazia (1981) and Gregor (1969); for Nazi Germany, see Moltmann (1986); For Fascist Spain see Stevens (1975). Pinochet's Chile is dealt with in Cristi and Dawson (1996) and in chapter 5 of this book; Brazil in De Azevedo (1979); China in Zuo (1991) and Demerath (1994). Demerath, also deals with pre-1945 Japan, as does Coleman (1969). Former Marxis-Leninist regimes are discussed in Luke (1987) and McDowell (1974).

5 Israel's civil religion would also fall under the category of state-directed civil religions. See Liebman and Don-Yehiha (1983). The authors argue that, subsequent to the establishment of the State of

Israel, after Zionist-socialism was displaced, a "civil religion of statism" developed whose goal was the support of the particular needs of state and national institutions. The authors trace the roots and evolution of three different kinds of civil religion in Israel and argue that all three consciously adopted and adapted traditional symbols of religious Judaism to suit or enhance particular politico-ideological goals. For some interesting material and ideas regarding Israel, see Zerubavel (1985). For an analysis of political religions in "new nations" see Apter (1963).

6 For an excellent and comprehensive description of authoritarianism in Spain, see Linz (1964); see also, O'Donnell, Schmitter, and Whitehead (1986).

7 As Willaime (1993: 574) notes, "l'Etat occupe un place centrale en raison de la spécifité française des rapports Etat/société. Contrairement à l'Angleterre où prédomina une vision principalement juridique et instrumentale de l'Etat, contrairement à l'Allemagne où la nation précède l'Etat."

8 Pinochet, in Chile, was heavily influenced by Franco and tried to imitate his style of sacred authoritarianism. He endowed his mission of *reconstrucción nacional* with divine characteristics, so much so, that one author has referred to the Chilean coup d'état as "le coup divin" (Bastien, 1974).

Chapter 5. Chile, 1973-1989: A Case Study

1 There is a vast literature covering both the Allende and the military regime. What follows is just a brief sample of it. For information on the social, political, and economic conditions that lead to the coup d'etat, see Alexander (1978); Valenzuela (1978); Sigmund (1977); and O'Brien (1976). For information on Chile, the Allende years, and the revolutionary process that unfolded under his regime see Oppenheim (1993); Falcoff (1991); Garretón and Moulián (1978); Roxborough, O'Brien, and Roddick (1977); Boorstein (1975); Sobel (1974). For an analysis of Chile's past and its legacy of Hispanic capitalism, see Loveman (1979). For studies on civil/military relations in Chile and the overthrow of Allende, see Michaels (1975). Finally, for those interested in Chile's transition to democracy see Tulchin and Varas (1991).

2 This chapter, with minor modifications, is part of a larger article, co-authored with Lorne Dawson, which originally appeared under the title "Civil Religion in Comparative Perspective: Chile under Pinochet (1973-1989)," in *Social Compass*, 43, 3 (Sept. 1996). Reprinted here by permission of Sage Publications.

3 For an analysis of the old origins and evolution of Chilean democracy, see Arturo Valenzuela (1990).

4 This ideological discourse was accompanied by widespread violation of human rights. In the first month after the coup an estimated 45,000

people were arrested. Thousands of Chileans went into exile; some 50,000 simply left and another 10,000 were authorized to leave the country (Sanders, 1981: 301). The *Vicaría de la Solidaridad* (Vicariate of Solidarity), the Catholic Church's organization that monitored human rights violations, recorded over 600 cases between 1975 and 1976 of persons "whose arrests were reported and verified," and who subsequently "disappeared," and whose remains were never found (Arriagada, 1988: 25).

5 Catholicism's record in the face of fascist regimes has often been reactionary. In Italy, Portugal, Spain, Brazil, and Argentina, Catholic bishops offered no resistance to the emergence of fascist regimes. A similar situation was observed in Germany, where only isolated clerics openly opposed Hitler (Smith, 1982: 285). Pius XII, the war-time pontiff, has been accused of failing to help the Jewish victims of the Holocaust, turning a blind eye to Hitler's atrocities against the Jews and other minorities. The Chilean Catholic Church is in a sense quite unique. After a short initial period of ambiguity, it became a strong voice (the only voice, in fact) openly condemning human rights violations.

6 Some movement in this direction was admittedly made in Arturo H. Chacón and Humberto S. Lagos's *Religión y Proyecto Político Autoritario* (1986) and Lagos and Chacón's *La Religión en las Fuerzas Armadas y de Orden* (1987). However, these brief analytic readings do not employ the concept of civil religion and lack a theoretical base.

7 I disagree with Hammond's conclusions. While it is true that a civil religion of the type one finds in the United States never developed in Mexico, it is no less true that one can infer, from Hammond's own article, that Mexico has the type of civil religion identified by Coleman (1969) as "secular nationalism." The problem is that Hammond's basic approach to Mexico's civil religion has been worked out primarily in relation to the American case. He has taken American civil religion as the paradigmatic model through which he evaluates Mexican civil religion. In so doing, he has drawn the mistaken conclusion that Mexico does not have a civil religion. To be sure, Mexico does not have an "American" civil religion, in the sense of having institutions imbued simultaneously with political and religious significance, but does have a strong civil religion in the form of secular nationalism.

8 Guzmán, who was, undoubtedly, the éminence grise of the military junta, was assassinated in 1999 by a left-wing terrorist group. For an excellent account of the role played by Guzmán during this period, see R. Cristi (2000).

9 For example, between 30 October and 11 December 1975, when Franco was on his sickbed, the pro-government, weekly magazine *Que Pasa* published several lengthy articles praising Franco and his leadership qualities for forging a "new Spain: *GREAT AND FREE*," and for building a new Spain on the "solid base of God's Law." During his government "the Spanish soul flourished [and] the road he walked reached

clear levels of divine presence." His approaching death, the article says, marks a "disheartening point for Christianity." Christianity is being deprived of hope for he was the most sublime champion of the Great Crusade of the twentieth century"—the fight against atheist Marxism (30 Oct. 1975, No. 236). Similar praises, filled with grandiose words and religious imagery, appeared in the issues of 20 November, 27 November, 4 December, and 11 December 1975 (author's translation).

Chapter 6. Civil Religion and the Spirit of Nationalism

1 The idea of nationalism is often linked to the emergence of the modern nation-state and popular sovereignty, but it was the French Revolution that provided its "first great manifestation." After 1789, nationalist ideas spread to central and eastern Europe, giving birth to different types of nationalism. Liberal versions, where Rousseau's approach certainly belongs, pointed to a democratic world order, while others, predicated upon "irrational and pre-enlightened" doctrines, tended towards chauvinism, fanaticism, and exclusiveness (Kohn, [1944] 1967: 3, 457). See also Bendix (1974) and Hayes (1960).

2 Both patriotism and nationalism promised, at first, increased freedom, dignity, and participation of the masses. Patriotism, originally equated with liberalism, was synonymous with interest in public good and the rule of law: "a patriot was the supporter of good government, an altruistic friend of liberty and mankind; fatherland was an ideal rather than a geographic concept, belonged more to the realm of civic morality than to that of national exclusiveness" (Kohn, [1944] 1967: 456). Nationalism meant popular participation in national affairs. It is in this sense that Rousseau encouraged and espoused patriotic sentiments.

3 What Rousseau proposes at a national (citizenship) level, to rekindle a patriotic spirit, Durkheim proposes at a school (student) level. To train students for collective life and future citizenship, and to instill in each child a "feeling of continuity" and belongingess, Durkheim recommends compiling "a history to record class achievements...keeping an honor book, and other souvenirs of past generations of students." By inculcating the sense of "class honor" and "class responsibility" educators would awaken and strengthen "the spirit of the group." To educate, was to nationalize and socialize the individual (Mitchell, 1990: 121-22).

4 Patriotism is for Rousseau the "most heroic of all passions." In his *Discourse on Political Economy*, in poetic and rather exalted language, he compares the love of the fatherland with the love of a mistress, and finds the former far more enriching. The love of the fatherland, "this sweet and lively sentiment, which joins the force of price to the complete beauty of virtue, gives virtue an energy that, without disfiguring it, makes it the most heroic of all passions." And he continues, "the love of the fatherland, a hundred times more lively and delicious than that of a mistress, can...be conceived only by experiencing it." It

is this love that has produced "many immortal actions" and "many great men" (Rousseau, [1755] 1984: 155).

5 Rousseau also envisioned a world where egoistic principles could be transcended. In *A Discourse on Political Economy* he advocates the idea of a universal general will of humanity—"the great city of the world becomes the body politic, whose general will is always the law of nature, and of which the different States and peoples are individual members" ([1758] 1973: 121).

6 In Durkheim's writings *society* appears to have a great diversity of meanings. Sometimes it refers to specific groups ranging from the family, tribe, or city-state to the nation, or even religious sects or occupational and professional groups or corporations. He uses the terms "'people,' 'nation,' 'state,' *la patrie*, and 'society,' synonymously, to denote a 'collective being' with a personality distinct from and superior to that of its individual members" (Mitchell, 1990: 118). Society also constitute a sacred meaning system (Schoffeleers and Meijers, 1978:5). At other times, its connotation is even more obscure and perhaps "more mysterious." It refers to a collection of "ideas, beliefs and sentiments of all sorts which realize themselves through individuals" (in Bellah, 1973b: ix). Bellah has noted that no other word in Durkheim's theory may be more difficult to grasp. In Bellah's view, to apprehend the many levels of meanings connoted by the word *society*, "would be almost equivalent to understanding the whole of Durkheim's thought" (Bellah, 1973b: ix).

7 Wuthnow sees this tension not *within* American civil religion but *between* different versions of it. The conservative version of American civil religion, "closely identified with the biblical faith," is explicitly nationalistic, celebrates capitalism, and grants the American nation a "special place in the divine order." The liberal version, by contrast, centres "less on the nation as such, and more on humanity in general." In this latter construct, America's mission is not conceived as "divine" and Americans are not seen as "a chosen people." Rather, if America can play a role on a global scale it is because "it has vast resources…, because it has caused many of the problems currently facing the world, and because it is, simply, part of the community of nations." Issues such as peace, economic, political, and international justice, world hunger, and human rights are given a special place in its agenda (Wuthnow, 1988a: 247-51).

8 I am referring here to cultural nationalism, which I distinguish from political nationalism. The former refers to loyalty or devotion to one's nation and cultural traditions. The latter politicizes the sense of national consciousness. In its political dimension, nationalism becomes territorial and exclusionary, and requires active participation of the state. It exalts one nation above all others, and places primary emphasis on promotion of its culture and interests as opposed to those of other nations or supranational groups.

9 Bellah has argued that Canada's lack of a revolutionary past, its strong ties with England, and the existence of Quebec, which is linguistically, ethnically and religiously distinct from the rest of the country, have "militated against not only the emergence of a Canadian civil religion but of any very clearly defined sense of national identity" (Bellah, 1980a: xiii).

10 I am indebted to Hudson's *Nationalism and Religion in America* (1970), and to Huntington's *American Politics: The Promise of Disharmony* (1981) for the information contained in this section.

11 Throughout the colonial period it seems to have been quite common to refer to America as our "British Israel," "our New English Israel," and eventually "our American Israel." Colonists believed that "they were a chosen and covenanted people, successors to Israel of old" (Hudson, 1970: 33-34). This is clearly reflected in the rise of Mormonism in the 1830s.

12 Wilson's model parallels Weber's distinction between two types of prophet—the exemplary prophet, and the emissary or ethical one. In the former case, preaching is not very important. What counts is the prophet's actual behaviour, which is to be taken as a model; in the latter, the prophet preaches a certain lifestyle, and followers have a moral responsibility or an "obligation to conform to it on pain of damnation" (Hamilton, 1995: 142).

13 Compare this with other nations where the political system has changed several times in the course of a century. For example, the Germans had five different systems in the twentieth century, while France, in two hundred years, has had five republics and several political systems (Huntington, 1981: 29). Between 1789 and 1870, alone, France had three monarchies, two empires, and two republics, which resulted in fourteen constitutions (Bellah, 1973b: xvi).

14 Wuthnow has noted that opinion polls show the consistent tendency of Americans to link "faith in their country" to "the state of the economy." The stronger the economy, the higher the public expression of satisfaction with the political machinery. Wuthnow notes that in a 1984 Gallup survey, when the economy was booming, 50 per cent of those polled "were satisfied with the way things were going in the United States." Yet five years earlier, when the economy was in recession, only 12 per cent gave this response. The same polls revealed a discrepancy between business managers or people with incomes over $40,000 and manual workers. The former group was "twice as likely to express satisfaction" than were people with low incomes (Wuthnow, 1988a: 266).

15 To be sure, nationalist tendencies under the Durkheimian/Bellah tradition are neither virulent nor belligerent, as I have already mentioned. But it goes without saying that in a non-democratic setting, a civil religion with strong nationalist overtones can be very disruptive not only to a particular nation but to world peace. Consider dictatorships such

as Napoleon's, Hitler's, or Stalin's, where "decisions for aggression and war" relied, to a large extent, on "patriotic mass support assured by dictatorial propaganda and duress" (Hayes, 1960: 175).

16 In line with my argument that historians, philosophers, and political scientists have been more sensitive than sociologists to the implications and ramifications of the civil religion concept, it should be noted that Hayes is a historian, not a sociologist, and so is Huntington, who, as I have already noted, also links the American creed with nationalism.

17 Consider American flag etiquette: no flag may fly higher than U.S. flag in the country; the U.S. flag may not be lowered in salute, at home or abroad, or before a foreign head of state; the U.S. flag may not touch the ground, or be shown or treated in disrepute, and so on.

18 One should remember, for example, the national pride, enthusiasm, and positive media coverage that the victory of the Gulf War received.

19 This is the type of civil religion that emerged during the American Civil War. The "American state identified its interests with those of its northern nation," and the Yankees successfully imposed "their culture, commercial interests," and ideology to every corner of the nation and to every new immigrant entering the promised land. Attempts by other groups to preserve their heritage, language, religion, and values were persistently thwarted through government policies and state action. As a result, white Anglo-Saxon America created its own history and "rendered invisible blacks, nisei, chicanos, and other peoples who were unlikely candidates for Puritan forefathers." By identifying the interests of the nation with the interests of the dominant social group, competition for social power was effectively dissolved. This is what Richardson has called "the method of nationalism," which, he notes, is "no different in America from elsewhere" (Richardson, 1974: 168-69).

20 For more on Nixon's civil religion, see Henderson (1972), Wimberley (1975), Donahue (1975), and Alley (1972). His civil religious discourse has been characterized as "priestly" (that is, more comforting than judgmental). Apparently, Nixon's political and religious rhetoric resonated well with the great majority of the voters, for he obtained in 1972 the second highest percentage of the popular vote ever achieved by a president. Nixon "was capable of establishing bases for both a political and religious identity with the 'new majority' in the electorate" (Donahue, 1975: 55-57, 60). Henderson (1972: xi) has described Nixon as illustrating perfectly the "curious inbreeding of patriotism and piety, the Protestant ethic, and liberal pragmatism that has been so pervasive in this nation's history." Nixon, he notes, vibrated "to the rhythms of American folk religion." He did this by systematically appropriating the vocabulary of the church—"faith, trust, hope, belief, spirit"—and applying these words not to a transcendent God but to his own nation, and worse, to his personal vision of what that nation should be (in Donahue, 1975: 60). Wimberley's data (1975)

show an association between civil religious orientation, especially the nationalistic arch-conservative aspects of Republicanism, and support for Nixon in 1972.

21 I reproduce here some passages of Nixon's inaugural address: "Above all else, the time has come for us to renew our faith in ourselves and in America. In recent years, that faith has been challenged. Our children have been taught to be ashamed of their country, ashamed of their parents, ashamed of America's record at home and its role in the world. At every turn, we have been beset by those who find everything wrong with America and little that is right....America's record in this century has been unparalleled in the world's history for its responsibility, for its generosity, for its creativity and for its progress....Let us be proud that in each of the four wars in which we have engaged in this century, including the one we are now bringing to an end, we have fought not for selfish advantage, but to help others resist aggression. Let us be proud that by our bold, new initiatives, and by our steadfastness for peace with honor, we have made a breakthrough toward creating in the world what the world has not known before....We shall answer to God, to history, and to our conscience for the way in which we use these years" (in Bellah, 1974b: 259-60).

22 Berger does not use the term civil religion but he describes forms of American cultural and political religion. Cultural religion is based on profoundly shared American values and it serves to reinforce cultural integration. Political religion, a manifestation of cultural religion but within the polity performs the function of social control (Berger, 1961: 39-72).

Conclusion: Durkheim versus Rousseau Revisited

1 I am heavily indebted to Williams's article in this section. I have borrowed and applied his interesting ideas on the role of religion proper to my analysis of civil religion.

2 It is worth bearing in mind that Bellah himself claims that American civil religion has been moulded in times of trial (Bellah, 1975: 1).

3 Bellah has argued that Japanese civil religion, while being very authoritarian in nature, has some "egalitarian components, even if relatively minor ones." The American case, while largely democratic, has "hierarchical components, even if largely confined to the background" (Bellah, 1980d: 30). I have borrowed Bellah's idea to make the distinction between civil and political religions.

4 The authors use this distinction in the context of the value systems of Soviet Russia and communist China. The relationship between voluntary compliance and imposed force is used as an indicator of the "truth" of a civil religion. In their view, Russian communism appeared to require an "unusual amount of centrally regulated 'force,'" while Maoism seemed to be "sufficiently *internalized*," show-

ing a strong tendency towards voluntary compliance (Anthony and Robbins, 1975). Yet history has proven that Maoism was, in this sense, no different than the Soviet system—it also required a strong regulated force to ensure compliance with the Chinese tenets of faith.

5 For a discussion of Richard Nixon's exploitation of civil religion during the 1970s in an effort to gather support for his Vietnam policy, see Linder and Pierard (1978). See also Donahue (1975) and Bennett (1979) for an analysis of the "dilemma of public morality" and potential abuses of American civil religion in public life.

6 It should be mentioned that Apter makes this argument with reference to political religions, which he finds solely in the developing nations.

7 It goes without saying that methods of socialization may be manipulated and even controlled by the state and political authorities. As Weber suggests, a particular religious ideology may be proliferated quite successfully "by an alliance between the carrying stratum and political rulers" (Hughey, 1983: 42). The government may utilize the educational process for inculcating those quasi unconscious feelings of self-identity and national solidarity. So in its institutionalized form, it too may be subject to a measure of manipulation, but its influence will be exerted in a non-compelling form.

8 This is taken from Durkheim's distinction between mechanical solidarity and organic solidarity. The former generates a "morality of constraint"; the latter yields a "morality of cooperation" (Selznick, 1992: 165 n. 30).

9 The importance of the religious-political link for an understanding of the civil religion phenomenon was recognized by Bellah from the very beginning. In his 1967 article he contended that "these questions are worth pursuing because they raise the issue of how civil religion is related to the political society, on the one hand, and to private religious organizations, on the other" (Bellah, 1967: 3). Bellah's focus, however, has been more on the religious dimension of civil religion rather than on its political manifestation.

10 For an excellent discussion of civil religion as movement ideology, see Williams and Alexander (1994). The authors analyze the rhetoric of late nineteenth-century American populism, which borrowed heavily from American civil religious discourse and symbolism. This allowed populism to gain a legitimate language and platform to challenge the status quo. The authors argue that the ideology of civil religion was as important to mobilization of supporters as were other factors such as economic or organizational features. For a discussion of civil religion in America as a revitalization movement, see Wilson (1979, the epilogue).

11 Markoff and Regan note that in France the post-Thermidor political elites wanted neither the mass mobilization of the revolution's early years, nor a government armed with the "vast emergency powers of the great Committee," nor an aristocratic or clerical alliance that

might reject the ideals of the revolution. Both the extreme Catholic and anti-Catholic versions of civil religion "were much too threatening, and hence a minimalist version" emerged that could be embraced by both groups (1982: 346).

12 See, for example, Ungar (1991) and Linder and Pierard, (1978).

13 Bear in mind that, for Durkheim, the moral reaffirmation of a society is achieved through rituals, ceremonies, and collective celebrations. He emphasizes practices rather than beliefs.

14 Abercrombie, Hill and Turner, in *The Dominant Ideology Thesis* (1980), contest the view that a dominant ideology successfully incorporates powerless groups into an existing social system, thereby perpetuating their subordination. They argue that a strong parallel exists between functionalist approaches to culture and Marxist accounts of dominant ideology. Neither a dominant ideology nor a dominant culture incorporate all social groups. The only important role they assign to the dominant ideology is that of binding the dominant class itself: "ideology has importance in explaining the coherence of the dominant class but not in the explanation of the coherence of a society as a whole" (3).

REFERENCES

Abercrombie, Nicholas, Stephen Hill, and Bryan S. Turner. (1980). *The Dominant Ideology Thesis*. London: George Allen & Unwin.

Adams, David S. (1987). "Ronald Reagan's 'Revival': Voluntarism as a Theme in Reagan's Civil Religion." *Sociological Analysis* 48, 1: 17-29.

Alexander, Robert J. (1978). *The Tragedy of Chile*. Westport, CT: Greenwood Press.

Allen, William J. (1960). *A History of Political Thought in the Sixteenth Century*. London: Methuen.

Alley, Robert S. (1972). *So Help Me God: Religion and the Presidency, Wilson to Nixon*. Richmond, VA: John Knox Press.

Anthony, Dick, and Thomas Robbins. (1975). "From Symbolic Realism to Structuralism." *Journal for the Scientific Study of Religion* 14, 4: 403-14.

_____. (1982). "Spiritual Innovation and the Crisis of American Civil Religion." *Daedalus: Journal of the American Academy of Arts and Sciences* 1 (Winter): 215-34.

Apter, David E. (1960). "Political Organization and Ideology." Pp. 326-47. In *Labor Commitment and Social Change in Developing Areas*. Ed. Wilbert E. Moore and Arnold S. Feldman. New York: Social Science Research Council.

_____. (1963). "Political Religion in the New Nations." Pp. 57-104. In *Old Societies and New States*. Ed. Clifford Geertz. London: Free Press.

Arriagada, Genaro. (1988). *Pinochet: The Politics of Power*. Trans. Nancy Morris with Vincent Escolano and Kristen A. Whitney. Boston: Unwin Hyman.

Bastien, Ovide. (1974). *Le coup Divin.* Montreal: Editions du Jour.

Beckford, James A. (1988). "The Restoration of Power to the Sociology of Religion." Pp. 13-37. In *Church-State Relations: Tensions and Transitions."* Ed. Thomas Robbins and Roland Robertson. New Brunswick, NJ: Transaction Books.

_____. (1989). *Religion and Advanced Industrial Society.* London: Unwin Hyman.

Beiner, Ronald. (1993). "Machiavelli, Hobbes, and Rousseau on Civil Religion." In *The Review of Politics* 55, 4: 617-38.

Bellah, Robert N. (1957). *Tokugawa Religion.* Glencoe: Free Press.

_____. (1967). "Civil Religion in America." *Daedalus: Journal of the American Academy of Arts and Sciences* 96: 1-21.

_____. (1968). "Response." In *The World Year Book of Religion. The Religious Situation.* Vol. 1. Pp. 388-93. Ed. Donald R. Cutler. Boston: Beacon Press.

_____. (1970). *Beyond Belief: Essays on Religion in a Post-Traditional World.* New York: Harper and Row.

_____. (1973a). "American Civil Religion in the 1970's." *Anglican Theological Review, Supplementary Series* 1: 8-20.

_____. (1973b). *Emile Durkheim on Morality and Society.* Chicago: University of Chicago Press.

_____. (1974a). "Civil Religion in America." Pp. 21-44. In *American Civil Religion.* Ed. Russell B. Richey and Donald G. Jones. New York: Harper and Row.

_____. (1974b). "American Civil Religion in the 1970s." Pp. 255-72. In *American Civil Religion.* Ed. Russell B. Richey and Donald G. Jones. New York: Harper and Row.

_____. (1974c). "Religion and Polity in America." *Andover Newton Quarterly* 15, 2: 107-21.

_____. (1975). *The Broken Covenant: American Civil Religion in Times of Trial.* New York: Seabury.

_____. (1976a). "Reponse to the Panel on Civil Religion." *Sociological Analysis* 37, 2: 153-59.

_____. (1976b). "Comment on 'Bellah and the New Orthodoxy.'" *Sociological Analysis* 37, 2: 167-68.

_____. (1978). "Religion and Legitimation in the American Republic." *Society* 15, 4: 16-23.

_____. (1980a). Introduction to *Varieties of Civil Religion* by Robert N. Bellah and Phillip E. Hammond. Pp. vii-xv. San Francisco: Harper and Row.

_____. (1980b). "Religion and the Legitimation of the American Republic." Pp. 3-23. In Robert N. Bellah and Phillip E. Hammond, *Varieties of Civil Religion.* San Francisco: Harper and Row.

_____. (1980c). "The Five Religions of Modern Italy." Pp. 86-118. In Robert N. Bellah and Phillip E. Hammond, *Varieties of Civil Religion.* San Francisco: Harper and Row.

_____. (1980d). "The Japanese and American Cases." Pp. 27-39. In Robert N. Bellah and Phillip E. Hammond, *Varieties of Civil Religion*. San Francisco: Harper and Row.

_____. (1985). *Habits of the Heart: Individualism and Commitment in American Life*. Berkeley: University of California Press.

_____. (1989). "Comment on 'Twenty Years After Bellah,'" *Sociological Analysis* 50, 2:147.

Bellah, Robert N., and Phillip E. Hammond. (1980). *Varieties of Civil Religion*. New York: Harper and Row.

Bendix, Reinhard. (1974). *Nation-Building and Citizenship*. Berkeley: University of California Press.

Beneyto, José María. (1983). *Politiche Theologie als Politische Theorie: Eine Untersuchung zur Rechts-und Staas Theorie Carl Schmitts und zu ihrer Wirkungsgeschichte in Spanian*. Berlin: Duncker and Humblot.

Bennet, William J. (1992). *The De-Valuing of America*. New York: Summit Books.

Bennett, Lance W. (1975). "Political Sanctification: The Civil Religion and American Politics." *Social Science Information* 14, 6: 79-102.

_____. (1979). "Imitation, Ambiguity, and Drama in Political Life: Civil Religion and the Dilemmas of Public Morality." *Journal of Politics* 4, 1: 107-33.

Berger, Peter L. (1961). *The Noise of Solemn Assemblies*. Garden City, NY: Doubleday Anchor.

_____. (1967). *The Sacred Canopy: Elements of a Sociological Theory of Religion*. Garden City, NY: Doubleday Anchor.

_____. (1973). "Religious Institutions." Pp. 303-46. In *Sociology*. Ed. N.J. Smelser. New York: Wiley.

Berger, P., and T. Luckmann. (1967). *The Social Construction of Reality*. London: Allen Lane.

Beyer, Peter. (1994). *Religion and Globalization*. London: Sage.

Billings, Dwight B., and Shaunna L. Scott. (1994). "Religion and Political Legitimation." In *Annual Review of Sociology* Vol. 20: 173-202. Ed. John Hagan.

Blanchard, D.A., and T.J. Prewitt. (1993). *Religious Violence and Abortion: The Gideon Project*. Gainesville: University of Florida Press.

Booenm, Kenneth A. (1980). "Comparative Measurement of Political Democracy." *American Sociological Review* 45, 3: 370-90.

Boorstein, Edward. (1977). *Allende's Chile*. New York: International.

Bourg, Carroll J. (1976). "A Symposium on Civil Religion." *Sociological Analysis* 37, 2: 141-49.

Bowden, Henry Warner. (1975). "A Historian's Response to the Concept of Civil Religion." *Journal of Church and State* 17: 495-505.

Braswell, George W. (1979). "Civil Religion in Contemporary Iran." *Journal of Church and State* 21, 1: 223-46.

Breslauer, Daniel S. (1993). *Judaism and Civil Religion*. Atlanta: Scholars Press.

Breytspraak, August W. (1973). *Toward a Post-Critical Sociology of Knowledge: A Study of Durkheim, Mannheim, Berger, and Polanyi*. Durham, NC: Duke University.

Brogan, Denis. (1968). "Commentary" In *The World Year Book of Religion. The Religious Situation*.Vol. 1. Pp. 356-60. Ed. Donald R. Cutler. Boston: Beacon Press.

Burns, Gene (1996). "Studying the Political Culture of American Catholicism." *Sociology of Religion* 57: 37-53.

Caplow, Theodore. (1994). "Tocqueville's Civil Religion: American Christianity and the Prospects for Freedom." *Journal for the Scientific Study of Religion* 33, 4: 394-95.

Cardoso, Fernando H. (1979). "On the Characterization of Authoritarian Regimes in Latin America." Pp. 33-57. In *The New Authoritarianism in Latin America*. Ed. David Collier. Princeton: Princeton University Press.

Casanova, José (1984). "Interpretations and Misinterpretations of Max Weber: The Problem of Rationalization." Pp. 141-53. In *Max Weber's Political Sociology: A Pessimistic Vision of a Rationalized World*. Ed. Ronald M. Glassman and Vatro Murvar. London: Westport.

_____. (1994). *Public Religions in the Modern World*. Chicago: University of Chicago Press.

Chacón, H. Arturo, and Humberto Lagos S. (1986). *Religión y Proyecto Político Autoritario*. Concepción, Chile: Programa Evangélico de Estudios Socio-Religiosos.

Cheal, David. (1978). "Religion and Social Order." *Canadian Journal of Sociology,* 3, 1: 61-69.

Cherry, Conrad. (1969). "Two American Sacred Ceremonies." *American Quarterly* 21: 739-54.

_____. (1970). "American Sacred Ceremonies." Pp. 303-16. In *American Mosaic*. Ed. Phillip E. Hammond and Benton Johnson. New York: Random House.

_____. (1971). *God's New Israel*. Englewood Cliffs, NJ: Prentice-Hall.

Clark, S.D. (1962). *The Developing Canadian Community*. Toronto: University of Toronto Press.

Cobban, Alfred. (1934). *Rousseau and the Modern State*. London: George Allen and Unwin.

Cole, G.D.H. (1973). Introduction to *The Social Contract and Discourses* by Jean-Jacques Rousseau. Pp. xi-xliv. London: J.M. Dent and Sons.

Cole, William A., and Phillip E. Hammond. (1974). "Religious Pluralism, Legal Development, and Societal Complexity: Rudimentary Forms of Civil Religion." *Journal for the Scientific Study of Religion* 13, 2: 177-89.

Coleman, John A. (1969). "Civil Religion." *Sociological Analysis* 30, 1: 67-77.

Coleman, Kenneth M., and Charles L. Davis. (1978). "Civil and Conventional Religion in Secular Authoritarian Regimes: The Case of Mexico." *Studies in Comparative International Development* 13, 1: 56-76.

Collier, David. (1979). Introduction to *The New Authoritarianism in Latin America*. Ed. David Collier. Princeton, NJ: Princeton University Press.

Collins, Randall. (1986). *Weberian Sociological Theory*. Cambridge: Cambridge University Press.

Constable, Pamela, and Arturo Valenzuela. (1991). *A Nation of Enemies: Chile under Pinochet*. New York: W.W. Norton.

Corradi, Juan E., Patricia Weiss Fagen , and Manuel Antonio Garretón. (1992). *Fear at the Edge: State Terror and Resistance in Latin America*. Berkeley: University of California Press.

Cristi, Marcela and Lorne Dawson. (1996). "Civil Religion in Comparative Perspective: Chile Under Pinochet (1973-1989)." *Social Compass* 43, 3: 319-38.

Cristi, Renato. (2000). El Pensamiento Politico de Jaime Guzmán: Autoridad y Libertad. Santiago, Chili: LOM Ediciones.

Cutler, Donald R., ed. (1968). *The World Year Book of Religion. The Religious Situation*. Vol. 1. Boston: Beacon Press.

De Azevedo, Thales. (1979). "La religion civile." *Archives de Sciences Sociales des Religions* 47, 1: 7-22.

DeGrazia, Victoria. (1981). *The Culture of Consent: Mass Organization of Leisure in Fascist Italy*. New York: Cambridge University Press.

DeLue, Steven M. (1997). *Political Thinking, Political Theory, and Civil Society*. Boston: Allyn and Bacon.

Demerath, N.J. (1994). "The Moth and the Flame: Religion and Power in Comparative Blur." *Sociology of Religion* 55, 2: 105-17.

Demerath, N.J., and Phillip E. Hammond. (1969). *Religion in Social Context*. New York: Random House.

Demerath, N.J., and N.C. Roof. (1976). "Religion: Recent Strands in Research." In *Annual Review of Sociology*. Vol. 2. Ed. Alex Inkeles, James Coleman, and Neil Smelser.

Demerath, N.J., and Rhys H. Williams. (1985). "Civil Religion in an Uncivil Society." *Annals of the American Academy* 480: 154-65.

_____. (1989). "Religion and Power in the American Experience." *Society* 26, 2: 29-38.

_____. (1992). *A Bridging of Faiths: Religion and Politics in a New England City*. Princeton, N.J. Princeton University Press.

Dewey, John. (1934). *A Common Faith*. New Haven, Yale University Press.

Diamond, Larry, Juan J. Linz, and Seymour Martin Lipset, eds. (1989). *Democracy in Developing Countries*. Vol. 4. Boulder, CO: Lynne Rienner.

Donahue, Bernard F. (1975). "The Political Use of Religious Symbols: A Case Study of the 1972 Presidential Campaign." *The Review of Politics* 37, 1: 48-65.

Drake, W. Paul, and Ivan Jaksic. (1993). "Introducción: Transformación y Transición en Chile, 1982-1990." In *El Difícil Camino Hacia la Democracia en Chile, 1982-1990*. Santiago: Flacso.

Durkheim, Emile. ([1893] 1964). *The Division of Labor in Society*. New York: Free Press.

_____. ([1895] 1938). *The Rules of the Sociological Method*. Trans. Sarah A. Solovay and John H. Mueller. Ed. George E.G. Catlin. New York: Free Press.

_____. ([1898] 1973). "Individualism and the Intellectuals." Pp. 43-57. In *Emile Durkheim: On Morality and Society*. Ed. by Robert N. Bellah. Chicago: University of Chicago Press.

_____. ([1898] 1975). "Individualism and the Intellectuals." Pp. 59-73. In *Durkheim on Religion: A Selection of Readings with Bibliographies*. Trans. Jacqueline Redding and W.S.F. Pickering. London: Routledge and Kegan Paul.

_____. ([1912] 1961). *The Elementary Forms of Religious Life*. Trans. Joseph Ward Swain. New York: Collier Books.

_____. ([1912] 1975). *"The Elementary Forms of the Religious Life: The Totemic System in Australia."* In *Durkheim on Religion. A Selection of Readings with Bibliographies*. Trans. Jacqueline Redding and W.S.F. Pickering. London: Routledge and Kegan Paul.

_____. ([1916] 1979). "The Moral Greatness of France and the School of the Future." Pp. 158-61. In *Durkheim: Essays on Morals and Education*. Ed. by W.S.F. Pickering. Trans. H.L. Sutcliffe. London: Routledge and Kegan Paul.

_____. ([1922] 1956). *Education and Sociology*. Trans. Sherwood Fox. Glencoe: Free Press.

_____. ([1925] 1961). *Moral Education*. Trans. Everett K. Wilson and Herman Schnurer. New York: Free Press.

_____. ([1925] 1975). "Moral Education." Pp. 190-201. In *Durkheim on Religion. A Selection of Readings with Bibliographies*. Trans. Jacqueline Redding and W.S.F. Pickering. London: Routledge and Kegan Paul.

_____. ([1938] 1986). "L'Evolution pédagogique en France." Pp.174-76. In *Durkheim on Politics and the State*. Ed. Anthony Giddens. Trans. W.D. Halls. Cambridge: Polity Press.

_____. ([1950] 1986). "Patriotism and Militarism." Pp. 194-204. In *Durkheim on Politics and the State*. Ed. Trans. W.D. Halls. Cambridge: Polity Press.

_____. ([1950] 1957). *Professional Ethics and Civic Morals*. London: Routledge.

_____. (1975). *Durkheim on Religion. A Selection of Readings with Bibliographies*. Trans. Jacqueline Redding and W.S.F. Pickering. London: Routledge and Kegan.

_____. (1986). *Durkheim on Politics and the State*. Ed. Anthony Giddens. Trans. W.D. Halls. Cambridge: Polity Press.

Edelman, Murray. (1964). *The Symbolic Uses of Politics*. Urbana: University of Illinois Press.

Engels, Friedrich. ([1891] 1978). Introduction to "The Civil War in France." Pp. 618-29. In *The Marx-Engels Reader*. 2nd ed. Ed. Robert C. Tucker. New York: W.W. Norton.

Evans, John H. (1996). "'Culture Wars' or Status Group Ideology as the Basis of U.S. Moral Politics." *International Journal of Sociology and Social Policy* 16, 1/2: 15-34.

Fairbanks, David J. (1981). "The Priestly Function of the Presidency: A Discussion of the Literature on Civil Religion and Its implications for the Study of Presidential Leadership." *Presidential Studies Quarterly* 11: 214-32.

Falcoff, Mark. (1991). *Modern Chile, 1970-1989: A Critical History.* New Brunswick, NJ: Transaction Publishers.

Falwell, Jerry, Ed Dobson, and Ed Hinson, eds. (1981). *The Fundamentalist Phenomenon: The Resurgence of Conservative Christianity.* Garden City, NY: Doubleday.

Fenn, Richard K. (1970). "The Process of Secularization: A Post-Parsonian View." *Journal for the Scientific Study of Religion* 9: 117-36.

———. (1972). "Toward a New Sociology of Religion." *Journal for the Scientific Study of Religion* 11: 16-32.

———. (1974). "Religion and the Legitimation of Social Systems." Pp. 143-61. In *Changing Perspectives in the Scientific Study of Religion.* Ed. Allan W. Eister. New York: John Wiley and Sons.

———. (1976). "Bellah and the New Orthodoxy." *Sociological Analysis* 37: 160-66.

———. (1978). *Toward a Theory of Secularization.* Society for the Scientific Study of Religion, Monograph Series No. 1. Storrs, CT: Society for the Scientific Study of Religion.

Fenton, Steve, Robert Reiner, and Ian Hamnett. (1984). *Durkheim and Modern Sociology.* Cambridge: Cambridge University Press.

Finke, Roger, and Rodney Stark. (1992). *The Churching of America, 1776-1992.* New Brunswick, NJ: Rutgers University Press.

Frohnen, Bruce. (1996). *The New Communitarians and the Crisis of Modern Liberalism.* Lawrence, KA: University Press of Kansas.

Gamoran, Adam. (1990). "Civil Religion in American Schools." *Sociological Analysis* 51, 3: 235-56.

Garretón, Manuel Antonio. (1989). *The Chilean Political Process.* Trans. Sharon Kellum in collaboration with Gilbert W. Merkx. Boston: Unwin Hyman.

Garretón, Manuel Antonio and Tomás Moulián. (1978). *Análisis conyuntural y proceso político: Las fases del conflicto en Chile.* San José, Costa Rica: Editorial Universitaria Centroamericana.

Garrett, William (1975). "The Religious Roots of American Civil Religion." Paper read at the Annual Meeting of the Association for the Sociology of Religion. San Francisco Hilton.

Geertz, Clifford. (1973). *The Interpretations of Culture.* New York: Basic Books.

Gehrig, Gail. (1981a). "The American Civil Religion Debate: A Source for Theory Construction." *Journal for the Scientific Study of Religion* 20, 1: 51-63.

———. (1981b). *American Civil Religion: An Assessment.* Society for the Scientific Study of Religion, Monograph Series No. 3. Romeoville, IL: Lewis University.

Gellner, Ernest. (1965). *Thought and Change.* Chicago: University of Chicago Press.

Gentile, Emilio. (1990). "Fascism as Political Religion." *Journal of Contemporary History* 25, 2-3: 229.

Gerth, H.H., and C. Wright Mills, eds. and trans. (1958). *From Max Weber: Essays in Sociology.* New York: Oxford University Press.

Giddens, Anthony. (1978). *Durkheim*. London: Harvester Press.

_____. (1981). *A Contemporary Critique of Historical Materialism*. London: Macmillan.

_____. (1982). *Profiles and Critiques in Social Theory*. London: Macmillan.

_____. (1986). Introduction to *Durkheim on Politics and the State*. Cambridge: Polity Press.

Gil, Federico. (1966). *The Political System of Chile*. Boston: Houghton Mifflin.

Giner, Salvador. (1993). "Religión Civil." *Revista española de investigaciones sociológicas* 61: 23-55.

Grabb, Edward, Douglas Baer, and James Curtis. (1999). "The Origins of American Individualism: Reconsidering the Historical Evidence." *Canadian Journal of Sociology* 24, 4: 511-33.

Green, F.C. (1955). *Jean-Jacques Rousseau: A Critical Study of His Life and Writings*. Cambridge: Cambridge University Press.

Gregor, A. James. (1969). *Ideology of Fascism: The Rationale of Totalitarianism*. New York: Free Press.

_____. (1974). *The Fascist Persuasion in Radical Politics*. Princeton, NJ: Princeton University Press.

Hadden, Jeffrey K. (1975). Review Symposium. Editor's Introduction. "The Sociology of Religion of Robert N. Bellah." *Journal for the Scientific Study of Religion* 14, 4: 385-414.

Hamilton, Malcolm B. (1995). *The Sociology of Religion*. London: Routledge.

Hammond, Phillip E. (1968). "Commentary." In *The World Year Book of Religion*. Vol. 1. *The Religious Situation*. Pp. 381-88. Ed. Donald R. Cutler. Boston: Beacon Press.

_____. (1974). "Religious Pluralism and Durkheim's Integration Thesis." Pp. 115-42. In *Changing Perspectives in the Scientific Study of Religion*. Ed. Allan W. Eister. New York: John Wiley and Sons.

_____. (1976). "The Sociology of American Civil Religion: A Bibliographic Essay." *Sociological Analysis* 37, 2: 169-82.

_____. (1980a). "The Conditions for Civil Religion: A Comparison of the United States and Mexico." Pp. 40-85. In Robert N. Bellah and Phillip E. Hammond, *Varieties of Civil Religion*. San Francisco: Harper and Row.

_____. (1980b). "The Rudimentary Forms of Civil Religion." Pp. 121-37. In Robert N. Bellah and Phillip E. Hammond, *Varieties of Civil Religion*. San Francisco: Harper and Row.

_____. (1980c). "Pluralism and Law in the Formation of American Civil Religion." Pp. 138-63. In Robert N. Bellah and Phillip E. Hammond, *Varieties of Civil Religion*. San Francisco: Harper and Row.

_____. (1980d). "Civility and Civil Religion: The Emergence of Cults." Pp. 188-99. In Robert N. Bellah and Phillip E. Hammond, *Varieties of Civil Religion*. San Francisco: Harper and Row.

_____. (1980e). "Epilogue: The Civil Religion Proposal." Pp. 200-205. In Robert N. Bellah and Phillip E. Hammond, *Varieties of Civil Religion*. San Francisco: Harper and Row.

_____. (1981). "The Shifting Meaning of a Wall of Separation: Some Notes on Church, State, and Conscience." *Sociological Analysis* 42, 3: 227-34.

_____. (1983). "Another Great Awakening?" In *The New Christian Right: Mobilization and Legitimation*. Ed. Robert C. Liebman and Robert Wuthnow. New York: Aldine.

Hayes, Carleton J.H. (1960). *Nationalism: A Religion*. New York: Macmillan.

Henderson, Charles P. (1972). *The Nixon Theology*. New York: Harper and Row.

_____. (1975). "Civil Religion and the American Presidency." *Religious Education* 70, 5: 473-85.

Henry, Maureen. (1979). *The Intoxication of Power: An Analysis of Civil Religion in Relation to Ideology*. London: D. Reidel.

Herberg, Will. (1955). *Protestant, Catholic, Jew*. New York: Doubleday.

_____. (1960). "Religion and Education in America." Pp. 101-25. In *Religious Perspectives in American Culture*. Ed. J.W. Smith and A.L. Jamison. Princeton, NJ: Princeton University Press.

_____. (1974). "America's Civil Religion: What It Is and When It Comes." Pp. 76-88. In *American Civil Religion*. Ed. Russell E. Richey and Donald G. Jones. New York: Harper and Row.

Hill, Michael, and Wiebe Zwaga. (1987). "Civil and Civic: Engineering a National Religious Consensus." *New Zealand Sociology* 2: 25-35.

Hudson, Winthrop. (1970). *Nationalism and Religion in America*. New York: Harper and Row.

Hughes, Richard T. (1980). "Civil Religion, the Theology of the Republic, and the Free Church Tradition." *Journal of Church and State* 22, 1: 75-87.

Hughey, Michael W. (1983). *Civil Religion and Moral Order: Theoretical and Historical Dimensions*. Westport, CT: Greenwood Press.

_____. (1984). "The Political Covenant: Protestant Foundations of the American State." *State, Culture and Society* 1, 1: 113-56.

_____. (1992). "Americanism and Its Discontents: Protestantism, Nativism, and Political Heresy in America." *International Journal of Politics, Culture and Society* 5, 4: 533-53.

Hunter, James Davison. (1991). *Culture Wars: The Struggle to Define America*. New York: Basic Books.

Huntington, Samuel P. (1981). *American Politics: The Promise of Disharmony*. Cambridge: Belknap Press of Harvard University Press.

Inkeles, Alex (1964). "The Totalitarian Mystique: Some Impressions of the Dynamics of Totalitarian Society." Pp. 87-108. In *Totalitarianism*. Ed. Carl J. Friedrich. New York: Grosset and Dunlap.

Jelen, Ted G. (1987). "The Effects of Religious Separation on White Protestants in the 1984 Presidential Election." *Sociological Analysis* 48: 30-45.

_____. (1993). "The Political Consequences of Religious Groups' Attitudes." *Journal of Politics* 55: 178-90.

_____. (1995). "Religion and the American Political Culture: Alternative Models of Citizenship and Discipleship." *Sociology of Religion* 56, 3: 271-84.

Jolicoeur, Pamela M., and Louis K. Nowles. (1978). "Fraternal Associations and Civil Religion: Scottish Rite Freemasonry." *Review of Religious Research* 20: 3-22.

Jones, Donald G., and Russell E. Richey. (1974). "The Civil Religion Debate." Pp. 3-18. In *American Civil Religion*. Ed. Russell E. Richey and Donald G. Jones. New York: Harper and Row.

Kalberg, Stephen. (1994). *Max Weber's Comparative-Historical Sociology*. Chicago, IL: University of Chicago Press.

Kathan, Boardman, and Nancy Fuchs-Kreimer. (1975). "Civil Religion in America: A Bibliography." *Religious Education* 5: 541-50.

Kavka, Gregory S. (1986). *Hobbesian Moral and Political Theory*. Princeton, NJ: Princeton University Press.

Kessler, Sanford. (1994). *Tocqueville's Civil Religion: American Christianity and the Prospects for Freedom*. Albany: State University of New York Press.

Kim, Andrew E. (1993). "The Absence of Pan-Canadian Civil Religion: Plurality, Duality, and Conflict in Symbols of Canadian Culture." *Sociology of Religion* 54, 3: 257-75.

Kohn, Hans ([1944] 1967). *The Idea of Nationalism: A Study in Its Origins and Background*. New York: Collier Books.

Kokosalakis, Nikos. (1985). "Legitimation, Power and Religion in Modern Society." *Sociological Analysis* 46, 4: 367-76.

Krinsky, Fred. (1968). *The Politics of Religion in America*. Beverly Hills: Glencoe Press.

Laeyendecker, L. (1982). "Publieke Godsdienst in Nederland." *Sociologische-Gids* 29: 346-65.

Lagos, S. Humberto, and Arturo Chacón H. (1987). *La Religión en las Fuerzas Armadas y de Orden*. Santiago, Chile: Programa Evangélico de Estudios Socio Religiosos.

Lamb, Matthew L. (1986). "Civil Religion and Political Theology: Politics and Religion Without Domination?" Pp. 154-68. In *Civil Religion and Political Theology*. Ed. Leroy S. Rouner. Notre Dame, IN: University of Notre Dame Press.

Lane, Christel. (1979). "Ritual and Ceremony in Contemporary Soviet Society." *Sociological Review* 27, 2: 253-78.

_____. (1981). *The Rites of Rulers: Ritual in Industrial Society. The Soviet Case*. Cambridge: Cambridge University Press.

Larraín, Jorge. (1979). *The Concept of Ideology*. London: Hutchinson.

Larson, Gerald James. (1995). *India's Agony over Religion*. Albany: State University of New York Press.

Levy, Guenther. (1974). *Religion and Revolution*. New York: Oxford University Press.

Liebman, Charles S., and Eliezer Don-Yehiya. (1983). *Civil Religion in Israel*. Berkeley: University of California Press.

Linder, Robert D., and Richard V. Pierard. (1978). *Twilight of the Saints: Biblical Christianity and Civil Religion in America*. Downers Grove, IL: Inter Varsity.

Linz, Juan J. (1964). "An Authoritarian Regime: Spain" Pp. 291-341. In *Cleavages, Ideologies and Party Systems*. Vol. 10. Ed. Eric Allardt and Yrjo Littunen. Helsinki: Academic Bookstore.

Linz, Juan J., and Alfred Stepan. (1978). *The Breakdown of Democratic Regimes*. Baltimore: Johns Hopkins University Press.

Lippmann, Walter. (1956). *The Public Philosophy*. New York: Mentor.

Lipset, Seymour Martin. (1963). *The First New Nation*. New York: Basic Books.

_____. (1986). "Historical Traditions and National Characteristics: A Comparative Analysis of Canada and the United States." *Canadian Journal of Sociology* 11, 2: 113-55.

Loveman, Brian. (1979). *Chile: The Legacy of Hispanic Capitalism*. New York: Oxford University Press.

Lowden, Pamela. (1996). *Moral Opposition to Authoritarian Rule in Chile, 1973-1990*. London: Macmillan.

Luke, Timothy W. (1987). "Civil Religion and Secularization: Ideological Revitalization in Post-Revolutionary Communist Systems." *Sociological Forum* 2, 1: 108-34.

Lukes, Steven. (1971). "Some Problems about Rationality." Pp. 194-213. In *Rationality*. Ed. Bryan Wilson. New York: Harper and Row.

_____. (1973). *Emile Durkheim, His Life and Work*. London: Allen Lane Penguin Press.

_____. (1975). "Political Ritual and Social Integration." In *Sociology*. Ed. N.J. Smelser. New York: Wiley.

Macfarlane, L.J. (1970). *Modern Political Theory*. London: Thomas Nelson and Sons.

Machiavelli, Niccolo. ([1513] 1985). *The Prince*. Trans. Harvey C. Mansfield. Chicago: University of Chicago Press.

Markoff, John, and Daniel Regan. (1982). "The Rise and Fall of Civil Religion: Comparative Perspectives" *Sociological Analysis* 42, 4: 333-54.

Marsden, George M. (1990). "Afterword: Religion, Politics, and the Search for an American Consensus." Pp. 380-90. In *Religion and American Politics*. Ed. Mark Noll. New York: Oxford University Press.

Martin, David. (1978). *A General Theory of Secularization*. New York: Harper and Row.

Marty, Martin E. (1959). *The New Shape of American Religion*. New York: Harper and Row.

_____. (1974). "Two Kinds of Two Kinds of Civil Religion." In *American Civil Religion*. Pp. 139-57. Ed. Russell E. Richey and Donald G. Jones. New York: Harper and Row.

_____. (1976). *A Nation of Behavers*. Chicago: University of Chicago Press.

Marx, Karl. ([1843] 1978). "On The Jewish Question." Pp. 26-52. In *The Marx-Engels Reader*. 2nd ed. Ed. Robert C. Tucker. New York: W.W. Norton.

_____. ([1844] 1978). "Contribution to the Critique of Hegel's Philosophy of Right." Pp. 53-65. In *The Marx-Engels Reader*. 2nd. ed. Ed. Robert C. Tucker. New York: W.W. Norton.

_____. ([1844] 1978). "For a Ruthless Criticism of Everything Existing." Pp. 12-15. In *The Marx-Engels Reader.* 2nd ed. Ed. Robert C. Tucker. New York: W.W. Norton.

_____. ([1848] 1978). "Manifesto of the Communist Party." Pp. 469-500. In *The Marx-Engels Reader.* 2nd ed. Ed. Robert C. Tucker. New York: W.W. Norton.

_____. ([1871] 1978). "The Civil War in France." Pp. 618-52. In *The Marx-Engels Reader.* 2nd ed. Ed. Robert C. Tucker. New York: W.W. Norton.

_____. ([1888] 1978). "Theses on Fuerbach." Pp. 143-45. In *The Marx-Engels Reader.* 2nd ed. Ed. Robert C. Tucker. New York: W.W. Norton.

_____. ([1932] 1978). "The German Ideology: Part I." Pp. 146-200. In *The Marx-Engels Reader.* 2nd ed. Ed. Robert C. Tucker. New York: W.W. Norton.

Masters, Roger D. (1968). *The Political Philosophy of Rousseau.* Princeton, NJ: Princeton University Press.

Mathisen, James A. (1989). "Twenty Years after Bellah: Whatever Happened to American Civil Religion?" *Sociological Analysis* 50: 129-46.

McDowell, Jennifer. (1974). "Soviet Civil Ceremonies." Journal for the Scientific Study of Religion 13, 1: 265-79.

McGuire, Meredith B. (1983). "Discovering Religious Power." *Sociological Analysis* 44, 1: 1-10.

_____. (1987). *Religion: The Social Context.* Belmont, CA: Wadsworth.

Mead, Sidney E. (1963). *The Lively Experiment: The Shaping of Christianity in America.* New York: Harper and Row.

————. (1974). "The Nation with the Soul of a Church." In *American Civil Religion.* Pp. 45-75. Ed. Russell E. Richey and Donald G. Jones. New York: Harper and Row.

_____. (1975). *The Nation with the Soul of a Church.* New York: Harper and Row.

Merquior, J.G. (1980). *Rousseau and Weber: Two Studies in the Theory of Legitimacy.* London: Routledge and Kegan Paul.

Michaels, Albert L. (1975). *Background to a Coup: Civil Military Relations in Twentieth-Century Chile and the Overthrow of Salvador Allende.* Special Studies Series. Council on International Studies. Buffalo: State University of New York.

Michaelson, Robert. (1970). *Piety in the Public Schools.* New York: Macmillan.

_____. (1971). "Is the Public School Religious or Secular?" Pp. 22-44. In *The Religion of the Republic.* Ed. Elwyn A. Smith. Philadelphia: Fortress Press.

Mitchell, Joshua. (1995). "Tocqueville's Civil Religion: American Christianity and the Prospects for Freedom." *Journal of Politics* 57, 3: 873-75.

Mitchell, Marion M. (1990). "Emile Durkheim and the Philosophy of Nationalism." Pp. 113-27. In *Emile Durkheim: Critical Assessments.* Vol. 4. Ed. Peter Hamilton. London: Routledge.

Mitzman, Arthur. (1969). *The Iron Cage: An Historical Interpretation of Max Weber.* New York: Grosset and Dunlap.

Moellering, R.L. (1973). "Civil Religion, the Nixon Theology and the Watergate Scandal." *Christian Century.* 26 Sept.

Moltmann, Jürgen. (1986). "Christian Theology and Political Religion." Pp. 41-58. In *Civil Religion and Political Theology.* Ed. Leroy S. Rouner. Notre Dame, IN: University of Notre Dame Press.

Mommsen, J. Wolfgang. (1984). *Max Weber and German Politics, 1890-1920.* Chicago: University of Chicago Press.

Mommsen, T. (1974). *The Age of Bureaucracy.* Oxford: Oxford University Press.

Moodie, Dunbar T. (1975). *The Rise of Afrikanerdom: Power, Apartheid, and the Afrikaner Civil Religion.* Berkeley: University of California Press.

Moore, Laurence R. (1986). *Religious Outsiders and the Making of Americans.* New York: Oxford University Press.

Morawska, Ewa. (1987). "Civil Religion versus State Power in Poland." Pp. 221-32. In *Church-State Relations: Tensions and Transitions.* Ed. Thomas Robbins and Roland Robertson. New Brunswick, NJ: Transaction Books.

Morris, Aldon D. (1984). *The Origins of the Civil Rights Movement.* New York: Free Press.

Neeman, R., and N. Rublin. (1996). "Ethnic Civil Religion: A Case Study of Immigrants from Rumania in Israel." *Sociology of Religion* 57 (summer): 195-212.

Neuhaus, Richard John. (1984). *The Naked Public Square: Religion and Democracy in America.* Grand Rapids, MI: Eerdmans.

_____. (1986). "From Civil Religion to Public Philosophy." Pp. 98-110. In *Civil Religion and Political Theology.* Ed. Leroy S. Rouner. Notre Dame, IN: University of Notre Dame Press.

Noone, John B. (1980). *Rousseau's Social Contract: A Conceptual Analysis.* Athens: University of Georgia Press.

Novak, Michael. (1976). *The Joy of Sports.* New York: Basic Books.

_____. (1992). *Choosing Presidents: Symbols of Political Leadership.* New Brunswick, NJ: Transaction Publishers.

O'Brien, Philip. (1976). *Allende's Chile.* New York: Praeger.

O'Donnell, Guillermo, Philippe C. Schmitter, and Laurence Whitehead, eds. (1986). *Transitions from Authoritarian Rule, Prospects for Democracy.* Baltimore: Johns Hopkins University Press.

Oppenheim, Lois Hecht. (1993). *Politics in Chile: Democracy, Authoritarianism, and the Search for Development.* Boulder, CO: Westview Press.

O'Toole, Roger. (1984). *Religion, Classic Sociologic Approaches.* Scarborough, ON: McGraw-Hill Ryerson.

Parsons, Talcott. (1963). "On the Concept of Political Power." *Proceedings of the American Philosophical Society* 197: 232-62.

_____. (1964). "Christianity and Modern Industrial Society." In *Religion, Culture, and Society.* Ed. L. Schneider, L. New York: Wiley

Pasquino, Gianfranco. (1986). "The Demise of the First Fascist Regime and Italy's Transition to Democracy: 1943-1948." Pp. 45-70. In *Transitions from Authoritarian Rule, Prospects for Democracy*. Ed. Guillermo O'Donnell, Philippe C. Schmitter, and Laurence Whitehead. Baltimore: Johns Hopkins University Press.

Peal, Norman Vincent. (1971). *One Nation under God*. Pawling, NY: Foundation for Christian Living.

Pfeffer, Leo. (1968). "Commentary." In *The World Year Book of Religion. The Religious Situation*. Vol. 1. Pp. 360-65. Ed. Donald R. Cutler. Boston: Beacon Press.

Pickering, W.S.F. (1975). *Durkheim on Religion*. Trans. Jacqueline Redding and W.S.F. Pickering. London: Routledge and Kegan Paul.

_____. (1979). Introduction to *Durkheim: Essays on Morals and Education*. Pp. 3-27. Trans. H.L. Sutcliffe. London: Routledge and Kegan Paul.

Pierard, Richard V., and Robert D. Linder. (1988). *Civil Religion and the Presidency*. Grand Rapids, MI: Zondervan.

Pinochet, Augusto. (1983). *Política, politiquería y demagogia*. Santiago, Chile: Renacimiento.

Purdy, Susan S. (1982). "The Civil Religion Thesis as It Applies to a Pluralistic Society: Pancasila Democracy in Indonesia (1945-1965)." *Journal of International Affairs*: 307-16.

Puryear, Jeffrey M. (1994). *Thinking Politics*. Baltimore: Johns Hopkins University Press.

Rawls, John. (1996). *Political Liberalism*. New York: Columbia University Press.

Regan, Daniel. (1976). "Islam, Intellectuals and Civil Religion in Malaysia." *Sociological Analysis* 37, 2: 95-110.

Remmer, Karen L. (1980). "Political Demobilization in Chile, 1973-1978." *Comparative Politics* 12 (April): 275-301.

_____. (1989). *Military Rule in Latin America*. Boston: Unwin Hyman.

Reynolds, Frank E. (1977). "Civic Religion and National Community in Thailand." *Journal of Asian Studies* 36, 2: 267-82.

Rhodes, James M. (1980). *The Hitler Movement: A Modern Millenarian Movement*. Standford, CA: Hoover Institution Press.

Rice, Daniel F. (1980). "Sidney E. Mead and the Problem of 'Civil Religion.'" *Journal of Church and State* 22, 1: 53-74.

Richardson, Herbert. (1974). "Civil Religion in Theological Perspectives." Pp. 161-84. In *American Civil Religion*. Ed. Russell E. Richey and Donald G. Jones. New York: Harper and Row.

Richey, Russell E., and Donald G. Jones, eds. (1974). *American Civil Religion*. New York: Harper and Row.

Richter, Melvin. (1960). "Durkheim's Politics and Political Theory." Pp. 170-210. In *Emile Durkheim, 1858-1917*. Ed. Kurth H. Wolf. Columbus: Ohio University Press.

Robbins, Thomas, Dick Anthony, Madeline Doucas, and Thomas Curtis. (1976). "The Last Civil Religion: Reverend Moon and the Unification Church." *Sociological Analysis* 37, 2: 111-26.

Rogers, Cornish. (1972). "Sports, Religion and Politics: The Renewal of an Alliance." *Christian Century* 5 (April): 392-94.

Roof, W.C., and W. McKinney. (1987). *American Mainline Religion: Its Changing Shape and Future.* New Brunswick, NJ: Rutgers University Press.

Rouner, Leroy S., ed. (1986). *Civil Religion and Political Theology.* Notre Dame: IN: University of Notre Dame Press.

Rousseau, Jean-Jacques. ([1750] 1973). "A Discourse on the Moral Effects of the Arts and Sciences." Pp. 3-26. In *The Social Contract and Discourses.* Trans. G.D.H. Cole. London: J.M. Dent and Sons.

_____. ([1758] 1973). "Discourse on Political Economy." Pp. 117-53. In *The Social Contract and Discourses.* Trans. G.D.H. Cole. London: J.M. Dent and Sons.

_____. ([1758] 1984). "Discourse on Political Economy." Pp. 139-82. In *Of the Social Contract or Principles of Political Right & Discourse on Political Economy.* Trans. Charles M. Sherover. New York: Harper and Row.

_____. ([1762] 1973). *The Social Contract and Discourses.* Trans. G.D.H. Cole. London: J.M. Dent and Sons.

_____. ([1762] 1984). *Of the Social Contract or Principles of Political Right & Discourse on Political Economy.* Trans. Charles M. Sherover. New York: Harper and Row.

_____. ([1762] 1911). *Emile.* Trans. Barbara Foxley. London: Dent.

Roxborough, Ian, Philip O'Brien , and Jackie Roddick. (1977). *Chile: The State and Revolution.* London: Macmillan.

Sandel, Michael J. (1996). *Democracy's Discontent: America in Search of a Public Philosophy.* Cambridge: Belknap Press of Harvard University Press.

Sanders, Thomas G. (1981). "Military Government and National Organization." In *Military Government and the Movement toward Democracy in Latin America.* Pp. 287-306. Ed. Howard Handelman and Thomas G. Sanders. Bloomington: Indiana University Press.

Schaff, Philip. (1888)."Church and State in the United States." *Papers of the American Historical Association,* 2, 4.

Schieder, Rolf. (1987). *Civil Religion: die religiose Dimension der politischen Kultur.* Guetersloh: Guetersloher Verlagshans G. Mohn.

Schmitt, Carl. (1985). *Political Theology.* Trans. George Schwab. Cambridge, Mass: MIT Press.

Schoffeleers, Mathew. (1978). "Clan religion and civil religion: on Durkheim's conception of God as a symbol of society." Pp. 11-51. In *Religion, Nationalism and Economic Action.* The Netherlands, Assen: Van Gorcum.

Schoffeleers, Mathew, and Daniel Meijers. (1978). *Religion, Nationalism and Economic Action.* The Netherlands, Assen: Van Gorcum.

Selznick, Phillip. (1992). *The Moral Commonwealth: Social Theory and the Promise of Community.* Berkeley: University of California Press.

Seneviratne, H.L. (1984). "Continuity of Civil Religion in Sri Lanka." *Religion* 14: 1-14.

Shanks, Andrew. (1995). *Civil Society, Civil Religion.* Oxford: Blackwell.

Sharot, Stephen. (1990). "Israel: Sociological Analyses of Religion in the Jewish State." *Sociological Analysis* 51 (supplement): 63-76.

Sherover, Charles M. (1984). Introduction and Notes to *Of The Social Contract or Principles of Political Rights and Discourse on Political Economy* by Jean-Jacques Rousseau. Pp. vii-xl. New York: Harper and Row.

Sigmund, Paul E. (1977). *The Overthrow of Allende and the Politics of Chile, 1964-1976*. Pittsburgh: University of Pittsburgh Press.

Sihvo, Jouko. (1991). "The Evangelical-Lutheran Church and State in Finland." *Social Compass* 38: 17-24.

Smith, Brian H. (1982). *The Church and Politics in Chile: Challenges to Modern Catholicism*. Princeton, NJ: Princeton University Press.

———. (1986). "Chile: Deepening the Allegiance of Working-Class Sectors to the Church in the 1970s." Pp. 156-86. In *Religion and Political Conflict in Latin America*. Ed. Daniel H. Levine. Chapel Hill: University of North Carolina Press.

Sobel, A. Lester. (1974). *Chile and Allende*. Ed. Lester A. Sobel. Intro. Jordan M. Young. New York: Facts on File.

Starobinski, Jean. (1982). *1798: The Emblems of Reason*. Charlottesville: University Press of Virginia.

Stauffer, Robert E. (1973). "Civil Religion, Technocracy, and the Private Sphere: Further Comments on Cultural Integration in Advanced Societies." *Journal for the Scientific Study of Religion* 12, 4: 415-25.

———. (1975). "Bellah's Civil Religion." *Journal for the Scientific Study of Religion* 14, 4: 390-95.

Stauffer, Robert E., William C. Shepherd, Dick Anthony, and Thomas Robbins. (1975). "The Sociology of Religion of Robert N. Bellah." *Journal for the Scientific Study of Religion* 14, 4: 385-414.

Stepan, Alfred. (1988). *Rethinking Military Politics: Brazil and the Southern Cone*. Princeton, NJ: Princeton University Press.

Stern, Fritz Richard. (1963). *The Politics of Cultural Despair: A Study in the Rise of the German Ideology*. Berkeley: University of California Press.

Stevens, Evelyn P. (1975). "Protest Movement in an Authoritarian Regime." *Comparative Politics* 7, 3: 361-82.

Stillman, Peter G. (1974). "The Concept of Legitimacy," *Polity* 10/11, 1: 33-56.

Strauss, Leo. (1973). *The Political Philosophy of Hobbes: Its Basis and Its Genesis*. Chicago: University of Chicago Press.

Suleiman, Susan R. (1982). *Authoritarian Fictions: The Ideological Novel as a Literary Genre*. New York: Columbia University Press.

Sullivan, William M. (1982). *Reconstructing Public Philosophy*. Berkeley: University of California Press.

Swidler, Ann. (1986). "Culture in Action: Symbols and Strategies." *American Sociological Review* 51: 273-86.

Takayama, Peter K. (1988). "Revitalization Movement of Modern Japanese Civil Religion." *Sociological Analysis* 48, 4: 328-41.

Thomas, Michael C., and Charles C. Flippen. (1972). "American Civil Religion: An Empirical Study." *Social Forces* 51, 2: 218-25.

Thompson, J. Earl. (1971). "The Reform of the Racist Religion of the Republic." Pp. 267-85. In *The Religion of the Republic*. Ed. Elwyn A. Smith. Philadelphia: Fortress Press.

Toolin, Cynthia. (1983). "American Civil Religion from 1789 to 1981: A Content Analysis of Presidential Inaugural Addresses." *Review of Religious Research* 25: 39-48.

Tucker, Robert C. (1978). *The Marx-Engels Reader*. 2nd ed. Ed. Robert C. Tucker. New York: W.W. Norton.

Tulchin, Jospeh S., and Augusto Varas. (1991). *From Dictatorship to Democracy: Rebuilding Political Consensus in Chile*. Boulder, CO: Lynne Rienner.

Turner, Bryan S. (1983). *Religion and Social Theory*. London: Sage Publications.

Ungar, Sheldon. (1991). "Civil Religion and the Arms Race." *Canadian Review of Sociology and Anthropology* 28, 4503-24.

Valenzuela, Arturo. (1978). "The Breakdown of Democratic Regimes: Chile." Part IV. Pp. 1-110. In *The Breakdown of Democratic Regimes*. Ed. Juan J. Linz and Alfred Stephan. Baltimore: Johns Hopkins University Press.

_____. (1990). "Chile: Origins, Consolidation, and Breakdown of a Democratic Regime." Pp. 39-86. In *Politics in Developing Countries*. Ed. Larry Diamond, Juan J. Linz, and Seymour Martin Lipset. Boulder, CO: Lynne Rienner.

Vaughan, Charles E., ed. ([1915] 1962). *The Political Writings of Jean-Jacques Rousseau*. 2 Vols. Oxford: Blackwell.

Villela, G. Hugo. (1979). "The Church and the Process of Democratization in Latin America." *Social Compass* 86: 261-83.

Wallace, Ruth A. (1973). "The Secular Ethic and the Spirit of Patriotism." *Sociological Analysis* 34, 1: 3-11.

_____. (1990). "Emile Durkheim and the Civil Religion Concept." Pp. 220-25. In *Emile Durkheim: Critical Assessments*. Vol. 4. Ed. Peter Hamilton. London: Routledge.

Warner, Lloyd W. ([1953] 1974). "An American Sacred Ceremony." Pp. 89-111. In *American Civil Religion*. Ed. Russell E. Richey and Donald G. Jones. New York: Harper and Row.

Weber, Max ([1905] 1930). *The Protestant Ethic and the Spirit of Capitalism*. Trans. Talcott Parsons. New York: Scribner's.

_____. ([1915] 1958). "Religious Rejections of the World and Their Directions." Pp. 343-59. In *From Max Weber: Essays in Sociology*. Trans. and ed. H.H. Gerth and C. Wright Mills. New York: Oxford University Press.

_____. ([1919] 1958). "Politics as a Vocation." Pp. 77-128. In *From Max Weber: Essays in Sociology*. Trans. and ed. H.H. Gerth and C. Wright Mills. New York: Oxford University Press.

_____. ([1921] 1958). "Wirtschaft und Gesellschaft" Pp. 196-264. In *From Max Weber: Essays in Sociology*. Trans. and ed. H.H. Gerth and C. Wright Mills. New York: Oxford University Press.

_____. ([1922] 1965). *The Sociology of Religion*. Trans. Ephraim Fischoff. London. Methuen.

Weigel, G. (1992). *The Final Revolution: The Resistance Church and the Collapse of Communism.* New York: Oxford University Press.

West, Ellis M. (1980). "A Proposed Neutral Definition of Civil Religion." *Journal of Church and State* 22, 1: 23-39.

Whitney, John R. (1968). "Commentary." In *The World Year Book of Religion. The Religious Situation.* Vol. 1. Pp. 365-80. Ed. Donald R. Cutler. London: Beacon Press.

Wierdsma, Andreas I. (1987). "Civil Religion in the Netherlands." *Sociologia-Neerlandica* 23: 31-44.

Willaime, Jean-Paul. (1993). "La religion civile à la française et ses meta-morphoses." *Social Compass* 40, 4: 571-80.

Williams, Rhys H. (1996). "Religion as Political Resource: Culture or Ideology? *Journal for the Scientific Study of Religion* 35, 4: 368-78.

Williams, Rhys H., and Susan M. Alexander. (1994). "Religious Rhetoric in American Populism: Civil Religion as Movement Ideology." *Journal for the Scientific Study of Religion* 33, 1:1-15.

Williams, Rhys H., and N.J. Demerath. (1991). "Religion and Political Process in an American City." *American Sociological Review* 56: 417-31.

Williams, Robin M. (1951). *American Society: A Sociological Interpretation.* New York: Alfred A. Knopf.

Williams, Stahl. (1981). *Symbols of Canadian Civil Religion, Nationality and the Search for Meaning.* Ann Arbor, MI: University Microfilms International.

Wilson, Brian. (1982). *Religion in Sociological Perspective.* Oxford: Oxford University Press.

Wilson, John F. (1971). "The Status of 'Civil Religion' in America." Pp. 1-21. In *The Religion of the Republic.* Ed. Elwyn A. Smith. Philadelphia: Fortress Press.

_____. (1974). "A Historian's Approach to Civil Religion." Pp. 115-38. In *American Civil Religion.* Ed. by Russell E. Richey and Donald G. Jones. New York: Harper and Row.

_____. (1979). *Public Religion in American Culture.* Philadelphia: Temple University Press.

_____. (1986). "Common Religion in American Society." Pp. 111-24. In *Civil Religion and Political Theology.* Ed. Leroy S. Rouner. Notre Dame, IN: University of Notre Dame Press.

Wimberley, Ronald C. (1976). "Testing the Civil Religion Hypothesis." *Sociological Analysis* 37: 341-52.

_____. (1980). "Civil Religion and the Choice for President: Nixon in '72.'" *Social Forces* 59: 44-61.

Wimberley, Ronald C., and James A. Christenson. (1980). "Civil Religion and Church and State." *Sociological Quarterly* 21 (winter): 35-40.

_____. (1981). "Civil Religion and other Religious Identities." *Sociological Analysis* 42: 91-100.

_____. (1982). "Civil Religion, Social Indicators, and Public Policy." *Social Indicators Research* 10: 211-23.

Wimberley, Ronald C., Donald A.Clelland, Thomas C. Hood, and C.M. Lipsey. (1976). "The Civil Religious Dimension: Is It There?" *Social Forces* 54, 4: 890-900.

Woocher, Jonathan S. (1986). *Sacred Survival: The Civil Religion of American Jews*. Bloomington: Indiana University Press.

Wuthnow, Robert. (1988a). *The Restructuring of American Religion*. Princeton, NJ: Princeton University Press.

_____. (1988b). "Divided We Fall: America's Two Civil Religions." *Christian Century* 115: 395-99.

_____. (1992). *Rediscovering the Sacred: Perspectives on Religion in Contemporary Society*. Grand Rapids, MI: William B. Eerdmans.

_____. (1994). *Producing the Sacred: An Essay on Public Religion*. Chicago: University of Illinois Press.

Zeldin, Mary-Barbara. (1969). "The Religious Nature of Russian Marxism." *Journal for the Scientific Study of Religion* 8, 1: 100-11.

Zerubavel, Eviatar. (1985). *The Seven Day Circle: The History and Meaning of the Week*. New York: Free Press.

Zuo, Jiping. (1991). "Political Religion: The Case of the Cultural Revolution in China." *Sociological Analysis* 52, 1: 99-110.

INDEX